Progressive Business Plan for a Senior Concierge Service

Copyright © 2018 by Progressive Business Consulting, Inc.
Pembroke Pines, FL 33027

Business and Marketing Plan Instructions

1. If you want the digital version of this plan, please send proof-of-purchase to Probusconsult2@yahoo.com

2. Complete the Executive Summary section, as your final step, after you have completed the entire plan.

3. Feel free to edit the plan and make it more relevant to your strategic goals, objectives and business vision.

4. We have provided all of the formulas needed to prepare the financial plan. Just plug in the numbers that are based on your particular situation. Excel spreadsheets for the financials are available on the microsoft.com website and www.simplebizplanning.com/forms.htm http://office.microsoft.com/en-us/templates/

5. Throughout the plan, we have provided prompts or suggestions as to what values to enter into blank spaces but use your best judgment and then delete the suggested values (?).

6. The plan also includes some separate worksheets for additional assistance in expanding some of the sections, if desired.

7. Additionally, some sections offer multiple choices and the word 'select' appears as a prompt to edit the contents of the plan.

8. Your feedback, referrals and business are always very much appreciated.

Thank you

Nat Chiaffarano, MBA
Progressive Business Consulting, Inc.
Pembroke Pines, FL 33027
ProBusConsult2@yahoo.com

NON-DISCLOSURE AGREEMENT

_____ (Company)., and _____ (Person Name), agrees:

_____ (Company) Corp. may from time to time disclose to _____ (Person Name) certain confidential information or trade secrets generally regarding Business plan and financials of _____ (Company) corp.

_____ (Person Name) agrees that it shall not disclose the information so conveyed, unless in conformity with this agreement. _____ (Person Name) shall limit disclosure to the officers and employees of _____ (Person Name) with a reasonable "need to know" the information and shall protect the same from disclosure with reasonable diligence.

As to all information which _____ (Company) Corp. claims is confidential, _____ (Company) Corp. shall reduce the same to writing prior to disclosure and shall conspicuously mark the same as "confidential," "not to be disclosed" or with other clear indication of its status. If the information which _____ (Company) Corp. is disclosing is not in written form, for example, a machine or device, _____ (Company) Corp. shall be required prior to or at the same time that the disclosure is made to provide written notice of the secrecy claimed by _____ (Company) Corp. _____ (Person Name) agrees upon reasonable notice to return the confidential tangible material provided by it by _____ (Company) Corp. upon reasonable request.

The obligation of non-disclosure shall terminate when if any of the following occurs:
(a) The confidential information becomes known to the public without the fault of _____ (Person Name), or;
(b) The information is disclosed publicly by _____ (Company) Corp., or ;
(c) a period of 12 months passes from the disclosure, or;
(d) the information loses its status as confidential through no fault of _____ (Person Name).

In any event, the obligation of non-disclosure shall not apply to information which was known to _____ (Person Name) prior to the execution of this agreement.

Dated: _____

_____
_____ (Company) Corp.
_____(Person Name)

"Progressive Business Plan for a Senior Concierge Service"

Copyright Notice

Copyright © 2018   Nat Chiaffarano, MBA
Progressive Business Consulting, Inc
All Rights Reserved.   **ISBN:** 9781980478423

This program is protected under Federal and International copyright laws. No portion of these materials may be reproduced, stored in a retrieval system or transmitted in any manner whatsoever, without the written consent of the publisher.

Limits of Liability / Disclaimer of Warranty

The author and the publisher of "Progressive Business Plan for a Senior Concierge Service", and all accompanying materials have used their best efforts in preparing this program. The author and publisher make no representations and warranties with respect to the accuracy, applicability, fitness or completeness of the content of this program. The information contained in this program is subject to change without notice and should not be construed as a commitment by the author or publisher.

The authors and publisher shall in no event be held liable for any loss or damages, including but not limited to special, incidental, consequential, or other damages. The program makes no promises as to results or consequences of applying the material herein: your business results may vary in direct relation to your detailed planning, timing, availability of capital and human resources, and implementation skills.

This publication is not intended for use as a source of legal, accounting, or professional advice. As always, the advice of a competent legal, accounting, tax, financial or other professional should be sought. If you have any specific questions about your unique business situation, consider contacting a qualified business consultant. The fact that an organization or website is referred to as a 'resource' or potential source of information, does not mean that the publisher or authors endorse the resource. Websites listed may also have been changed since publication of the book.

Senior Concierge Service
Business Plan
_____ (date)

Business Name: _____
Plan Time Period: 2018 - 2020

Founding Directors:
Name: _____
Name: _____

Contact Information:
Owner: _____
Address: _____
City/State/Zip: _____
Phone: _____
Cell: _____
Fax: _____
Website: _____
Email: _____

Submitted to: _____
Date: _____
Contact Info: _____

This document contains confidential information. It is disclosed to you for informational purposes only. Its contents shall remain the property of _____ (business name) and shall be returned to _____ when requested. This is a business plan and does not imply an offering of securities.

Senior Concierge Service Business Plan: Table of Contents

Section	Description	Page
1.0	**Executive Summary**	____
1.1.0	Tactical Objectives	____
1.1.1	Strategic Objectives	____
1.2	Mission Statement	____
1.2.1	Core Values Statement	____
1.3	Vision Statement	____
1.4	Keys to Success	____
2.0	**Company Summary**	____
2.1	Company Ownership	____
2.2	Company Licensing and Liability Protection	____
2.3	Start-up To-do Checklist	____
2.4.0	Company Location	____
2.4.1	Company Facilities	____
2.5.0	Start-up Summary	____
2.5.1	Inventory	____
2.5.2	Supply Sourcing	____
2.6	Start-up Requirements	____
2.7	SBA Loan Key Requirements	____
2.7.1	Other Financing Options	____
3.0	**Products and Services**	____
3.1	Service Descriptions	____
3.1.1	Product Descriptions	____
3.2	Alternate Revenue Streams	____
3.3	Production of Products and Services	____
3.4	Competitive Comparison	____
3.5	Sale Literature	____
3.6	Fulfillment	____
3.7	Technology	____
3.8	Future Products and Services	____
4.0	**Market Analysis Summary**	____
4.1.0	Secondary Market Research	____
4.1.1	Primary Market Research	____
4.2	Market Segmentation	____
4.3	Target Market Segment Strategy	____
4.3.1	Market Needs	____
4.4	Buying Patterns	____
4.5	Market Growth	____

Section	Description	Page
4.6	Service Business Analysis	____
4.7	Barrier to Entry	____
4.8	Competitive Analysis	____
4.9	Market Revenue Projections	____
5.0	**Industry Analysis**	____
5.1	Industry Leaders	____
5.2	Industry Statistics	____
5.3	Industry Trends	____
5.4	Industry Key Terms	____
6.0	**Strategy and Implementation Summary**	____
6.1.0	Promotion Strategy	____
6.1.1	Grand Opening	____
6.1.2	Value Proposition	____
6.1.3	Positioning Statement	____
6.1.4	Distribution Strategy	____
6.2	Competitive Advantage	____
6.2.1	Branding Strategy	____
6.3	Business SWOT Analysis	____
6.4.0	Marketing Strategy	____
6.4.1	Strategic Alliances	____
6.4.2	Monitoring Marketing Results	____
6.4.3	Word-of-Mouth Marketing	____
6.5	Sales Strategy	____
6.5.1	Customer Retention Strategy	____
6.5.2	Sales Forecast	____
6.5.3	Sales Program	____
6.6	Merchandising Strategy	____
6.7	Pricing Strategy	____
6.8	Differentiation Strategies	____
6.9	Milestone Tracking	____
7.0	**Website Plan Summary**	____
7.1	Website Marketing Strategy	____
7.2	Development Requirements	____
7.3	Sample Frequently Asked Questions	____
8.0	**Operations**	____
8.1	Security Measures	____
9.0	**Management Summary**	____
9.1	Owner Personal History	____

Section	Description	Page
9.2	Management Team Gaps	____
9.2.1	Management Matrix	____
9.2.2	Outsourcing Matrix	____
9.3	Employee Requirements	____
9.4	Job Descriptions	____
9.4.1	Job Description Format	____
9.5	Personnel Plan	____
9.6	Staffing Plan	____
10.0	**Business Risk Factors**	____
10.1	Business Risk Reduction Strategies	____
10.2	Reduce Customer Perceived Risk Strategies	____
11.0	**Financial Plan**	____
11.1	Important Assumptions	____
11.2	Break-even Analysis	____
11.3	Projected Profit and Loss	____
11.4	Projected Cash Flow	____
11.5	Projected Balance Sheet	____
11.6	Business Ratios	____
12.0	**Business Plan Summary**	____
13.0	**Potential Exit Strategies**	____
	Appendix	____
	Helpful Resources	____

1.0 Executive Summary

Industry Overview

The elderly population is growing steadily as baby boomers age, creating a solid market for senior concierge services. This new service provides home companionship, errands, light housework, transportation to appointments or social events and many, many more services. These companies or individuals offer services by the hour, the day and sometimes even weekly for respite type care. These are non-medical services but most companies offer referrals for when a more serious need arises. The featured value in these providers is not only extending independence for seniors who need support, but also the comfort and peace of mind that comes with knowing the senior has someone to contact when the family caregiver is not available.

Recently, the industry has been on a steady rise, with industry revenues of $220 million in 2012. IBIS expects the concierge industry to see an uptick, with annual revenue projected to grow to $264 million by 2017. As of 2013, the industry continues to increase at an annual five-year growth rate of 3.2% to 658 total companies. The gradual increase is attributed to a decrease in "leisure time" among individuals, the greater need for pre-screened and pre-qualified service providers, the desire of businesspersons to focus on their entrepreneurial activities, the desire by seniors to remain active and participate in travel plans, and the increasing aging of the population.

The industry is also thriving because of the cost savings they are able to deliver to seniors. According to data collected by the National Private Duty Association (NPDA) in 2011, the average cost of one nursing home resident was $69,715 and the average annual cost of one assisted-living facility resident was $36,372. So not only does a senior care concierge service help the elderly to continue to live on in their homes with their families on their own terms, but it also costs a lot less.

Business Overview:

_____ (company name) will provide a full range of services to senior and home-bound individuals in the _____ (city) metro area. Our mission is to provide support, friendship, transportation and outings for those whose families can't be with their loved ones around the clock. We will focus on relationship development that enables seniors to maintain social connection and fulfillment. Some of our most frequently requested services will include: lunch outings, shopping trips, theater, and beauty salon or medical appointments. Most importantly, _____ (company name) will provide a compassionate buddy for your loved one and a reliable, trustworthy support system.

The company has an experienced management team, and a well-developed business strategy. This business plan will include a strategic marketing plan, with a focus on the development of differentiation and growth strategies, and a sales plan.

Actual financial performance will be tracked closely and adjusted when necessary to ensure that full profit potential is realized.

The Company:
The business _____ (will be/was) incorporated on _____ (date) as a _____ (Corporation/LLC), in the state of _____ and intends to register for Sub-chapter 'S' status or federal tax purposes. This will effectively shield the owner(s) from personal liability and double taxation. The company was started by _____ (business owner name), who is the majority owner and a past _____ (indicate relevant business experience or achievements).

_____ (company name) will be a home-based business. The staff will consist of Mr./Ms. _____, working full-time for the company. The company plans to hire ____ (#) _____ (part-time/full-time) employees by the end of year one. The company plans to offer higher wages, profit sharing and a continuous employee training program to attract quality individuals and insure the delivery of superior services. We will assist seniors so that they do not have to abandon the familiarity of their home or the camaraderie of their neighbors, friends and family.

Our Services: (select)
_____ (company name) will provide a wide range of services for our customers. Our major concierge service categories are as follows:

Companionship	Medication reminders
Check food supply	Assist with apparel
Home safety check / fall prevention	Bring in mail / newspaper
Remove trash	Errand Services
Correspondence Handling	Housekeeping
Kitchen Duties	Transportation
Arrange Appointments	Care Coordination
Connections to other Services/Professionals	Patient Advocacy
Companion Care	Senior Massages

Marketing Plan:
With the help of this aggressive marketing plan, _____ (company name) expects to experience steady growth. _____ (company name) plans to attract its customers through the use of local newspaper advertisements, circulating flyers to surrounding businesses and major employers, a systematic series of direct mailings, news releases in newspapers, a website, educational seminars, online directories, traditional and online Yellow Page ads, word-of-mouth marketing, and a referral program. Additionally, the plan is to be a contributor to the community through outreach events.

We will provide printed materials with large print and senior photos and testimonials to potential clients. We will also use phone calls and face to face marketing because research indicates that seniors respond well to these marketing methods. We will also market our services to their caregivers, because some seniors do not make decisions on their own due to forgetfulness and illnesses such as dementia. Additionally, since most people work full time jobs, taking care of elderly family members can be a burden, and therefore, those family members will be more inclined to enlist our services.

The Market:
We will service the needs of seniors and their families, who recognize the value of having someone else do tasks that they cannot physically accomplish or they do not have the time for, or after a cost/benefit analysis, realize that it is not worth their time to perform the task. Currently in _____ (city) there are ___ (# or no) other concierge style companies, primarily servicing seniors. We will primarily focus on seniors because they require a specialized set of skills and have the potential to provide both larger sales volume and more consistent business.

Critical Risks
Management recognizes there are several internal and external risks inherent in our business concept. Quality, selection, responsiveness, value pricing and convenience will be key factors in the consumers' decision to utilize our senior concierge services. Consumers must be willing to accept our one-stop services and become repeat and referral customers in order for our company to meet its sales projections. Building a loyal and trusting relationship with our customers and referral partners will be a key component to the success of _____ (company name).

Customer Service
We will take every opportunity to help the customer, regardless of what the revenue might be. We will outshine our competition by doing something "extra" and offering added-value services in a timely manner. We will take a long-term perspective and focus on the client's possible lifetime value to our business. By giving careful consideration to customer responsiveness, _____'s (company name) goal will be to meet and exceed every service expectation. Quality service, and quick and informed responsiveness will be the philosophy guiding a customer-centric approach to our senior concierge service.

Competitive Edge
_____ company name) will take the client/concierge service matching process to a new level of detail by having new clients fill out in-depth profiles, documenting precisely their likes, dislikes, preferences and the type of concierge services they require. Then a member of our staff will visit the client's home, where they will have a 'meet and greet' to evaluate the proposed relationship, ensuring that both the assigned service facilitator and client feel comfortable with the new concierge service arrangement.

Other competitive advantages will include:
1. 24 Hour Availability, 7 days a week, 365 days per year.
2. No Minimum Hourly Requirement for services.
3. Free In-Home Consultation or complimentary assessment by a geriatric care manager to build a customized service plan that fits the client's needs and budget.
4. All of our caregivers are fully bonded, insured, and covered through worker's compensation insurance.
5. Perform extensive interviews, reference checks, and state and national criminal history background checks to ensure that our clients receive the highest quality of

dedicated caregivers.
6. Real Time Care Schedules and Task Updates can be seen with a simple login at any time via the internet.
7. We will assist our clients in finding ways to pay for our services. Examples include:
   - Reverse Mortgages
   - VA Benefits
   - Long-term care insurance
   - State and Local Programs, such Medicaid

Differentiation Strategy
We will take the caregiver matching process to the next level by pairing a smart, empathetic Activity Specialist with a senior who shares his or her interests and passions. As an auxiliary service to physical care, our two- to three-hour sessions, led by carefully screened and matched Activity Specialists will stimulate and enhance cognitive and social interactions, while giving immediate family members some welcome respite from continuing care.
Example: http://leconciergesf.com/wpbdm-directory/sf-senior-services

Mission Statement   **(optional)**
Our mission is to enable seniors to maintain an independent lifestyle, by addressing the following customer pain points or unmet needs and wants, which will define the opportunity for our business: _____
In order to satisfy these unmet needs and wants, we will propose the following unique solutions, which will create better value for our customers: _____
Our mission is to enrich the lives of our clients by delivering concierge services that allow seniors to maintain an independent and dignified lifestyle.

Services
The company will offer a complete range of solutions for seniors who need assistance and security in their own homes, including: companionship, meal prep and light housework, supervision, personal care, transportation and errands.

The Management Team
_____ (company name) will be led by _____ (owner name) and _____ (co-owner name). ____ (owner name) has a _____ degree from _____ (institution name) and a _____ background within the industry, having spent ____ (#) years with ____ (former employer name or type of business). During this tenure, ___ (he/she) helped grow the business from $_____ in yearly revenue to over $___. ____ (co-owner name) has a ___ background, and while employed by __ was able to increase operating profit by __ percent. These acquired skills, work experiences and educational backgrounds will play a big role in the success of our senior concierge service. Additionally, our president, _____ (name), has an extensive knowledge of the _____ area and has identified a niche market opportunity to make this venture highly successful, combining his ___ (#) years of work experience in a variety of businesses. _____ (owner name) will manage all aspects of the business and service development to ensure effective customer

responsiveness while monitoring day-to-day operations. Qualified and trained clerks personally trained by _____ (owner name) in customer service skills will provide additional support services. Support staff will be added as seasonal or extended hours mandate.

Past Successful Accomplishments

_____ (company name) is uniquely qualified to succeed due to the following past successes:

1. **Entrepreneurial Track Record**: The owners and management team have helped to launch numerous successful ventures, including a _____.

2. **Key Milestones Achieved**: The founders have invested $___ to-date to staff the company, build the core technology, acquire starting inventory, test market the _____ (product/service), realize sales of $_____ and launch the website.

Start-up Funding

_____ (owner name) will financially back the new business venture with an initial investment of $_____ and will be the principal owner. Additional funding in the amount of $_____ will be sought from _____, a local commercial bank, with a SBA loan guarantee. This money will be needed to start the company. This loan will provide start-up capital, financing for a selected site lease, remodeling renovations, inventory purchases, pay for permits and licensing, staff training and certification, equipment and working capital to cover expenses during the first year of operation.

Financial Plan:

Our start-up costs will include all of the equipment needed for the home-based office, legal fees, website build, and start-up marketing campaign. The projected growth rate for our company is over _____ (100?) % per year, with operating margins ranging between ____ (65?) % and ____ (75?) %. We expect to earn approximately $_____ in revenues based on sales of $_____ by year _____. The company plans to bill our clients on either an hourly rate or a monthly membership plan fee.

Financial Profile Summary

Key Indicator	2018	2019	2020
Total Revenue			
Expenses			
Gross Margin			
Operating Income			
Net Income			
EBITDA			

EBITDA = Revenue - Expenses (excluding tax, interest, depreciation and amortization)
EBITDA is essentially net income with interest, taxes, depreciation, and amortization added back to it, and can be used to analyze and compare profitability between companies and industries because it eliminates the effects of financing and accounting decisions.

Gross Margin (%) = (Revenue - Cost of Goods Sold) / Revenue
Net Income = Total revenue - Cost of sales - Other expenses - Tax

Exit Strategy

If the business is very successful, __(owner name) may seek to sell the business to a third party for a significant earnings multiple. Most likely, the Company will hire a qualified business broker to sell the business on behalf of __ (company name). Based on historical numbers, the business could generate a sales premium of up to __(#) times earnings.

Summary

Through a combination of a proven business model and a strong management team to guide the organization, _____ (company name) will be a long lasting, profitable business. We believe our ability to create future product and service opportunities and growth will only be limited by our imagination and our ability to attract talented people who understand the concept of branding.

1.1 Key Strategic Objectives   (select - 3)

Every objective will specify quantifiable results and involve activities that can be easily tracked. They will also be realistic, tied to specific marketing strategies and serve as a good benchmark to evaluate our business plan implementation success.

1. To be an active networking participant and productive member of the community by _____ (date).
2. Create over _____ (50?) % of business revenues from repeat customers by _____ (date).
3. Achieve an overall customer satisfaction rate of ____ (99?) % by _____ (date).
4. Get a business website designed, built and operational by _____ (date), which will include an online shopping cart for web purchases.
5. Achieve total sales revenues of $_____ in _____ (year).
6. Realize gross margins higher than _____ (75?) percent by _____ (date).
7. Achieve net income more than ___ (10?) percent of net sales by the ____ (#) year.
8. Build pricing programs based on the assumption of a _____ (10?) percent profit.
9. To create a service-based company whose primary goal is to exceed customers' expectations.
10. To secure at least ____ (#) of the top 20 local businesses as corporate clients.
11. Increase overall sales by _____ (20?) percent from prior year.
12. To increase the number of clients served by ____ (20?) % per year through superior performance and word-of-mouth referrals.
13. Generate ____ (#) new individual clients per month.
14. To develop a sustainable home-based business that is capable of surviving on its own cash flow by the end of year _____.
15. To have ___ (15?) clients within our first year of business.

1.2 Mission Statement

Our Mission Statement is a written statement that spells out our organization's overall goal, provides a sense of direction and acts as a guide to decision making for all levels of management. In developing the following mission statement, we will encourage input from employees, volunteers, and other stakeholders, and publicize it broadly in our website and other marketing materials.

Our mission is to provide quality non-medical services for seniors in their own homes or in an assisted living environment, so they can live a safe, happy and independent life.

Our goal is to provide professional, enthusiastic, quality services to meet our customer's needs whatever they may be. _____ (company name), strives to be the best choice of clients by helping to ease their daily burden. Our mission is to assist our clients with concierge, personal and virtual assistant services in order for them to manage their individual needs. Through consistent, predictable professionalism, _____ (company name), will ensure a worry and hassle-free day at a reasonable price.

To create a company that provides peace of mind for seniors or their families who may be located in a different city, or busy with the demands of their daily lives.

Keeping in tune with the needs of the market, utilizing the latest technology and trends, all while ensuring the client receives the individual attention they deserve, is the daily mission of _____ (company name). We will use relationship building techniques to identify and serve the ideal senior target audience within a ____ (#) mile radius of _____ (city). We will foster a workplace where employees take pride in and ownership of their contributions and empowers them to realize some compensation in the form of pay-for-performance benefits.

1.2.1 Mantra

We will create a mantra for our organization that is three or four words long. Its purpose will be to help employees truly understand why the organization exists. Our mantra will serve as a framework through which to make decisions about product and business direction. It will boil the key drivers of our company down to a sentence that defines our most important areas of focus and resemble a statement of purpose or significance.
Our Mantra is _____

1.2.2 Core Values Statement

The following Core Values will help to define our organization, guide our behavior, underpin operational activity and shape the strategies we will pursue in the face of various challenges and opportunities:
    Being respectful and ethical to our customers and employees.
    Building enduring relationships with clients.
    Seeking innovation in our industry.

Practicing accountability to our colleagues and stakeholders.
Pursuing continuous improvement as individuals and as a business entity.
Performing tasks on time to satisfy the needs of our internal and external clients,
Taking active part in the organization to meet the objectives and the establishment of continuous and lasting relationships.
Offering professional treatment to our clients, employees, shareholders, and the community.
Continuing pursuit of new technologies for the development of the projects that add value for our clients, employees, shareholders, and the community.

1.3 Vision Statement

The following Vision Statement will communicate both the purpose and values of our organization. For employees, it will give direction about how they are expected to behave and inspires them to give their best. Shared with customers, it will shape customers' understanding of why they should work with our organization.

____ (company name) will strive to become one of the most respected and favored Senior Concierge Services company in the area. It is our desire to become a landmark in _____ (city), ____ (state), that is known, not only for our quality service, customer friendliness and exacting professionalism, but also for community and charity involvement.

_____ (company name) is dedicated to operating with a constant enthusiasm for learning about concierge software advancements, being receptive to implementing new ideas, and maintaining a willingness to adapt to changing senior market needs and wants. Our Vision is to practice accountability and embrace change, while seeking knowledge and growth through learning. Our Vision is to be the premier lifestyle management company of choice in _____ (region), comprising the city of _____, in the senior concierge industry.

1.4 Keys to Success

In broad terms, the success factors relate to providing what our clients want and doing what is necessary to be better than our competitors. The following critical success factors are areas in which our organization must excel in order to operate successfully and achieve our objectives:

1. Recruiting employees with a passion for Senior Concierge Service, share the company mission and the same concern for helping seniors to lead fulfilling lives.
2. Networking aggressively within the community, as word of mouth will be our most powerful advertising asset.
3. Implementing and maintaining an organized, consistent means of lead generation, lead tracking and follow-up to turn referral leads into clients.
4. The flexibility to respond to changing customer buying habits and needs.
5. Offering free educational seminars to businesses to demonstrate our expertise.

6. Communicating with potential customers through direct mail, postcards, print advertising, an easy-to-use website, seminars, articles, and e-newsletters.
7. Offering a wide variety of Senior Concierge Services to individuals and families.
8. A business model that offers multiple revenue streams from the sale of products and services.
9. Keeping overhead expenses budgeted and under control.
10. The use of software technology and website design to develop loyal clients.
11. A detailed customer service plan
12. The establishment of client plan contract options and vendor agreements.
13. A start-up focus on a target market niche, such as office support services.
14. An in-depth of knowledge of your town, and the ability to research and find answers.
15. The screening, hiring, educating, supporting and mentoring of great employees.
16. Maximize the return on your core resources and capabilities, while being receptive to changing customer demands.
17. Target many different kinds of clients, form individuals to corporate clients.
18. Vendor contacts are key in the personal service business.
19. Build a file of people you can call on to help you meet your client's needs.
20. Must establish and meet service performance standards.
21. Must be proactive in exceeding customer expectations.
22. Must keep clients informed as to the status of service performance.
23. Invoices must be submitted in an accurate and timely manner.
24. Must deliver superior value to secure more client personal information.
25. Must develop the understanding and ability to ask for the right client information at the right time.
26. Concierge staff must develop one-to-one relationships with individual users of the service.
27. Effective database management of client profile, preferences, expectations and transaction data records.
28. Must make the number one priority the protecting of the client's interests and privacy.
29. Must practice effective vendor management and partnership sales.
30. Must be able to provide clients with remote, integrated access to the concierge service across all the new touch points, including mobile and email.
31. Develop a network of well-connected contacts.
32. The personal qualities of flexibility, resourcefulness, organization, multi-tasking, trustworthiness, approachability, likeability, and time management.
33. Develop a detailed customer service plan.
34. Work with lawyer to create client contracts, partnership agreement and vendor agreements.
35. Decide upon range of support services and price point range.
36. Hold focus groups, conduct one-on-one interviews or conduct surveys to connect with the seniors in the area to determine their needs and wants.
37. Hire a virtual assistant who accepts hourly pay or per-project pay, as needed.
38. Research the market to see how your skills can fit with a senior service demand.

39. Use data from the U.S. Census Bureau and other government agencies to learn about the number of elderly people living in the area and about the types of housing they inhabit.
40. Evaluate potential competition and look to fill a service void.
41. Get first aid and CPR training.
42. Have clear policies and procedures for conducting banking transactions and pharmacy pick-ups, such as placing medications in a locked box in the trunk until delivered to the client and securing and handing-off detailed documentation.
43. Remember that your client is the person you are providing service to; if a client and family member disagree, confirm the power of attorney or other legal right of the family member to make decisions before going against the wishes of a client.
44. Develop an emergency plan to help maintain composure and obtain the appropriate assistance during possible emergency situations.
45. Develop membership packages with different listed service options, time and distance limits, and frequencies.
46. Focus on finding potential customers in senior apartment complexes, adult daycares, and retirement communities.
47. Know everything there is to know about filing your business tax returns as an independent contractor.
    Resource: www.thepennyhoarder.com/smart-money/independent-contractor-taxes/?aff_id=76&aff_sub2=elderconcierge05232017

2.0 Company Summary

_____ (company name) will be a _____ (sole-proprietorship/corporation/LLC) that will offer an unlimited Senior Concierge Service for individuals and families. It will be incorporated under the laws of _____ (state) and will be located in _____ (city), _____ (state).

In the profitable and rapidly growing Senior Concierge Services industry, _____ (company name) will stand out as a leader in customer service and innovative service offerings. A strong customer focus, fast completed job turnaround, and a broad service line will enable our business to steadily develop a large and loyal customer base.

_____ (company name) will enrich the lives of _____ area seniors with a range of non-medical services that enable them to maintain an independent and dignified lifestyle in the comfort of their own home. We will offer a complete range of solutions for seniors who need assistance and care in their own homes, including: companionship, meal preparation and light housework, supervision, personal care, transportation, errands, catering and relocation. The company has been designed to assist the elderly with instrumental activities of daily living that had once been easy, but now are overwhelming. Our company will enable seniors to age in place, so they keep the familiarities and comfort of their present home.

Sales are expected to reach $_____ within the first year and to grow at a conservative rate of _____ (10?) to _____ (15?) percent during the next two to five years.

The company is expected to make a profit in the _____ (second?) month, and will grow steadily each consecutive month. To stimulate growth, the company will introduce a steady stream of new services. The specific products and services added will depend on consumer trends, projected profit margins, customer draw and overall company direction. The business will be based out of the owner's home, and within 12 months, we plan to add _____ (#) additional employees.

A senior errand service offers just one basic service, which is running errands. But as a senior's concierge business, we will provide seniors with more personal assistance than just errands. As a senior concierge service, we will offer between 10 and 20 additional personalized services to our clients.

Business Operation:
_____ (company name) will open for business on _____ (date) and will maintain the following business hours:
    Monday through Thursday: _____
    Friday: _____
    Saturday: _____
    Sunday: _____

We will also maintain extended holiday hours and be available on an appointment basis.

Business Policies:

The company will invest in customer relationship management software (CRM) and a point of sales (POS) system to track sales and collect customer information, including names, address, email address and other pertinent information, including personal preferences, likes/dislikes, and key dates. This information will be used with email, e-newsletter and direct mail campaigns to build custom marketing programs, establish customer loyalty and drive revenue. The company will offer a 30-day contract cancellation policy to build trust with customers and to improve client retention. Our business serves the following areas in _____ (state): _____ (city) _____ (city) and _____ (city).

Concierge Sales Model:

Our concierge professionals will spend ____ (40?) % of their time building rapport and trust with the client, ____ (30?) % identifying needs and wants, ____ (20?) % presenting possible solutions and ____ (10?) % closing the deal.

2.0.1 Traction (optional)

We will include this section because investors expect to see some traction, both before and after a funding event and investors tend to judge past results as a good indicator of future projections. It will also show that we can manage our operations and develop a business model capable of funding inventory purchases. Traction will be the best form of market research.

Period   _____
Product/Service Focus   _____
Our Sales to Date: _____
Our Number of Users to Date: _____
Number of Repeat Users   _____
Number of Pending Orders: _____
Value of Pending Orders: _____
Reorder Cycle Period: _____
Key Reference Sites   _____
Mailing List Subscriptions   _____
Competitions/Awards Won   _____
Notable Product Reviews   _____
Actual Percent Gross Profit Margin   _____
Industry Average: GPM   _____
Actual B/(W) Industry Average   _____

Note: Percent Gross Profit Margin equals the sales receipts less the cost of goods sold divided by sales receipts multiplied by 100.

2.1 Company Ownership

_____ (company name) is a _____ (Sole-proprietorship /Corporation/LLC) and is registered to the owner, _____ (owner name). It will be registered as a Subchapter S, with ownership _____ (owner name) ____ % and _____ (owner name) ____ %. The owner is a _____ (year) graduate of _____ (institution name), in ____ (city, ____ (state), with a _____ degree. The owner has ____ years of experience as a _____, performing the following roles: _____.
His/her accomplishments include _____.

Ownership Breakdown:

Shareholder Name	Responsibilities	Number and Class of Shares	Percent Ownership

The remainder of the issued and outstanding common shares are retained by the Company for __ (future distribution / allocation under the Company's employee stock option plan).

Shareholder Loans

The Company currently has outstanding shareholder loans in the aggregate sum of $_____. The following table sets out the details of the shareholder loans.

Shareholder Name	Loan Amount	Loan Date	Balance Outstanding

Directors

The Company's Board of Directors, which is made up of highly qualified business and industry professionals, will be a valuable asset to the Company and be instrumental to its development. The following persons will make up the Board of Directors of the Company:

Name of Person	Educational Background	Past Industry Experience	Other Companies Served

2.2 Company Liability Protection

The business will consider the need to acquire the following types of insurances. This will require extensive comparison shopping, through several insurance brokers, listed with our state's insurance department:
1. Workman's Compensation,

2. Business Policy: Property & Liability Insurance
3. Health insurance.
4. Commercial Vehicle Insurance
5. Professional Liability (Errors and Omissions Insurance)

Workman's compensation covers employees in case of harm attributed to the workplace. The property and liability insurance protects the building from theft, fire, natural disasters, and being sued by a third party. Employee health insurance will be provided for the full-time employees. Professional Liability Insurance is important when a business is involved with contracts. Life and Disability Insurance may be required if a bank loan is obtained.

Liability Insurance includes protection in the face of day-to-day accidents, unforeseen results of normal business activities, and allegations of abuse or molestation, food poisoning, or exposure to infectious disease.
Property Insurance - Property Insurance should take care of the repairs less whatever deductible you have chosen.
Loss of Income Insurance will replace our income during the time the business is shut-down. Generally, this coverage is written for a fixed amount of monthly income for a fixed number of months.
Product Liability Insurance covers injuries caused by products that are designed, sold or specified by the business.

To help save on insurance cost and claims, management will do the following:
1. Stress employee safety in our employee handbook.
2. Screen employees with interview questionnaires and will institute pre-employment drug tests and comprehensive background checks.
3. Videotape our equipment and inventory for insurance purposes.
4. Create an operations manual that shares safe techniques.
5. Limit the responsibilities that we choose to accept in our contracts.
6. Consider the financial impact of assuming the exposure ourselves.
7. Establish loss prevention programs to reduce the hazards that cause losses.
8. Consider taking higher deductibles on anything but that which involves liability insurance because of third-party involvement.
9. Stop offering services that require expensive insurance coverage or require signed releases from clients using those services.
10. Improve employee training and initiate training sessions for safety.
11. Require Certificate of Insurance from all subcontractors.
12. Make staff responsible for a portion of any damages they cause.
13. We will investigate the setting-up of a partial self-insurance plan.
14. Convince underwriters that our past low claims are the result of our ongoing safety programs and there is reason to expect our claims will be lower than industry averages in the future.
15. At each renewal, we will develop a service agreement with our broker and get their commitment to our goals, such as a specific reduction in the number of incidents.
16. We will assemble a risk control team, with people from both sides of our

business, and broker representatives will serve on the committee as well.
17. When an employee is involved in an accident, we will insist on getting to the root cause of the incident and do everything possible to prevent similar incidents from re-occurring.
18. At renewal, we will consult with our brokers to develop a cost-saving strategy and decide whether to bid out our coverage for competitive quotes or stick with our current carrier.
19. We will set-up a captive insurance program, as a risk management technique, where our business will form its own insurance company subsidiary to finance its retained losses in a formal structure.
20. Review named assets (autos and equipment), drivers and/or key employees identified on policies to make sure these assets and people are still with our company.
21. As a portion of our business changes, that is, closes, operations change, or outsourcing occurs, we will eliminate unnecessary coverage.
22. We will make sure our workforce is correctly classified by our workers' compensation insurer and liability insurer because our premiums are based on the type of workers used.
23. We will become active in Trade Organizations or Professional Associations, because as a benefit of membership, our business may receive substantial insurance discounts.
24. We will adopt health specific changes to our work place, such as adopting a no smoking policy at our company and allow yoga or weight loss classes to be held in our break room.
25. We will consider a partial reimbursement of health club membership as a benefit.
26. We will find out what employee training will reduce rates and get our employees involved in these programs.

The required business insurance package will be provided by _____ (insurance carrier name). The business will open with a ____ (#) million-dollar liability insurance policy, with an annual premium cost of $ _____.

All required licenses to own and operate a small business of this type will be obtained through the local city and county government offices.

The concierge business will need to acquire the following special licenses to operate:
- A sales tax license is required through the State Department of Revenue.
- A County and/or City Occupational License.

Note: In most states, you are legally required to obtain a business license, and a dba certificate. A business license is usually a flat tax assessment and a percentage of Your gross income. A dba stands for Doing Business As, and it is the registration of Your trade name if you have one. You will be required to register your trade name Within 30 days of starting your business. Instead of registering a dba, you can simply form an LLC or Corporation and it will have the same effect, namely register business name.

Resources:
Workers Compensation Regulations
> http://www.dol.gov/owcp/dfec/regs/compliance/wc.htm#IL

New Hire Registration and Reporting
> www.homeworksolutions.com/new-hire-reporting-information/

State Tax Obligations
> www.sba.gov/content/learn-about-your-state-and-local-tax-obligations

Resource:
www/sba.gov/content/what-state-licenses-and-permits-does-your-business-need

Note: Check with your local County Clerk and state offices or Chamber of Commerce to make sure you follow all legal protocols for setting up and running your business.
Note: To find out about your local business licensing office, visit SBA.gov. This government website compiles information on business licenses and permits at the state level.

Resources:

Production Insurance	www.productioninsurance.com
Insurance Information Institute	www.iii.org/individuals/business/
National License Directory	www.sba.gov/licenses-and-permits
Concierge Association Insurance	www.iceaweb.org
American Family Insurance	www.amfam.com
ICLMA	www.iclma.org
USA.gov	www.usa.gov/Topics/Seniors.shtml
Independent Insurance Agents & Brokers of America	www.iiaa.org
Find Law	http://smallbusiness.findlaw.com/starting-business/starting-business-licenses-permits/starting-business-licenses-permits-guide.html
Business Licenses	www.iabusnet.org/business-licenses
National Association of Surety Bond Producers	www.nasbp.org
Legal Zoom	www.legalzoom.com

2.3   Start-up To-Do Checklist

1. Describe your business concept and model, with special emphasis on planned multiple revenue streams and services to be offered.
2. Create Business Plan and Opening Menu of Products and Services.
3. Determine our startup costs of Senior Concierge Service business, and operating capital and capital budget needs.
4. Seek and evaluate alternative financing options, including SBA guaranteed loan, equipment leasing, social networking loan (www.prosper.com) and/or a family loan (www.virginmoney.com).
5. Do a name search: Check with County Clerk Office or Department of Revenue and Secretary of State to see if the proposed name of business is available.
6. Decide on a legal structure for business.
    Common legal structure options include Sole Proprietorship, Partnership,

Corporation or Limited Liability Corporation (LLC).
7. Make sure you contact your State Department of Revenue, Secretary of State, and the Internal Revenue Service to secure EIN Number and file appropriate paperwork. Also consider filing for Sub-Chapter S status with the Federal government to avoid the double taxation of business profits.
8. Protect name and logo with trademarks, if plan is to go national.
9. Find a suitable location with proper zoning.
10. Research necessary permits and requirements your local government imposes on your type of business. (Refer to: www.business.org)
11. Call for initial inspections to determine what must be done to satisfy Fire Marshall and Building Inspector requirements.
12. Adjust our budget based on build-out requirements.
13. Negotiate lease or property purchase contract.
14. Obtain a building permit.
15. Obtain Federal Employee Identification Number (FEIN).
16. Obtain State Sales Tax ID/Exempt Certificate.
17. Open a Business Checking Account.
18. Obtain Merchant Credit Card Account.
19. Obtain City and County Business Licenses
20. Create a prioritized list for equipment, furniture and décor items.
21. Comparison shop and arrange for appropriate insurance coverage with product liability insurance, public liability insurance, commercial property insurance and worker's compensation insurance.
22. Locate and purchase all necessary equipment and furniture prior to final inspections.
23. Get contractor quotes for required alterations.
24 Manage the alterations process.
25. Obtain information and price quotes from possible distributors.
26. Set a tentative opening date.
27. Install 'Coming Soon' sign in front of building and begin word-of-mouth advertising campaign.
28. Document the preparation, project and payment process flows.
29. Create your accounting, purchasing, payroll, marketing, loss prevention, employee screening and other management systems.
30. Start the employee interview process based on established job descriptions and interview criteria.
31. Contact and interview the following service providers: uniform service, security service, trash service, utilities, telephone, credit card processing, bookkeeping, cleaning services, etc.
32. Schedule final inspections for premises.
33. Correct inspection problems and schedule another inspection.
34. Set a Grand Opening date after a month of regular operations to get the bugs out of the processes.
35. Make arrangements for website design.
36. Train staff.
37. Schedule a couple of practice lessons for friends and interested prospects.

38. Be accessible for direct customer feedback.
39. Distribute comment cards and surveys to solicit more constructive feedback.
40. Remain ready and willing to change your business concept and offerings to suit the needs of your actual customer base.

2.3.1   EMPLOYER RESPONSIBILITIES CHECKLIST

1. Apply for your SS-4 Federal Employer Identification Number (EIN) from the Internal Revenue Service. An EIN can be obtained via telephone, mail or online.
2. Register with the State's Department of Labor (DOL) as a new employer. State Employer Registration for Unemployment Insurance, Withholding, and Wage Reporting should be completed and sent to the address that appears on the form. This registration is required of all employers for the purpose of determining whether the applicants are subject to state unemployment insurance taxes.
3. Obtain Workers Compensation and Disability Insurance from an insurer. The insurance company will provide the required certificates that should be displayed.
4. Order Federal Tax Deposit Coupons – Form 8109 – if you didn't order these when you received your EIN. To order, call the IRS at 1-800-829-1040; you will need to give your EIN. You may want to order some blanks sent for immediate use until the pre-printed ones are complete. Also ask for the current Federal Withholding Tax Tables (Circular A) – this will explain how to withhold and remit payroll taxes, and file reports.
5. Order State Withholding Tax Payment Coupons. Also ask for the current Withholding Tax Tables.
6. Have new employees complete an I-9 Employment Eligibility Verification form. You should have all employees complete this form prior to beginning work. Do not send it to Immigration and Naturalization Service – just keep it with other employee records in your files.
7. Have employees complete aW-4 Employees Withholding Allowance Certificate.

2.4.0   Company Location

_____ (company name) will be located in the _____ (complex name) in _____ (city), ___ (state). It is situated on a _____ (turnpike/street/avenue) just minutes from _____ (benchmark location), in the neighborhood of _____. It borders a large parking lot which is shared by all the businesses therein.

The location has the following advantages:
　　It is easy to locate and accessible to a number of major roadways.
　　Good visibility
　　Plentiful parking.
　　Proximity to _____ and _____ growth areas.
　　Reasonable rent.

Convenient access to both consumers and commercial accounts.

2.4.1   Company Facilities

_____ (company name) signed a _____ (#) year lease for _____ (#) square foot space. The cost is very reasonable at $____/sq. foot. We also have the option of expanding into an additional _____ sq. ft. of space or subletting our space. The facilities will include office space for the principals, outside sales rep and bookkeeper, conference room, restrooms and storage area.

2.5.0   Start-up Summary

Start-up costs for the Senior Concierge Service business will be financed through a combination of owner investment and a short-term bank loan. The start-up costs for this company are approximately $ _____ and can be broken down in the following major categories:

			Estimate
1.	Office Equipment	$_____	($5000?)
	Includes computer system, fax machine, cellular phones, answering machine/voice mail, pager, etc.		
2.	Software for website, accounting and contact management	$_____	($1000?)
2.	Office Fixtures	$_____	($2000?)
	Includes electronic cash register, work tables, accounting software, desks, filing cabinets, fixtures, furniture, etc.		
3.	Office Supplies Inventory	$_____	($1000?)
4.	Working Capital	$_____	($3000?)
	For day-to-day operations, including payroll, internet access, insurance, accounting services, etc.		
5.	Home Office Remodeling	$_____	($2000?)
	Includes architect, lighting update, flooring, etc.		
6.	Start-up Marketing/Advertising Expenses	$_____	($5000?)
7.	Rent and Utility Deposits	$_____	($1000?)
8.	Contingency Fund	$_____	
9.	Other	$_____	
	Includes website design, legal expenses, etc.		
Total:		$_____	

The company will require $_____ in initial cash reserves and additional $_____ in assets. The start-up costs are to be financed by the equity contributions of the owner in the amount of $_____, as well as by a ____ year commercial loan in the amount of $_____. The funds will be repaid through earnings.

The required business insurance package will be provided by _____(insurance carrier name). The business will open with a ____ (#) million-dollar Business Liability Insurance Policy, with an annual premium cost of $ ____. The company will also explore

Employee Dishonesty Bonds to protect the business from dishonest acts by employees. All required licenses to own and operate a small business of this type will be obtained through the local city and county government offices.

The legal fees will be used for the formation of the business entity, as well as for the generation of standard client contracts.

The advertising costs are based on the need to communicate our range of services to perspective clients. The bulk of our advertising will be communications to corporations. Additionally, as we achieve an increase in clients, there will be a need to hire more employees and incur training costs for each employee. We will not bring on new employees initially, and therefore, the start-up costs do not reflect this expense.
The start-up infrastructure costs to pursue business include the following:
1. Call center building.
2. Web development
3. Information partnering
4. Software program development
5. Staff recruitment and training.
6. Promotional overheads.

2.5.1 Inventory

Inventory:	Supplier	Qty	Unit Cost	Total
Packaging Supplies				
Business Forms/Contracts				
Concierge Products/Supplies				
Cleaning Supplies				
Office Supplies				
Computer Supplies				
Marketing Materials				
Misc. Supplies				
Totals:				

2.5.2 Supply Sourcing

Initially, _____ (company name) will purchase all of its equipment from _____ and supplies from _____, the _____ (second/third?) largest supplier in _____ (state), because of the discount given for bulk purchases. However, we will also maintain back-up relationships with two smaller suppliers, namely _____ and _____. These two suppliers have competitive prices on certain products.

2.5.3 Supplier Assessments

We will use the following form to compare and evaluate suppliers, because they will play a major role in our procurement strategies and significantly contribute to our profitability.

	Supplier #1	Supplier #2	Compare
Supplier Name			
Website			
Address			
Contacts			
Annual Sales			
Distribution Channels			
Memberships/Certifications			
Quality System			
Positioning			
Pricing Strategy			
Payment Terms			
Discounts			
Delivery Lead-time			
Return Policy			
Rebate Program			
Technical Support			
Core Competencies			
Primary Product			
Primary Service			
New Products/Services			
Innovative Applications/Uses			
Competitive Advantage			
Capital Intensity			
State of Technology			
Capacity Utilization			
Price Volatility			
Vertical Integration			
References			
Overall Rating			

2.5.4 Equipment Leasing

Equipment Leasing will be the smarter solution allowing our business to upgrade our equipment needs at the end of the term rather than being overly invested in outdated equipment through traditional bank financing and equipment purchase. We also intend to explore the following benefits of leasing some of the required equipment:

1. Frees Up Capital for other uses.
2. Tax Benefits
3. Improves Balance Sheet
4. Easy to add-on or trade-up
5. Improves Cash Flow
6. Preserves Credit Lines
7. Protects against obsolescence
8. Application Process Simpler

Our leasing strategy will also be shaped by the following factors:
1. Estimated useful life of the equipment.

2. How long our business plans to use the equipment.
3. What our business intends to do with the equipment at the end of the lease.
4. The tax situation of our business.
5. The cash flow of our business.
6. Our company's specific needs for future growth.

List Any Leases:

Leasing Company	Equipment Description	Monthly Payment	Lease Period	Final Disposition

Resource:
Innovative Lease Services   http://www.ilslease.com/equipment-leasing/
This company was founded in 1986 and is headquartered in Carlsbad, California. It is accredited by the Better Business Bureau, a longstanding member of the National Equipment Finance Association and the National Association of Equipment Leasing Brokers and is the official equipment financing partner of Biocom.

2.5.5   Funding Source Matrix

Funds Source	Amount	Interest Rate	Repayment Terms	Use

2.5.6   Distribution or Licensing Agreements (if any)

Note: These are some of the key factors that investors will use to determine if we have a competitive advantage that is not easily copied.

Licensor	License Rights	License Term	Fee or Royalty

2.5.7   Trademarks, Patents and Copyrights (if any)

Our trademark will be virtually our branding for life. Our choice of a name for our business is very important. Not only will we brand our business and services forever, but what may be worthless today will become our most valuable asset in the years to come. A trademark search by our Lawyer will be a must, because to be told down the road that we must give up our name because we did not bother to conduct a trademark search would be a devastating blow to our business. It is also essential that the name that we choose suit the expanding product or service offerings that we plan to introduce.

Note: These are some of the key factors that investors will use to determine if we have a competitive advantage that is not easily copied.

___

Resources: Patents/Trademarks www.uspto.gov / Copyright www.copyright.gov

2.5.8 Innovation Strategy (optional)

____ (company name) will create an innovation strategy that is aligned with not only our firm's core mission and values, but also with our future technology, supplier, and manufacturing strategies. The objective of our innovation strategy will be to create a sustainable competitive advantage. Our education and training systems will be designed to equip our staff with the foundations to learn and develop the broad range of skills needed for innovation in all of its forms, and with the flexibility to upgrade skills and adapt to changing market conditions. To foster an innovative workplace, we will ensure that employment policies facilitate efficient organizational change and encourage the expression of creativity, engage in mutually beneficial strategic alliances and allocate adequate funds for research and development. Our radical innovation strategies include _____ to achieve first mover status. Our incremental innovation strategies will include modifying the following _____ (products/services/processes) to give our customers added value for their money.

Resource: https://hbr.org/2015/04/the-5-requirements-of-a-truly-innovative-company

2.5.9 Summary of Sources and Use of Funds

Sources:
Owner's Equity Investment	$ _____
Requested Bank Loans	$ _____
Total:	$ _____

Uses:
Capital Equipment	$ _____
Beginning Inventory	$ _____
Start-up Costs	$ _____
Working Capital	$ _____
Total:	$ _____

2.5.9.1 Funding to Date

To date, _____'s (company name) founders have invested $_____ in _____

(company name), with which we have accomplished the following:
1. _____ (Designed/Built) the company's website
2. Developed content, in the form of ___ (#) articles, for the website.
3. Hired and trained our core staff of __(#) full-time people and ___ (#) part-time people.
4. Generated brand awareness by driving ___ (#) visitors to our website in a ___(#) month period.
5. Successfully _____ (Developed/Test Marketed) ___ (#) new products/services, which compete on the basis of _____.
6. _____ (Purchased/Developed) and Installed the software needed to _____ (manage _____ operations?)
7. Purchased $ _____ worth of _____ (supplies)
8. Purchased $ _____ worth of _____ equipment.

2.6 Start-up Requirements

Start-up Expenses:		Estimates
Legal		400
Accountant		300
Accounting Software Package		3000
Licenses & Permits		300
Office Supplies		300
Marketing Materials		3000
Advertising (2 months)		2000
Contact Management Software		200
Consultants		2000
Insurance (first six months)		800
Rent (2 months security)		3000
Rent Deposit		1500
Utility Deposit		600
DSL Installation/Activation		100
Telephone System Installation		200
Telephone Deposit		200
Credit Card (Zon) Machine		300
Cash Register		1000
Expensed Office Equipment		
Facility Planner/Design		1000
Website Design		2500
Home Renovations/Buildout		2000
Installation Expenses		
Used Delivery Van		7000
Signs		
Other		

Total Start-up Expenses _____ (A)

Start-up Assets:
    Cash Required _____ (T)
    Start-up Equipment _____ (Refer to Below List)
    Start-up Inventory _____
    Other Current Assets _____
    Long-term Assets _____
Total Assets _____ **(B)**
Total Requirements _____ (A+B)

Start-up Funding
Start-up Expenses to Fund _____ (A)
Start-ups Assets to Fund _____ (B)
Total Funding Required: _____ **(A+B)**

Assets
Non-cash Assets from Start-up _____
Cash Requirements from Start-up _____ (T)
Additional Cash Raised _____ (S)
Cash Balance on Starting Date _____ (T+S=U)
Total Assets: _____ **(B)**

Liabilities and Capital
Short-term Liabilities:
Current Borrowing _____
Unpaid Expenses _____
Accounts Payable _____
Interest-free Short-term Loans _____
Other Short-term Loans _____
Total Short-term Liabilities _____ **(Z)**

Long-term Liabilities:
Commercial Bank Loan _____
Other Long-term Liabilities _____
Total Long-term Liabilities _____ **(Y)**

Total Liabilities _____ (Z+Y = C)

Capital
Planned Investment
Owner _____
Family _____
Other _____

Additional Investment Requirement _____
Total Planned Investment _____ **(F)**
Loss at Start-up (Start-up Expenses) (-)_____ **(A)**
Total Capital (=)_____ **(F+A=D)**

Total Capital and Liabilities _____ **(C+D)**
Total Funding _____ (C+F)

2.6.1 Start-up Equipment List

Equipment Type	Model No.	New/ Used	Lifespan	Quantity	Unit Cost	Total Cost
Computer system						
Printer						
Scanner						
Zip Drive						
Fax machine						
Phone system						
Broadband Internet Connection						
Answering machine						
Blackberry PDS Phone						
Accounting Software						
Microsoft Office Software						
Scheduling Software						
Digital Camera						
Cell Phone						
Wheelchair-accessible Van						
Paper Shredder						
Credit Card Processor						
Other						
Total:						

2.6.2 Key On-the-Go Service Providers

1. Verizon Wireless   Wireless internet service.
2. www.PrintMe.com   Print of fax from any device.
3. www.GoToMyPC.com Computer remote access
4. www.efax.com   Local efax number to send and receive faxes.

2.7.0 SBA Loan Key Requirements

In order to be considered for an SBA loan, we must meet the basic requirements:
1. Must have been turned down for a loan by a bank or other lender to qualify for most SBA Business Loan Programs. 2. Required to submit a guaranty, both personal and business, to qualify for the loans. 3. Must operate for profit; be engaged in, or propose to do business in, the United States or its possessions; 4. Have reasonable owner equity to invest; 5. Use alternative financial resources first including personal assets.

All businesses must meet eligibility criteria to be considered for financing under the SBA's 7(a) Loan Program, including: size; type of business; operating in the U.S. or its possessions; use of available of funds from other sources; use of proceeds; and repayment. The repayment term of an SBA loan is between five and 25 years, depending on the lift of the assets being financed and the cash needs of the business.
Working capital loans (accounts receivable and inventory) should be repaid in five to 10 years. The SBA also has short-term loan guarantee programs with shorter repayment terms.

A Business Owner Cannot Use an SBA Loan:

To purchase real estate where the participant has issued a forward commitment to the developer or where the real estate will be held primarily for investment purposes. To finance floor plan needs. To make payments to owners or to pay delinquent withholding taxes. To pay existing debt, unless it can be shown that the refinancing will benefit the small business and that the need to refinance is not indicative of poor management.

SBA Loan Programs:
Low Doc: www.sba.gov/financing/lendinvest/lowdoc.html
SBA Express   www.sba,gov/financing/lendinvest/sbaexpress.html
Basic 7(a) Loan Guarantee Program
    For businesses unable to obtain loans through standard loan programs. Funds can be used for general business purposes, including working capital, leasehold improvements and debt refinancing.
    www.sba.gov/financing/sbaloan/7a.html
Certified Development Company 504 Loan Program
    Used for fixed asset financing such as purchase of real estate or machinery.
    www. Sba.gov/gopher/Local-Information/Certified-Development-Companies/
MicroLoan 7(m) Loan Program
    Provides short-term loans up to $35,000.00 for working capital or purchase of fixtures.
    www.sba.gov/financing/sbaloan/microloans.html

2.7.1 Other Financing Options

1. Grants:
Health care grants, along with education grants, represent the largest percentage of grant giving in the United States. The federal government, state, county and city governments, as well as private and corporate foundations all award grants. The largest percentage of grants are awarded to non-profit organizations, health care agencies, colleges and universities, local government agencies, tribal institutions, and schools. For profit organizations are generally not eligible for grants unless they are conducting research or creating jobs.

    A. Contact your state licensing office.
    B. Foundation Grants to Individuals: www.fdncenter.org
    C. US Grants www.grants.gov
    D. Foundation Center www.foundationcemter.org
    E. The Grantsmanship Center www.tgci.com
    F. Contact local Chamber of Commerce
    G. The Catalog of Federal Domestic Assistance is a major provider of business grant money.
    H. The Federal Register is a good source to keep current with the continually changing federal grants offered.
    I. FedBizOpps is a resource, as all federal agencies must use FedBizOpps to notify the public about contract opportunities worth over $25,000.
    J. Fundsnet Services http://www.fundsnetservices.com/
    K. SBA Women Business Center
    www.sba.gov/content/womens-business-center-grant-opportunities

Local Business Grants
Check with local businesses for grant opportunities and eligibility requirements. For example, Bank of America sponsors community grants for businesses that endeavor to improve the community, protect the environment or preserve the neighborhood.
Resource:
www.bankofamerica.com/foundation/index.cfm?template=fd_localgrants

Green Technology Grants
If you install green technology in the business as a way to reduce waste and make the business more energy efficient, you may be eligible for grant funding. Check your state's Economic Development Commission. This grant program was developed as part of the American Recovery and Reinvestment Act.
Resource: www.recovery.gov/Opportunities/Pages/Opportunities.aspx

2. Friends and Family Lending www.virginmoney.com
3. National Business Incubator Association www.nbia.org/
4. Women's Business Associations www.nawbo.org/
5. Minority Business Development Agency www.mbda.gov/

6. Social Networking Loans www.prosper.com
7. Peer-to-Peer Programs www.lendingclub.com
8. Extended Credit Terms from Suppliers 30/60/90 days.
9. Community Bank
10. Prepayments from Customers
11. Seller Financing: When purchasing an existing Senior Concierge Service.
12. Business Funding Directory www.businessfinance.com
13. FinanceNet www.financenet.gov
14. SBA Financing www.sbaonline.sba.gov
15. Use retirement funds to open a business without taxes or penalty. First, establish a C-corporation for the new business. Next, the C-corporation establishes a new retirement plan. Then, the owner's current retirement funds are rolled over into the C-corporation's new plan. And last, the new retirement plan invests in stock of the C-corporation. Warning: Check with your accountant or financial planner. Resource: http://www.benetrends.com/
16. Business Plan Competition Prizes
www.nytimes.com/interactive/2009/11/11/business/smallbusiness/Competitions-table.html?ref=smallbusiness
17. Unsecured Business Cash Advance based on future credit card transactions.
18. Micro-Loans www.accionusa.org/
19. Private Investors/Angels
20. Kick Starter www.kickstarter.com
21. Tech Stars www.techstars.org
22. Capital Source www.capitalsource.com
 www.msl.com/index.cfm?event=page.sba504
Participates in the SBA's 504 loan program. This program is for the purchase of fixed assets such as commercial real estate and machinery and equipment of a capital nature, which are defined as assets that have a minimum useful life of ten years. Proceeds cannot be used for working capital.
23. Commercial Loan Applications www.c-loans.com/onlineapp/
24. Sharing assets and resources with other non-competing businesses.
25. Angel Investors www.angelcapitaleducation.org
26. The Receivables Exchange http://receivablesxchange.com/
27. Bootstrap Methods: Personal Savings/Credit Card/Second Mortgages
28. Community-based Crowd-funding www.profounder.com
29. On Deck Capital http://www.ondeckcapital.com/
Created the Short-Term Business Loan (up to $100,000.00) for small businesses to get quick access to capital that fits their cash flow, with convenient daily payments.
31. Royalty Lending www.launch-capital.com/
With royalty lending, financing is granted in return for future revenue or company performance, and payback can prove exceedingly expensive if a company flourishes.
32. Stock Loans Southern Lending Solutions, Atlanta. GA.
 Custom Commercial Finance, Bartlesville, OK
A stock loan is based on the quality of stocks, Treasuries and other kinds of

investments in a businessperson's personal portfolio. Possession of the company's stock is transferred to the lender's custodial bank during the loan period.

33. Lender Compatibility Searcher   www.BoeFly.com
34. Strategic Investors
    Strategic investing is more for a large company that identifies promising technologies, and for whatever reason, that company may not want to build up the research and development department in-house to produce that product, so they buy a percentage of the company with the existing technology.
35. Bartering
36. Small Business Investment Companies   www.sba.gov/INV
37. Cash-Value Life Insurance
38. Employee Stock Option Plans   www.nceo.org
39. Venture Capitalists   www.nvca.org
40. Initial Public Offering (IPO)
41. Meet investors through online sites, including LinkedIn (group discussions), Facebook (BranchOut sorts Facebook connections by profession), and CapLinked (enables search for investment-related professionals by industry and role).
42. SBA Community Advantage Approved Lenders
    www.sba.gov/content/community-advantage-approved-lenders
43. Small Business Lending Specialists
    https://www.wellsfargo.com/biz/loans_lines/compare_lines
    http://www.bankofamerica.com/small_business/business_financing/
    https://online.citibank.com/US/JRS/pands/detail.do?ID=CitiBizOverview
    https://www.chase.com/ccp/index.jsp?pg_name=ccpmapp/smallbusiness/home/page/bb_business_bBanking_programs
44. Startup America Partnership   www.s.co/about
    Based on a simple premise: young companies that grow create jobs. Once startups apply and become a Startup America Firm, they can access and manage many types of resources through a personalized dashboard.
45. United States Economic Development Administration   www.eda.gov/
46. Small Business Loans   http://www.iabusnet.org/small-business-loans
47. Tax Increment Financing (TIF)
    A public financing method that is used for subsidizing redevelopment, infrastructure, and other community-improvement projects. TIF is a method to use future gains in taxes to subsidize current improvements, which are projected to create the conditions for said gains. The completion of a public project often results in an increase in the value of surrounding real estate, which generates additional tax revenue. Tax Increment Financing dedicates tax increments within a certain defined district to finance the debt that is issued to pay for the project. TIF is often designed to channel funding toward improvements in distressed, underdeveloped, or underutilized parts of a jurisdiction where development might otherwise not occur. TIF creates funding for public or private projects by borrowing against the future increase in these property-tax revenues.
48. Gust   https://gust.com/entrepreneurs
    Provides the global platform for the sourcing and management of early-stage investments. Gust enables skilled entrepreneurs to collaborate with the smartest

investors by virtually supporting all aspects of the investment relationship, from initial pitch to successful exit.

49. Goldman Sachs 10,000 Small Businesses   http://sites.hccs.edu/10ksb/
50. Earnest Loans   www.meetearnest.com
51. Biz2Credit   www.biz2credit.com
52. Funding Circle   www.fundingcircle.com
    A peer-to-peer lending service which allows savers to lend money directly to small and medium sized businesses
53. Lending Club   www.lendingclub.com
54. Equity-based Crowdfunding   www.Indiegogo.com
                            www.StartEngine.com
                            www.SeedInvest.com
55. National Funding   www.nationalfunding.com
    Their customers can to get working capital, merchant cash advances, credit card processing, and, equipment leasing.
56. Quick Bridge Funding   www.quickbridgefunding.com
    Offers a flexible and timely financing program to help assist small and medium sized businesses achieve their goals.
57. Kabbage   www.kabbage.com
    The industry leader in providing working capital online.

Resource: www.sba.gov/category/navigation-structure/starting-managing-business/starting-business/local-resources

http://usgovinfo.about.com/od/moneymatters/a/Finding-Business-Loans-Grants-Incentives-And-Financing.htm

3.0 Products and Services

In this section, we will not only list all of our planned products and services, but also describe how our proposed products and services will be differentiated from those of our competitors and solve a real problem or fill an unmet need in the marketplace.

Services:

_____ (company name) will provide a wide range of services for our customers. We will target seniors and their families. Seniors often have mobility problems and are seeking to improve the life balance. We plan to utilize specialized software to help our clients keep track of preferences, to-do lists and issue personal email reminders.

We will offer the following assortment of senior concierge services:

Entertainment Shopping:

Dining reservations & suggestions	Concert, sports & theatre tickets
Adult education classes	Spas & salon suggestions
Party ideas & planning	Day trip ideas
Flowers	Gift baskets
Gift ideas	Locate hard to find items
Purchase items	Research & compare products
Plan summer vacation	

City Specific Information

Complete retail business profiles	Laundry & dry cleaning services
Pet care & dog walkers	Movers & storage
Internet & wireless services	Utility comparison
Referrals for household services	

Senior Errands

Pick up & drop off laundry	Wait at home service
Package shipping	Dry cleaning drop-offs
Merchandise exchange	DMV Line waits
Meal pick-up	Mail drop-off
Grocery shopping	Pick up prescriptions
Procure theater tickets	Video returns
Sending and checking emails	Mailing letters
Watering plants	Taking care of pets
Notary Services	

Transportation Services (We will take the client to):

- Grocery	- Doctor Visits
- Beauty Salon	- Pharmacy

Pet Care

- Walking	- Boarding

    - Vet Visits   - Pet Feeding

Luxury Services
- Private Jet Charter   - Vacation Booking
- Wine Concierge

Daily Care
- Daily visits   - Daily calls
- Doctor communication   - Wellness Watch

Car Maintenance
- Detailing   - Maintenance
- Insurance Monitoring

Personal Appearance
- Exercise   - Massage
- Makeup Application

Continuing Education
- Cell Phone Training   - Computer Training
- Letter Writing

Relocation Assistance
Relocation Consultations   Life Management Needs Assessment
Simplicity Budget Requirements   Family Needs
Pre-Visit Area Orientation   Area Orientation Booklets
Home Finding Assistance   Country, Language, & Area
Orientation   Cultural Transition
Full Global / Domestic Relocation   Relocation Adjustment
Transitional Services

Personal & Virtual Assistants
Bill paying   Personal shopping

Real Property Management
House Sitting   House Cleaning
Storm Boarding   House Repairs
Vacation home checking   Pet sitting
Light housekeeping   Plant care
Maid service   Hang art

Party Planning
Networking events   Socializing Events

Resources:
https://seniorservicebusiness.com/start-your-senior-concierge-business-with-these-40-

profitable-services/
Examples: http://parentyourparents.com/services/

3.0.1 Service Descriptions

In creating our service descriptions, we will provide answers to the following types of questions:
1. What does the service do or help the customer to accomplish?
2. Why will people decide to buy it?
3. What makes it unique or a superior value?
4. How expensive or difficult is it to make or copy by a competitor?
5. How much will the service be sold for?

House Sitting Service
Many retirees look for an opportunity to travel to warmer climates during the winter. We will provide a house sitter to manage the property and gardens while the retirees are visiting family. We will care for their exotic plants, accept deliveries, water the gardens, sort mail, and generally care for the home while the seniors are away.

Home Staging Service
We will help seniors to prepare their homes for sale. Our Home Staging Service will help seniors to get top dollar for their homes. A professionally staged home will sell faster and for more money. We will tackle the preparation of a home for sale. This service will include: Clean Out Garages, Clean the House, Pack Up Excess Items, Organize, De-Clutter, De-Personalize, Sort Household Contents, and Coordinate Home Repairs and Painting Services.

Transportation Service
Many community transportation systems, such as public and para-transit (specialized transportation service for persons who are unable to use regular public transportation due to a disability or health-related condition), are not considered senior friendly because many seniors can't walk to a bus stop, can't easily get into or out of a van, or can't afford a taxi. We will provide seniors with reliable, comfortable transportation with sensitive, responsible drivers who will wait for them at the doctor's office, escort them when shopping and running errands, and most important, be where they're supposed to be on time so the client is not left waiting. Note: This service will require additional insurance and bonding.

Senior Transitional Services
We will offer this service for non-medical issues and logistics. We will be there to assist with admission or discharge planning, transportation services, packing up belongings, picking up prescriptions or stocking the refrigerator for a client's return home. We will coordinate with treatment facilities or at-home care providers to make sure everything is in order. We will take all the time we need to make sure our clients are comfortable and comforted in their new surroundings.

Referral Service
We will first check the references of all vendors, and then ask them to sign a contract in which they agree to pay us a yearly fee to participate in the service, plus a _____ (10?) % commission on any business that results in a sale. We will match the needs of our seniors to a large group of highly-trained professionals who offer the following services:

Massage Therapy	Acupuncture Therapy
Physical Therapy	In-Home Hairdressing & Makeup
Medication/Interaction Review	Nutrition Counseling
Personal Food Preparation	Investment/Financial Services
Counseling/Psychotherapy	Chiropractic Care
Elder Law Services	Medical Services
Organization	Moving Services
Handyman Services	Lawn Services
Pet Care	House Cleaning
Home Modifications	Chair Lifts/Assistive Devices
Bookkeeping Services	Homemaker Services
Evaluate Assisted Living Facilities	Senior Matchmaking Services

Our referral list will be thoroughly checked to make certain each is a reputable provider of senior care services and adheres to the highest standards of business practice. We will follow up each referral to be certain the work met the client's expectations. We will also periodically use customer satisfaction surveys to check to make sure that the client's needs are still being properly served.

Well-being Services
Our Well-being services will help seniors to navigate the health care system, pay bills, and compare insurance programs and providers. The service will also engage in patient advocacy and record keeping, book medical appointments, date reminders, and transportation, and order medication and monitor conditions.

Companionship Services
This service provides supportive companionship services in an effort to maintain the independence of persons ___ (60?) years of age and older who are homebound and dependent on a caregiver for support. This service will provide companionship activities for a client in his or her home. The companion may also accompany the client and provide transportation to access services outside of the home.

Senior Care Management Planning Services
We will develop and implement customized, creative and informed senior care planning solutions for our clients. We will have the expertise to asses, design a plan of care, coordinate services, provide family support, and much more at a fraction of the cost traditionally charged by Geriatric Care managers. Every prospective client will get a free consultation with our lead care manager, who will work with the individual and their family, trustee or guardian to put together a comprehensive care plan. Based on the unique personality and needs of the client. We will develop a plan and determine which concierge is the best match. The assigned concierge will then provide flexible and

continuous communication between the client, their family or guardian to ensure exceptional, personalized care. Our care plans will be customized to meet individualized needs, and cover the following areas: care coordination, care supervision, advocacy, observation and reporting, and problem solving.

3.0.2 Our Service Plans

1. **Specific Need Care**
   This service will be designed to meet the needs of the client or their loved ones through preplanning based on specific needs. The service is completely customized and outlines the dates and times of requested services.

2. **Guaranteed Care**
   This service will be pre-purchased in refillable "blocks" of hours that can be used at any time. This will ensure that the client has the concierge service available when needed.

3. **Now Service**
   This service is designed to meet the client's needs in the moment. We will run an isolated or one-time errand for the client or take them where they need to go upon receiving the request.

3.1 Recap of Service Benefits

- Achieve a significant reduction and elimination of stress.
- Do the upfront research to locate and interview service providers who provide first class service.
- Provide relevant information and education concerning available services, events and activities in the Metropolitan Area.
- Handle unexpected emergencies.
- Facilitate many of your personal activities which allow you to focus on your strategic life and personal interests.
- Put your senior concierge to work for you to handle your routine chores or unpleasant tasks.
- Provide temporary assistance when you need it for the number of hours that you need per month or annually.
- Honor our strict confidential service agreement to ensure exclusive confidentiality to our clients.
- Schedule family vacations, dinner reservations, purchasing tickets on client's behalf while providing an elite caregiver to not only transport, but accompany the client throughout their special event.
- Enable attendance at the symphony, play, theater event, charity event, museums, and

more.
Attend a ceremony honoring the individual or a charitable event for a favorite organization.
Lunching out to favorite restaurants.
Accompany client to the spa; arrange a therapeutic massage, pedicure, or manicure.
Assistance with pet appointments and needs for grooming and care.
Assist with or doing retail shopping, personal shopping for gifts, clothing, etc.
Accompany on a trip out of town to visit family or friends.
Arrange for individualized transport for travel.
Assistance for dinner out with family or a special family gathering/reunion.

3.2 Production of Products and Services

We will use the following methods to locate the best suppliers for our business:
- Attend trade shows to spot upcoming trends, realize networking opportunities and compare prices.

- Subscribe to appropriate trade magazines, journals, newsletters and blogs.

Senior Magazine
AARP Magazine
Living Well Magazine			www.livingwellmag.com
Girl Friendz Magazine	www.girlfriendzmag.com/2011/08/senior-concierge-services/

- Join our trade association to make valuable contacts, get listed in any online directories, and secure training and marketing materials.

The International Concierge and Lifestyle Management Association   http://iclma.org/
 The world's leading professional association designed to support concierge and lifestyle management professionals looking to build a strong business.

Aging 2.0		https://www.aging2.com/
A San Francisco-based organization that promotes entrepreneurship and innovation in the longevity market.

Resource: http://www.seniorconciergeservices.net/RESOURCES.html

3.3 Competitive Comparison

_____ (company name) does not have to pay for under-utilized staff or facilities. Our flexible employee scheduling procedures and use of part-timers ensure that the company is never overstaffed during slow times. We will also adopt a pay-for-performance compensation plan, and use independent commissioned sales reps and referral incentives to generate new business.

We will reinvest major dollars every year in professional and educational materials. We will attend frequent seminars to bring clients the finest selection of services, and industry trend information.

We also have an extremely flexible schedule, which is designed to meet client needs. Our prices are competitive with other local Senior Concierge Services that offer far less in the way of membership benefits, plan options, innovative services, etc. We will offer clients a 100% Satisfaction Guarantee and continuously monitor client feedback with customer satisfaction surveys.

3.4   Sales Literature

____ (company name) has developed sales literature that illustrates a professional organization with vision. ____ (company name) plans to constantly refine its marketing mix through a number of different literature packets. These include the following:
- direct mail with introduction letter and product price sheet.
- product information brochures
- press releases
- new product/service information literature
- email marketing campaigns
- website content
- corporate brochures

A copy of our corporate informational brochure is attached in the appendix of this document. This brochure will be available to provide referral sources, leave at seminars, and use for direct mail purposes.

3.5   Fulfillment

The key fulfillment and delivery of services will be provided by our director/owner, and certified store associates. The real core value is the industry expertise of the founder, and staff experience and company training programs.

3.7   Technology

___(company name) will employ and maintain the latest technology to enhance its office management, inventory management, payment processing, task time logging, customer profiling and record keeping systems.

Resources:
VA Manager   www.virtualassistantmanager.com/concierge_software.php
Task Manager   www.goconcierge.net/home/

Outright.com
The cost is way below what it costs to pay a bookkeeper, around $12 a month, and it has a built-in scheduling feature that can track work hours and prepare an invoice for a client. It even reminds users when taxes are due, or when a deduction is missed, like the 55 cents per mile for business mileage.

Mobile POS Systems

Vend www.vendhq.com/
A retail POS software, inventory management, ecommerce & customer loyalty for iPad, Mac and PC. Easily manage & grow your business in the cloud.

Shopkeep www.shopkeep.com
Charges a monthly fee of $49 per register. It customizes service for retail, quick service, restaurants and bars with features including inventory monitoring, staff management and customer marketing. Administrators can monitor business stats through an online back-end, which also syncs with an iOS app for iPhone. Shopkeep's system can also be integrated with MailChimp to manage emails to a customer listserv and Quickbooks accounting software for an additional fee.

LevelUp www.thelevelup.com/
LevelUp charges a 1.95% rate for every transaction, as well as $50 per scanner, which plugs into most POS systems or the $100 LevelUp Tablet. The scanner reads a QR code displayed on a customer's smartphone or uses near field communication technology to allow the customer to pay with the likes of ApplePay or Google Wallet. LevelUp reminds customers when they have not visited the businesses after a set period of time and provides a rewards program. Customers also have the option of leaving feedback for the owner through the LevelUp app.

Revel http://revelsystems.com/
An award-winning iPad Point of Sale solution for single and multi-location businesses.

Mobile Phone Credit Card Reader https://squareup.com/pos
Square, Inc. is a financial services, merchant services aggregator and mobile payments company based in San Francisco, California. The company markets several software and hardware products and services, including Square Register and Square Order. Square Register allows individuals and merchants in the United States, Canada, and Japan to accept offline debit and credit cards on their iOS or Android smartphone or tablet computer. The app supports manually entering the card details or swiping the card through the Square Reader, a small plastic device which plugs into the audio jack of a supported smartphone or tablet and reads the magnetic stripe. On the iPad version of the Square Register app, the interface resembles a traditional cash register.

Google Wallet https://www.google.com/wallet/
A mobile payment system developed by Google that allows its users to store debit cards, credit cards, loyalty cards, and gift cards among other things, as well as redeeming sales promotions on their mobile phone. Google Wallet can be used NFC to make secure

payments fast and convenient by simply tapping the phone on any PayPass-enabled terminal at checkout.

Apple Pay http://www.apple.com/apple-pay/
A mobile payment and digital wallet service by Apple Inc. that lets users make payments using the iPhone 6, iPhone 6 Plus, Apple Watch-compatible devices (iPhone 5and later models), iPad Air 2, and iPad Mini 3. Apple Pay does not require Apple-specific contactless payment terminals and will work with Visa's PayWave, MasterCard's PayPass, and American Express's ExpressPay terminals. The service has begun initially only for use in the US, with international roll-out planned for the future.
Resource: www.wired.com/2016/01/shadow-apple-pay-google-wallet-expands-online-reach/

WePay https://www.wepay.com/
An online payment service provider in the United States. WePay's payment API focuses exclusively on platform businesses such as crowdfunding sites, marketplaces andsmall business software. Through this API, WePay allows these platforms to access its payments capabilities and process credit cards for the platform's users.

Chirpify
Connects a user's PayPal account with their Twitter account in order to enable payments through tweeting.

Article: www.prnewswire.com/news-releases/tips-to-leverage-mobile-payments-in-your-marketing-strategy-300155855.html

3.8 Future Products and Services

_____ (company name) will continually expand services based on industry trends and changing client needs. We will not only solicit feedback via surveys and comments cards from clients on what they need in the future, but will also work to develop strong relationships with all our clients.

We plan to develop specialized Concierge Service packages targeted on the following niche markets:
1. New Mothers
2. Homemakers
3 Academics
4. Country Club Members

We plan to combine Business Center Services with a Corporate Concierge Service business. The Business Center Service will offer the following kinds of services:
1. Photocopying
2. Video Conferencing
3. Phone Answering
4. PowerPoint Presentations

We also plan to introduce our own line of gift baskets for all of our clients and offer our services via the purchase of our Concierge Certificates.

Specialty Programs

We plan to develop the following types of programs, which will be of vital importance to seniors and their families:

1. Medical Alert Program
2. Family Caregiver Training Programs: a series of online learning materials developed to understand what's happening, what to expect and what you can do.
3. Holiday Service Program: assistance with writing cards, shopping, decorating, preparing special traditional family recipes and much more.
4. Trip Planning Program
5. In-home Assessment Program: includes a written report and recommendations
6. Clutter Organization and Management Programs: includes clutter reduction strategies.

Senior Concierge Service Brokerage

We will refer pre-screened senior service providers for a referral fee and/or we will charge these vetted service providers a monthly fee to be included in our preferred senior services database. For our member clients, we will offer matchmaker and referral services for the following types of specialized service providers:

- Care Management Services
- Private Duty Caregivers
- Senior Expert Shippers and Packers
- Geriatric Medicine
- Senior Nutrition Specialists
- Orthopedic Surgery
- Home Health Care
- Physical, Occupational & Speech Therapy
- Medical Supplies
- Elder Law & Estate Planning
- Financial Planning
- Senior Social Workers
- Drug Interaction Checkers
- Transportation Services
- Organization and Moving Services
- Senior Relocation Specialists
- Fraud Prevention Advisors
- Senior Image and Style Consultants
- Pharmaceutical & Infusion Services
- Life Alert Systems
- Long Term Care Insurance
- Veteran Benefits
- Medicare & Medicaid
- Senior Technology Advisors and Trainers
- Social Security Benefits
- Real Estate Services

Senior Massage Service
We will specialize in massage for seniors to create a secondary revenue stream. This specialized form of massage will be appropriate for many seniors. Deeply restorative and relaxing, it will significantly relieve aches, pains, and stiffness, as well as many health conditions associated with aging.
Source:
http://www.eastbaysmartsenior.com/?p=1250

VIP Membership Program
We will use the following tactics to encourage customers to join our VIP Membership Program:
1. Offer immediate special benefits, such as reduced pricing and exclusive offers.
2. Add customers to our database to receive free monthly e-newsletter with coupons.
3. Develop a quiz that uncovers customer needs and assistance preferences.
4. Make membership joining easy via our website and mobile apps, and card sized application forms.

This program will produce the following benefits:
1. There will be less of a need to reacquire existing customers as more customers will remain in the active status.
2. There will be less need to experiment with inventory choices, because the quiz will help to develop a composite profile of customer needs and wants.
3. More customers will be motivated to make their first purchase, because the first purchase discount will reduce much of their perceived purchase risk.

Localization
Localization (also referred to as "l10n") is the process of adapting a product or content to a specific locale or market. This is also known as the "Theory of Local Relevance", which means that we need to get grounded in and familiar with the communities we operate within. The aim of localization is to give a service the look and feel of having been created specifically for a target market, no matter their language, culture, or location. As a senior concierge service provider, we will customize our offerings to local markets or consumer communities that are growing more focused in terms of ethnicity, wealth, lifestyle, and values. We will roll out different types of vehicle designs, service lines, and alternative approaches to pricing, marketing, staffing, and customer service. Localization and the resulting customization will encourage local experimentation, which will be difficult for competitors to track, let alone replicate. When well executed, localization strategies will provide a durable competitive edge.

Resources:
Globalization and Localization Association   www.gala-global.org
GALA is comprised of members worldwide who specialize in localization, translation, internationalization, and globalization. Every day they help companies, non-profit organizations, and governments communicate effectively to global audiences. They do

this by making sure the content of their clients' communications is culturally sensitive and presented in languages that their audiences understand.

Subscription Box Program
We will develop a subscription program or maintenance plan to generate a steady cash flow. We will try to up-sell customers on a quarterly or semi-annual subscription for oil changes or an annual servicing of the complete exhaust system, including the removal of any salt deposits or rust stops or the patching of any leaks. To improve the chances for customer acceptance of our subscription program, we will do the following:
1. Charge very competitively for our services so the customer realizes a savings for their steady business.
2. Enable hassle-free, automatic monthly Credit Card payments.
3. Do not require a long-term contract or commitment from customers so they are free to terminate the subscription at any time without any hassles or penalties.
4. Use an upfront survey to determine what types of products are more highly desired by specific clients.

Examples:
http://packagesthatcare.com/?utm_source=senioradvisor&utm_medium=email&utm_content=ptcintro&utm_campaign=sa20

Resources:
http://www.digitalbusinessmodelguru.com/
www.senioradvisor.com/blog/senior-products/senior-gifts/packages-that-care/

Expand Range of Services
To become more vital to our good clients, we will become the equivalent of a one stop destination, and offer the following related home services:
1. Snow Removal
2. Yard Maintenance
3. Small odd jobs
4. Dog walking
5. Dog Sitting
6. Window Washing
7. Home Check Service
8. Travel Companion

Service Packages
These service packages will be popular with our senior concierge clients, such as a 10 or 20-hour package for the month at a fixed, slightly reduced price. Offering a package will allow us to plan our schedule more efficiently, as well as improve cash flow, as packages will be paid in advance. We will charge extra for after-hours work or working on holidays, or for rush jobs that need to be done immediately.

4.0 Market Analysis Summary

Our Market Analysis will serve to accomplish the following goals:
1. Define the characteristics and needs and wants of the target market.
2. Serve as a basis for developing sales, marketing and promotional strategies.
3. Influence the e-commerce website design.

_____ (company name) will focus on the following distinct groups:
1. Seniors
2. Families

The biggest challenge facing our company is the perceived notion by the public that Senior Concierge Services are for wealthy people. We will use client testimonials to help correct this misconception.

Corporations hire concierges for their employees because it allows them to have some personal maintenance taken care of during normal business hours. The company also benefits in the following ways:
1. Better employee retention.
2. Keeping the employee at work during the day, yields more productivity and value generation for the company.

Residential property managers will hire us as a full-service Concierge for their hotel or residential properties that cater to people over the age of 55. The on-site or off-site Concierge Desk will put them ahead of their competition and enhances the lives of senior residents.

Currently in _____ (city name), there are ____ (#) Senior Concierge Service providers. We will be targeting senior community centers because the market is under-served, and it can provide larger sales volume and more consistent work.

Our success will be heavily dependent on our development of a network of pre-screened vendor connections.

4.1 Market Research

We will research demographic information for the following reasons:
1. To determine which segments of the population, such as Hispanics and the elderly, have been growing and may now be underserved.
2. To determine if there is a sufficient population base in the designated service area to realize the company's business objectives.
3. To consider what products and services to add in the future, given the changing demographic profile and needs of our service area.

We will pay special attention to the following general demographic trends:

1. Population growth has reached a plateau and market share will most likely be increased through innovation and excellent customer service.
2. Because incomes are not growing, and unemployment is high, process efficiencies and sourcing advantages must be developed to keep prices competitive.
3. The rise of non-traditional households, such as single working mothers, means developing more innovative and personalized programs.
4. As the population shifts toward more young to middle aged adults, ages 30 to 44, and the elderly, aged 65 and older, there will be a greater need for child-rearing and geriatric mobile support services.
5. Because of the aging population, increasing pollution levels and high unemployment, new 'green' ways of dealing with the resulting challenges will need to be developed.

We will collect the demographic statistics for the following zip code(s):
_____

We will use the following sources: www.census.gov, www.zipskinny.com, www.city-data.com, www.demographicsnow.com, www.freedemographics.com, www.ffiec.gov/geocode, www.esri.com/data/esri_data/tapestry and www.claritas.com/claritas/demographics.jsp. This information will be used to decide upon which targeted programs to offer and to make business growth projections.
Resource: www.sbdcnet.org/index.php/demographics.html

Snapshots of consumer data by zip code are also available online:
http://factfinder.census.gov/home/saff/main.html?_lang=en
http://www.esri.com/data/esri_data/tapestry.html
http://www.claritas.com/MyBestSegments/Default.jsp?ID=20

1. **Total Population**   _____
2. **Number of Households**   _____
3. **Population by Race:**   White ____% Black ____%
                                  Asian Pacific Islander ____% Other ____%
4. **Population by Gender**   Male ____% Female ____%
5. **Income Figures:**   Median Household Income $_____
                                  Household Income Under $50K ____%
                                  Household Income $50K-$100K ____%
                                  Household Income Over $100K ____%
6. **Housing Figures**   Average Home Value - $_____
                                  Average Rent $_____
7. **Homeownership**:   Homeowners   %_____
                                  Renters   %_____
8. **Education Achievement**   High School Diploma   %_____
                                  College Degree   %_____
                                  Graduate Degree   %_____
9. **Stability/Newcomers**   Longer than 5 years   %_____
10. **Marital Status**   ___% Married ___% Divorced ___% Single
                                  ___% Never Married ___% Widowed ___% Separated

11.	Occupations	___%Service ___% Sales ___% Management ___% Construction ___% Production ___% Unemployed ___% Below Poverty Level
12.	Age Distribution	___% 20-29 ___% 30-39 ___% 40-49 ___% 50-59 ___% 60-69 ___% 70-79 ___% 80+ years
13.	Prior Growth Rate	_____ % from _____ (year)
14.	Projected Population Growth Rate	_____ %

Secondary Market Research Conclusions:
This area will be demographically favorable for our business for the following reasons:
_____
_____

Resource:
www.allbusiness.com/marketing/segmentation-targeting/848-1.html
http://www.sbdcnet.org/industry-links/demographics-links
http://factfinder2.census.gov/faces/nav/jsf/pages/index.xhtml

4.1.1   Survey Market Research

We will use the following survey questions to develop an Ideal Customer Profile of our client base, so that we can better target our marketing communications and develop our member programs.

The surveys will also be used to gauge the level of interest by prospects and determine what services they would like to see provided.

1. What is the primary benefit you will receive from using our Senior Concierge Services, versus a competing service provider?
2. What is your zip-code? _____
3. Are you single, divorced, separated, widowed or married? _____
4. Are you male or female? _____
5. What is your age? _____
6. What is your approximate income? _____
7. Do you have children? If Yes, what are their ages? _____
8. What are your favorite magazines? _____
9. What is your favorite local newspaper? _____
10. What is your favorite radio station? _____
11. What are your favorite television programs? _____
12. What organizations are you a member of? _____
13. How frequently do/would you use the services of a concierge?
14. Please prioritize the importance of the following factors when choosing a Senior Concierge Service

Scale: 1 to 10   ____ Price   ____ One-stop services
                  ____ Flexibility   ____ Service Quality
                  ____ Overall Value   ____ Design Creativity
                  ____ Inquiry Responsiveness   ____ References
                  ____ Response Timeliness   ____ On Budget

15. In what area of your life would a concierge/errand service be of the most help?
16. What types of errands do you need handled?
17. How much would you expect to pay for this type of timesaver service?
18. Would you like to see this service offered as part of a benefits package at work?
19. How would you prefer to be charged for the service?
    ___ hourly rate ___ monthly member fee ___ combination
20. Describe your experiences with other senior concierge providers.
21. What can we do to improve/differentiate our Senior Concierge Service offerings?
22. What is the best way for us to market our senior concierge services?
23. How did you first hear about senior concierge services?

Comments: _____

We very much appreciate your participation in this survey. If you provide your name, address and email address, we will sign you up for our e-newsletter and enter you into our monthly drawing for a free _____.

Name   Address   Email

4.1.2   Voice of the Customer

To develop a better understanding of the changing needs and wants of our Senior Concierge Service customers, we will institute the following ongoing listening practices:

1. Focus Groups
   Small groups of customers will be invited to meet with a facilitator to answer open-ended questions about priority of needs and wants.
2. Individual Interviews
   We will conduct face-to-face personal interviews to understand customer thought processes, selection criteria and entertainment preferences.
3. Customer Panels
   A small number of customers will be invited to answer open-ended questions on home décor trends on a regular basis.
4. Customer Tours
   We will invite customers to visit our store to discuss how our processes and services can better serve them.
5. Visit Customers
   We will observe customers as they actually use our products to uncover the pains and problems they are experiencing during usage.

6. Trade Show Meetings
   Our trade show booth will be used to hear the concerns of our customers.
7. Toll-free Numbers
   We will attach our phone number to all products and sales literature to encourage the customer to call with problems or positive feedback.
8. Customer Surveys
   We will use surveys to obtain opinions on closed-ended questions, testimonials, constructive feedback, and improvement suggestions.
9. Mystery Shoppers
   We will use mystery shoppers to report on how our employees treat our customers.
10. Salesperson Debriefing
    We will ask our salespeople to report on their customer experiences to obtain insights into what the customer faces, what they want and why they failed to make a sale.
11. Customer Contact Logs
    We will ask our sales personnel to record interesting customer revelations.
12. Customer Serviceperson's Hotline
    We will use this dedicated phone line for service people to report problems.
13. Discussions with competitors.
14. Installation of suggestion boxes to encourage constructive feedback. The suggestion card will have several statements customers are asked to rate in terms of a given scale. There are also several open-ended questions that allow the customer to freely offer constructive criticism or praise. We will work hard to implement reasonable suggestions to improve our service offerings as well as show our commitment to the customer that their suggestions are valued.

4.2 Market Segmentation

Market segmentation is a technique that recognizes that the potential universe of users may be divided into definable sub-groups with different characteristics. Segmentation enables organizations to target messages to the needs and concerns of these subgroups. We will segment the market based on the needs and wants of select customer groups. We will develop a composite customer profile and a value proposition for each of these segments. The purpose for segmenting the market is to allow our marketing/sales program to focus on the subset of prospects that are "most likely" to purchase our senior concierge products and services. If done properly this will help to insure the highest return for our marketing/sales expenditures.

_____ (company name) clients can be divided into the following general groups:
1. Seniors
2. Families

Also, being solicited will be professional service providers like law firms and medical practices. The needs of the employees and clients in all of these types of organizations are fairly similar.

The tasks for the seniors will range considerably, but the primary need is for errands to be run when other family members are at work or otherwise unavailable.

Residential property managers of assisted living and residential care facilities will hire us as a full-service Concierge for their hotel or residential properties. The on-site or off-site Concierge Desk will service the needs of senior residents.

The other major group of clients are seniors. This group has similar needs to the employees of companies, but we will be contracting with them directly. This group can be further broken down into the following categories:
1. Those still at work and do not have the time to accomplish the needed tasks.
2. Those that have done a cost-benefit analysis and decide the benefits outweigh the costs.
3. Those who are not from _____ (city), but need to get something done in _____ (city).
4. Those who are physically incapable of performing the required tasks.

The most likely individuals to use a Senior Concierge Service share the following characteristics:
1. Time-pressured.
2. Affluent retirees.
3. Dual income households.
4. Working moms
5. The sick and handicapped.
6. Seniors
7. Divorced men and women.
8. One-person businesses
9. Travelers/Vacationers

We help seniors to maximize their time. Many of our senior adults have their very own to-do list, which will make them receptive to our referral service. Our concierge services will create more time for community involvement, daily shopping, healthy exercise, interest development, travel and much more.

We will also target airports and hotels where large numbers of strangers enter our town. These are great places to concentrate our marketing efforts as they are filled with seniors in need of services in our area. Vacationers, typically rent homes in resort areas, and require Senior Concierge Services because they do not have the time to establish local connections. They often require the services of personal chefs to satisfy strict dietary requirements and physical therapists.

Composite Ideal Customer Profile:
By assembling this composite customer profile, we will know what customer needs and wants our company needs to focus on and how best to reach our target market. We will use the information gathered from our customer research surveys to assemble the following composite customer profile:

Ideal Customer Profile

Who are they?

age _____
gender _____
occupation _____
location: zip codes _____
income level _____
marital status _____
ethnic group _____
education level _____
family life cycle _____
number of household members _____
household income _____
homeowner or renter _____
association memberships _____
leisure activities _____
hobbies/interests _____
core beliefs _____
Where are they located (zip codes)? _____
Most popular product/service purchased? _____
Lifestyle Preferences? Trendsetter/Trend follower/Other _____
How often do they buy? _____
What are most important purchase factors? Price/Brand Name/Quality/Financing/Sales Convenience/Packaging/Other_____

What is their key buying motivator? _____
How do they buy it? Cash/Credit/Terms/Other_____
Where do they buy it from (locations)? _____
What problem do they want to solve? _____
What are the key frustrations/pains that
these customers have when buying? _____
What search methods do they use? _____
What is preferred problem solution? _____

Table: Market Analysis

		Annual Sales Dollars		
Potential Customers	**Growth**	2017	2018	2019
Senior Friendly Corporations	10%			
Dual-income Families	10%			
Seniors	10%			
Other	10%			
Totals:	**10%**			

Resource: www.disabled-world.com/disability/statistics/senior-american-statistics.php

Helpful Resources:
U.S. Census Bureau Statistics   www.census.gov
U.S. Dept. of Labor/Bureau of Labor Statistics   www.bls.gov/data/home.htm
Encyclopedia of Associations: Trade and Professional Organizations

Dun & Bradstreet Company Profiles
Standard & Poor's Company Profiles

4.3 Target Market Segment Strategy

Our target marketing strategy will involve identifying a group of customers to which to direct our senior concierge products and services. Our strategy will be the result of intently listening to and understanding customer needs, representing customers' needs to those responsible for product production and service delivery, and giving them what they want. In developing our targeted customer messages, we will strive to understand things like: where they work, worship, party and play, where they shop and go to school, how they spend their leisure time, what magazines they read and organizations they belong to, and where they volunteer their time. We will use research, surveys and observation to uncover this wealth of information to get our product details and brand name in front of our customers when they are most receptive to receiving our messaging.

Target Market Worksheet   (optional)

Product Benefits: Actual factor (cost effectiveness, design, performance, etc.) or perceived factor (image, popularity, reputation, etc.) that satisfies what a customer needs or wants. An advantage or value that the product will offer its buyer.

Products Features: One of the distinguishing characteristics of a product or service that helps boost its appeal to potential buyers. A characteristic of a product that describes its appearance, its components, and its capabilities. Typical features include size and color.

Product or Service	**Product/ Service Benefits**	**Product/ Service Features**	**Potential Target Markets**

_____ (company name) intends to target seniors who need service, but do not have the time or physical ability to perform the necessary tasks. We are focusing on community centers because they have a large number of seniors who find a Senior Concierge Service to be a vital lifestyle support system.

Additionally, an employer of seniors would prefer to pay our service to perform the employee's task, as this would allow the employee to remain productive at work. We will offer corporations a discount off our standard hourly rate or a fixed priced contract for a certain number of senior concierge service hours. This will save us the marketing costs of pursing individual clients. We will invoice the corporation on a monthly basis, thus, also saving the labor costs of preparing many individual invoices.

We will target the following niche markets:

1. Hospitals
2. Condos/Apartment Buildings
3. Local Neighborhoods
4. Physical Therapists/Trainers
5. Assisted Living Facilities
6. Seniors Residential Communities
7. Nursing Homes
8. Residential Care Facilities
9. Senior Community Centers
10. Rehabilitation Clinics
11. Support Groups
12. Pharmacies
13. Physicians
14. Church Groups
15. Discharge Planners
16. Libraries
17. Retirement Communities

Target Seniors

We will be a unique personal-service business, offering seniors who are at home, or in an apartment in the ____ County area, a full range of non-medical services that support and enable seniors to continue living independently and safely. Our services will range from accompanying seniors to doctor, manicure, hair, pet appointments; to the mall for shopping; to restaurants for meals; escort to airports; oversee household repairs and other needs.

Target Affluent Seniors

Pew's research shows that affluent and well-educated seniors have become Internet users at substantially higher rates than those in lower income and education brackets. Their research states that, "Among seniors with an annual household income of $75,000 or more, 90% go online and 82% have broadband at home. According to Pew, "Once seniors join the online world, digital technology often becomes an integral part of their daily lives. These older Internet users also have strongly positive attitudes about the benefits of online information in their personal lives." 94% of seniors who use the Internet agree "the Internet makes it much easier to find information today than in the past." We will make it easy for our site and services to be found. This is where SEO will come into play. We will use keywords that people searching for senior concierge use within our site and social media posts and examine and adjust our SEO plan each month. We will also focus on the high-level, personal attention that our agency can provide.
Source: http://corecubed.com/blog/entry/marketing-home-care-how-to-reach-high-net-worth-seniors

Target Senior Travelers

We will enable a traveler visiting a foreign country to obtain in real-time, necessary information, solving the conventional problem that it is inconvenient for a foreigner to hire an interpreter or to obtain necessary information. A client from a foreign country can be contracted and registered through the Internet. The client will be able to in advance access our system to apply for Senior Concierge Service. We will announce on a Web page the content of the application by the foreigner client to the service, providing registered members with competent services in foreign languages.

Target Country Clubs

We will target country clubs because the majority of members are affluent seniors who respect the opinions of other club members. We will seek permission to submit articles to their club newsletter.

Target Pain Management/Rehabilitation Professionals
We will target this group because they work with seniors who have mobility challenges. We will place ads in their trade association journals and offer to speak at their networking events.

Target Hearing and Eyeglass Centers
Target Podiatrists
We will target these medical professionals because they treat problems that are common to most seniors. We will visit these practices and seek to establish a mutual referral relationship with management. We will make them aware of our transport, and prescription pick-up and monitoring services.

Target Hospitals
We will target hospital because we are often engaged by hospitals to accompany patients or clients to and from their residence. We are able to, for instance, communicate with doctors and our clients to ensure proper discharge instructions are followed.

Target Trustees
We will target elder and estate planners and make them aware of our senior concierge services for referral purposes. The Trustee is responsible for investing trust assets during the term of the Trust, making distributions to beneficiaries and filing tax returns. Sometimes the Trustee must make decisions that aren't popular with the beneficiaries in order to follow the provisions of the Trust. A Trustee's job often is more difficult and with more potential for conflict than being Executor.
Resources:
www.elderlawfirm.com/serving-as-executor-or-trustee/
http://info.legalzoom.com/duties-trust-administrator-20450.html

Target Legal Guardians
We will target guardianship attorneys and the County's Guardianship Commissioner and ask about the role we can play, because guardians have the authority to manage the assets of senior citizens, and to choose where they live, whom they associate with, and what medical treatment they receive. Guardian law allows the court to appoint someone to make legal and welfare decisions for them. A legal guardian may be appointed as a limited decision-maker or an all-purpose decision-maker. As an example, nursing home residents may need a general legal guardian to make all their welfare decisions for them.

Target Guardianship Lawyers
Guardianship lawyers advise about the appropriate legal guardianship for particular circumstances. They also help with guardianship forms and other legal paperwork and represent the guardian once one is appointed.
Resources:

https://www.avvo.com/guardianship-lawyer.html
http://family.findlaw.com/guardianship.html
https://attorneys.lawinfo.com/conservatorships/new-york/new-york/
www.neighborhoodchristianlawyer.com/Profiles/Stoops-LaCourse-PLLC4/
    Guardianship.aspx

Target Elder Law Attorneys

Elder Law attorneys use a variety of legal tools and techniques to meet the goals and objectives of their clients. Elder Law attorneys typically work with other professionals in various fields to provide their clients quality service and ensure their needs are met. Using this holistic approach, for example, an Elder Law attorney will address general estate planning issues and will counsel clients about planning for incapacity with alternative decision-making documents. This attorney will also assist clients in planning for possible long-term care needs, including nursing home care. Locating the appropriate type of care, coordinating private and public resources to finance the cost of care, and working to ensure the client's right to quality care are all part of the Elder Law practice. We will make the owners of Elder Law practices, aware of our senior concierge services by visiting their offices and circulating our sales brochures. Elder Law encompasses the following different fields of law:

1. Preservation/transfer of assets seeking to avoid spousal impoverishment when a spouse enters a nursing home.
2. Conservatorships and guardianships
3. Estate planning, including planning for the management of one's estate during life and its disposition on death through the use of trusts, wills and other planning documents.
4. Probate
5. Administration and management of trusts and estates

Resources:
https://www.eldercaredirectory.org/elder-law.htm
www.naela.org/Public/About_NAELA/Public_or_Consumer/Find_an_Elder_Lawyer/
    Find_an_Elder_Lawyer.aspx

Article:
www.newyorker.com/magazine/2017/10/09/how-the-elderly-lose-their-rights

Target Caregivers

We will target caregivers because some seniors do not make decisions on their own due to forgetfulness and illnesses such as dementia. Since most people work full time jobs, taking care of elderly family members can be a burden. Therefore, those family members will be more inclined to enlist our services. We will reach caregivers through their local church groups and social clubs.

Target Adult Day Care Centers

We will distribute our sales brochures and offer to give free seminars on the service options available through senior concierge services.

Target Assisted Living Facilities
These facilities provide a home for seniors who need the types of support services that we provide. We will seek permission to conduct education seminars on how to evaluate the benefits of our concierge services and circulate flyers with discount coupons.

Target Apartment Complexes and Condos
We will target the property managers of these complexes because many seniors downsize to these types of smaller residences. We will seek to make informative presentations at their community meetings.

Target Over-55 Communities
We will ask about running a small classified ad in their monthly newsletter offering our senior concierge services.

Target Hotels and Resorts
We will help the baby boomer guests at local hotels and resorts to experience the attractions and culture of the peoples beyond the gates of these facilities. We will sub-contract our services through the hotel or resort and help the guests to create a truly memorable stay and provide a reason for a return visit.

Target Community Center Managers
We will ask for permission to present an informational seminar about the benefits of working with senior concierge service providers. We will explain how the many advances in health care and communications technologies have allowed senior citizens to be independent and stay independent into their later years.

Target Retirement Communities
We will distribute our flyers in retirement communities and offer to give free seminars on the evolution of senior concierge services and their helpful role in society.

Target Existing Customers
We will target existing customers because they are the bedrock foundation of our business and are:
    Generally, less price sensitive.
    Likely to offer more opportunity for repeat business.
    Offer the potential for recommendations and referrals.
    Are generally more loyal.

Target Realtors
We will target Realtors because they often work with seniors who are having challenges caused by living on their own, and are considering downsizing to a more manageable situation. We will make Realtors aware that we specialize in assisting clients as they move from their home to a care facility, or vice versa.

Target Local Ethnic Groups
Ongoing demographic trends suggest that, in the coming decades, programs will be

serving a population of people which is increasingly diverse in economic resources, racial and ethnic background, and family structure. According to The Kline Group, a market research company, the U.S. is becoming more of a multicultural and mixed nation, where the Hispanic, Black, Asian and multicultural populations are collectively growing two to three times the rate of the White population. Our plan is to reach out to consumers of various ethnic backgrounds, especially Hispanics, who comprise nearly 13 percent of the country's total population. In addition to embarking on an aggressive media campaign of advertising with ethnic newspapers and radio stations, we will set up programs to actively recruit bilingual employees and make our store more accessible via signage printed in various languages based on the store's community. We will accurately translate our marketing materials into other languages. We will enlist the support of our bilingual employees to assist in reaching the ethnic people in our surrounding area through a referral program. We will join the nearest _____ (predominate ethnic group) Chamber of Commerce and partner with _____ (Hispanic/Chinese/Other?) Advocacy Agencies. We will also develop programs that reflect cultural influences and brand preferences.

Target Agencies that Support Seniors
We will contact the following agencies and organizations, and ask how we can play and role and get into their communications loop with seniors:

- AARP
- Administration on Aging (AOA) - Federal government info
- Eldercare Locator - Find information for seniors by geographical area
- Family Caregiver Alliance
- Medicare Info
- National Council on Aging
- Senior Living Map - Locate assisted living facilities, etc.
- Seniornet - Assistance with computers and technology

Helpful Resources:
U.S. census Bureau Statistics   www.census.gov
U.S. Dept. of Labor/Bureau of Labor Statistics   www.bls.gov/data/home.htm

4.4   Market Growth

We will assess the following general factors that affect market growth:
                                              Current Assessment
1. Interest Rates   _____
2. Government Regulations   _____
3. Perceived Environment Impact   _____
4. Consumer Confidence Level   _____
5. Population Growth Rate   _____
6. Unemployment Rate   _____
7. Political Stability   _____

8. Currency Exchange Rate _____
9. Innovation Rate _____
10. Home Sales _____
11. Gasoline Prices _____
12. Overall Economic Health _____

By 2020, nearly 14 million people in the United States will be over the age of 85, and 84 percent of them will want to continue living at home. To do that, more than half will need assistance with daily living activities.

There are over 47 million seniors in America today, and that number is growing by 10,000 every single day! That means lots of new customers for a senior concierge service.

4.4.1 Market Needs

The U.S. population is aging rapidly now that the first Baby Boomers started turning 65 as of 2011. Around 10,000 people turn 65 every day in the United States. By the year 2030, the U.S. government projects there will be 72 million people 65 years or older, representing 20 percent of the U.S. population. Millions of people will be living in their personal homes, retirement homes, apartments, and other types of living arrangement. This is the ideal time to start a senior concierge business with unlimited growth potential to serve this growing niche market.

There are 61.6 million caregivers, according to the 2011 AARP study "Valuing the Invaluable: The Growing Contributions and Costs of Family Caregiving," and one-third of them described their responsibilities as "highly stressful." And, nearly three-fourths of caregivers say their role has caused them to be late for work, take leaves of absence or had other negative impacts on their job performance.

According to AARP, 75 percent of adult children think about their parents' ability to live independently as they get older. In fact, 82 percent of seniors want to stay in their own homes even if they begin to need day-to-day assistance.

Nine out of ten older Americans want to stay in their homes for as long as possible and the 'Village' movement is capturing the imagination of the Boomers. Senior residents of these retirement communities are organizing services for themselves that will allow them to continue to live comfortably in their homes and communities as they age. (Refer to 'Villages' definition in Industry Terms Section).

Research indicates that:
- 5.4 million American are living with Alzheimer's disease.
- One in eight older Americans has Alzheimer's disease.

4.5   Service Business Analysis

In the _____ metro area, there are _____ (#) businesses that fall into the general category of Senior Concierge or Personal Assistant Services.

Medium to large size companies that offer a Senior Concierge Service to their older employees typically create an in-house solution. But, companies continue to struggle to find ways in which they can offer perks to their mature employees at reasonable costs.

Additionally, there is pressure from stakeholders to become more efficient and profitable. This pressure will contribute to the company's use of concierges, as efficiencies can be accomplished by having the baby boomer employees present at work, creating value for the business, rather than out of the office, pursing personal maintenance tasks or attending to family matters.

Although there is a large amount of overlapping between the needs of most senior adults, especially in physically or mentally disabled clients, research reveals that in areas such as travel, baby boomers (55 to 64), retirees (65 to 75) and the very mature (75-plus) have different needs that must be considered. For example, healthy, active grandparents usually in the baby boomer range are increasingly taking their grandchildren on trips. This has created the need to conduct more individualized needs assessments.

4.6   Buyer Characteristics/Patterns

A Buying Pattern is the typical manner in which /buyers consumers purchase goods or services or firms place their purchase orders in terms of amount, frequency, timing, etc. In determining buying patterns, we will need to understand the following:
- Why consumers make the purchases that they make?
- What factors influence consumer purchases?
- The changing factors in our society.

According to research, the top-five requests from concierge service providers were as follows:
1. Postal services, including mailing letters and packages, and purchasing stamps
2. Food pick up/delivery
3. Automobile service, such as taking cars to get oil changes
4. Courier services, such as delivering items anywhere within a 35-mile radius.
5. Information research for trip/vacation/hospital event planning.

To better service the needs of our clients, we will develop a Senior Concierge Client Profile for each client and then a composite profile of the ideal client. The profile will record the following information:
1. Contact information   2.   Personal Service Information

3. Demographic Information   4. Entertainment Preferences
5. Recreation/Hobby Interests   6. Favorites
7. Interests   8. Area Preferences
9. Personal Service Preferences   10. Travel Preferences
11. Health Issues   12. Description of Current Tasks
13. Restaurant Preferences   14. Payment Information

4.7 Competitive Analysis

Competitor analysis in marketing and strategic management is an assessment of the strengths and weaknesses of current and potential competitors. This analysis will provide both an offensive and defensive strategic context through which to identify our business opportunities and threats.

Competitive factors include breadth and depth of available stock, product knowledge, customer service, expense management, marketing programs, employee training and productivity, management of detailed customer information in databases, extended hours of operation, incoming and outgoing delivery efficiencies, customer loyalty programs, pricing, and branded reputation.

Additionally, we are aware of the importance of cultivating personal relationships with our neighborhood residents, so we can develop a long-term loyal customer base.

We will conduct good market intelligence for the following reasons:
1. To forecast competitors' strategies.
2. To predict competitor likely reactions to our own strategies.
3. To consider how competitors' behavior can be influenced in our own favor.

Our current competitors are listed under "errands and miscellaneous service" headings in the yellow pages and they primarily target _____(individuals) as opposed to _____ (corporations). While some corporations have in-house concierges, they are less efficient at providing the service than we are. We can provide Senior Concierge Services to companies and their families at a lower rate because this is our core competency, and we have worked hard to develop process efficiencies.

Resource:
We will check with 'The International Concierge & Lifestyle Management Network' database to see what companies are operating in our area.
Source: https://iclmnet.wildapricot.org/The-Directory

Competitive analysis conducted by the company owners has shown that there are _____ (# or no other?) Senior Concierge Service providers currently offering the same combination of products and services in the _____ (city) area. However, the existing competitors offer only a limited range of traditional Senior Concierge Services. In fact, of these, _____ (# or none) of the competitors offered a range of Senior Concierge

Services comparable with what _____ (company name) plans to offer to its customers.

Competitor	What We Can Do and They Can't	What They Can Do and We Can't

Self-assessment

Competitive Rating Assessment: 1 = Weak ....5 = Strong

	Our Company	Prime Competitor	Compare
Our Location			
Our Facilities			
Our Products			
Our Services and Amenities			
Our Management Skills			
Our Training Programs			
Our Research & Development			
Our Company Culture			
Our Business Model			
Our Distribution System			
Overall Rating			

Rationale: _____

The following Senior Concierge Service providers are considered direct competitors:

Competitor	Address	No. of Locations	Primary Focus	Secondary Prod/Svcs	Strengths	Weaknesses

Indirect Competitors include the following:
Examples: professional organizers, errand running companies, house-sitters, etc.

_____
_____

Alternative Competitive Matrix

Competitor Name:	Us			

Comparison Items:

Types of Services				
Times Available				
Yrs in Business				
Target Market				
Additional Services				
Bonded & Insured				
Package Options				
Pricing Strategy				
Marketing Strategy				

Sales Revenues _____
Reputation _____
Website _____
Number of Employees _____
Comments _____

Competitor Profile Matrix

	Our	Competitor 1		Competitor 2		Competitor 3	
Critical Success Factors	Score	Rating	Score	Rating	Score	Rating	Score
Advertising							
Product Quality							
Service Quality							
Price Competition							
Management							
Financial Position							
Customer Loyalty							
Brand Identity							
Market Share							
Total							

We will use the following sources of information to conduct our competition analysis:

1. Competitor company websites.
2. Mystery shopper visits.
3. Annual Reports (www.annual reports.com)
4. Thomas Net (www.thomasnet.com)
5. Trade Journals and Associations
6. Local Chamber of Commerce
7. Sales representative interviews
8. Research & Development may come across new patents.
9. Market research surveys can give feedback on the customer's perspective
10. Monitoring services will track a company or industry you select for news. Resources: www.portfolionews.com www.Office.com
11. Hoover's www.hoovers.com
12. www.zapdata.com (Dun and Bradstreet) You can buy one-off lists here.
13. www.infousa.com (The largest, and they resell to many other vendors)
14. www.onesource.com (By subscription, they pull information from many sources)
15. www.capitaliq.com (Standard and Poors).
16. Obtain industry specific information from First Research (www.firstresearch.com) or IBISWorld, although both are by subscription only, although you may be able to buy just one report.
17. Get industry financial ratios and industry norms from RMA (www.rmahq.com) or by using ProfitCents.com software.
18. Company newsletters
19. Industry and Market Research Consultants

20. Local Suppliers and Distributors
21. Customer interviews regarding competitors.
22. Analyze competitors' ads for their target audience, market position, product features, benefits, prices, etc.
23. Attend speeches or presentations made by representatives of your competitors.
24. View competitor's trade show display from a potential customer's point of view.
25. Search computer databases (available at many public libraries).
26. Competitor Yellow Book Ads.
27. www.bls.gov/cex/ (site provides information on consumer expenditures nationally, regionally, and by selected metropolitan areas).
28. www.sizeup.com
29. Business Statistics and Financial Ratios   www.bizstats.com

4.8 Market Revenue Projection

For each of our chosen target markets, we will estimate our market share in number of customers, and based on consumer behavior, how often do they buy per year? What is the average dollar amount of each purchase? We will then multiply these three numbers to project sales volume for each target market.

Target Market	Number of Customers	No. of Purchases per Year	Average Dollar Amount per Purchase	Total Sales Volume
	A x	B x	C =	D
_____				
_____				
_____				

Using the target market number identified in this section, and the local demographics, we have made the following assessments regarding market opportunity and revenue potential:

Potential Revenue Opportunity from Concierge Program:
Revenue Opportunity =
_____ (#) Likely Local Senior Consumers x $_____ average annual purchases = $_____.

Or…

	No. of Clients Per Week	(x) Avg. Sale	(=) Weekly Income
Services	_____	_____	_____
Product Sales	_____	_____	_____
Other	_____	_____	_____
Total:			_____

Annualized: (x) 52
Annual Revenue Potential: _____

Recap:

Month   Jan Feb Mar Apr May Jun Jul Aug Sep Oct Nov Dec   Total

Products

_____

_____

Services

_____

_____

Gross Sales: _____

(-) Returns   _____

Net Sales   _____

Revenue Assumptions:

1. The sources of information for our revenue projection are:
   _____

2. If the total market demand for our product/service = 100%, our projected sales volume represents ____% of this total market.

3. The following factors might lower our revenue projections:
   _____

4.9 Barriers to Entry   (select)

_____ (company name) will benefit from the following combination of barriers to entry, which cumulatively present a moderate degree of entry difficulty or obstacles in the path of other Senior Concierge Service businesses wanting to enter our market.

1. Business Experience.   2. Community Networking
3. Referral Program   4. People Skills
5. Marketing Skills   6. Vendor Relationships
7. Operations Management   8. Cash Flow Management
9. Website Design   10. Organization Skills
11. Time Management Skills   12. Patience
13. Listening Skills   14. Empathy

In addition to strong management and entrepreneurial skills, we will need to recruit and train service providers with the following skills:

1. Honesty and integrity.
2. Patience.
3. Versatility and flexibility
4. Interpersonal skills.
5. Reliability and punctuality.

6. Compassion and encouragement
7. Knowledge about various services available to seniors.

4.9.1 Porter's Five Forces Analysis

We will use Porter's five forces analysis as a framework for the industry analysis and business strategy development. It will be used to derive the five forces which determine the competitive intensity and therefore attractiveness of our market. Attractiveness in this context refers to the overall industry profitability.

Competitors	The degree of rivalry is moderate in this segment, but less when compared to the overall concierge service category. Major competitors include: _____
Substitutes	Substitutes are high for this industry. These include other senior concierge services, family members and errand services.
Buyer Power	Buyer power is moderate in this business. Buyers are sensitive to quality and pricing as the segment attempts to capitalize on the pricing and quality advantage.
Supplier Power	Supplier power is moderate in the industry. Services can be obtained from a number of vendors. A high level of operational efficiency for managing suppliers can be achieved.
Threat of New Entrants	Relatively high in this segment. The business model can be easily copied.

Conclusions: _____ (company name) is in a competitive field and has to move fast to retain its competitive advantage. The key success factors are to develop operational efficiencies, innovative packaged offers, cost-effective marketing plans and customer service excellence.

5.0 Concierge Industry Analysis

The Senior Concierge Service business has grown rapidly in the United States, driven by seniors who are physically overwhelmed by basic tasks, the lack of children support, because of long distance relocations and the need to maintain dual income households.

Clients typically look for the following benefits from Senior Concierge Services:
1. Reduced injuries and turnover.
2. Saving time and attention for work tasks by taking care of personal tasks through the Senior Concierge Service.
3. Reduced stress translates into improved mental health, increased productivity and reduced health care costs.
4. It costs less than providing these dedicated services in-house.
5. A cost-effective quality of life management tool.

5.1 Key Industry Statistics

Companies that provide personal Senior Concierge Services typically find that the percentage of employees within the organization that use the service averages about 30 percent, and member satisfaction levels exceed 95 percent.

According to published studies, businesses that offer work and life balance programs, have experienced up to a 50 percent increase in staff retention levels.

67% would hire a personal assistant over a life coach to help complete your daily tasks, according to WD/AOL online Survey.   Woman's Day, August 2, 2005

In 2000, 26 of Fortune Magazine's "100 Best Companies to Work For" offered personal Senior Concierge Services versus 15 companies in 1998.

57% of businesses offer some type of on-site personal service, such as an ATM, dry cleaner or travel agency.   Hewitt 2001
There are approximately 5,000 hotel concierges in the United States.

According to a study of the U.S. work force released by the Families and Work Institute (statistics found online at www.entrepreneurmag.com):
   The average worker spends 44 hours per week on the job.
   85% of workers have daily family responsibilities to go home to.
   78% of married workers have spouses who are also employed.
   70% of all parents feel that they don't spend enough time with their children.
   Weekends are consumed by errands and housekeeping.

There are nearly 16 million two-income families in the United States.
Source: U.S. Bureau of Labor.

According to Genworth's 2013 Cost of Care Survey, the national median hourly rate for home care was $19 per hour. In contrast, the national median cost of a one-bedroom residence in an assisted living community was $3,300 per month.
Resource:
www.genworth.com/dam/Americas/US/PDFs/Consumer/corporate/Florida_gnw.pdf

5.2 Industry Trends

We will determine the trends that are impacting our consumers and indicate ways in which our customers' needs are changing and any relevant social, technical or other changes that will impact our target market. Keeping up with trends and reports will help management to carve a niche for our business, stay ahead of the competition and deliver products that our customers need and want.

1. A growing number of employers are realizing that personal Senior Concierge Services can meet a variety of diverse employee needs.
2. Te *SHRM 2000 Benefits Survey* found that four percent of employers polled offer Senior Concierge Services. Among companies with 5,000 or more employees, that figure jumps to 15%.
3. Expect low-margin Senior Concierge Services to begin to morph into high-fee, high-value consulting services, seamlessly serving the personal and professional needs of the wealthy.
4. Senior Concierge Service providers will bring in specialists to help execute each assigned task, and manage the project in an objective, independent manner, not typical of some concierge firms, which have created conflicts of interest by steering clients to "preferred" suppliers.
5. Senior Concierge Services with more affluent members are offering wine, art, investment and real estate   consultancy.
6. There is a resurgence in the popularity of the apartment concierge.
7. Increased technology will play a vital role in the services market; enabling customers to place orders online or via mobile phones will further enhance the experience, freeing up their time to manage the delicate balance between work and home.
8. The growing popularity of personalized lifestyle management services.
9. Concierge business owners are taking a new approach to the business through the use of independent contractors such as personal chefs, personal trainers, massage therapists and much more. This will allow the concierge business to offer more upscale and elite services.
10. The concierge company will become the point of contact for every integral part of personal services that are offered its clients.
11. The growing trend is to use more software to create more value-added services, such as build stated client preference profiles, discern lifestyle patterns from historical transaction records, incorporate a reminder service, communicate electronically with vendors and, ultimately, to anticipate client needs.

12. The trading by clients of more personal details for more personalized concierge services.
13. Today's concierge clients are looking for efficiency and knowledge.
14. As boomers and their parents age, more are choosing to stay in their homes, prompting a brisk business for remodelers, specialized concierge-like services and home health agencies.
15. 'Senior Villages' are offering fee-based concierge services to facilitate the next generation of aging in place and aging well -- steps beyond the more passive senior center.

5.3 Concierge Business Model

The concierge business model is dependent on the following revenue streams:
1. Monthly customer subscription fees.
2. Commissioned sales, referral fees or response fees from brokered products and services.
3. A la carte or hourly rates for services performed.
4. Market research and aggregated sales data analysis.
5. Premium permission marketing income from vendors.
6. Improved rates of new customer acquisition.
7. Better customer retention.
8. Vendor screening services

5.5 Industry Terms

We will use the following term definitions to help our company to understand and speak the common language of our industry, and aid efficient communication.

Activities of Daily Living (ADLs)
Include the basic tasks essential for day-to-day functioning, such as bathing, dressing, grooming, eating, mobility and toileting. Many seniors who require help with such activities are largely independent but may require help with one or two ADLs. In many cases, the importance of scheduling these activities is critical, informal care arrangements may not be adequate.

Assisted Living Facilities
A housing option for older adults who need some assistance with the activities of daily living, but do not require the kind of 24-hour nursing and medical care provided by a skilled nursing facility. In 2006, the national average base rate for assisted living facilities was $7,000 per month. Many facilities charge a base rate for facilities and offer services on an a-la-carte basis.

Concierge Medical Practice
High-touch, personalized practices that give patients 24/7 access to doctors who keep close tabs on their care generally cost a few thousand dollars a year.

Companionship Services
Companions visit isolated and homebound elders for conversation, reading, and light errands. May also be termed "friendly visitor" services.

Continuing-care Retirement Community
Amenities may include gourmet restaurants, infinity pools, gyms, spas, concierges and health care for life. This type of community promises "aging in place," typically allowing residents to live independently as long as they can and giving them access to more care-- on the same campus--when, and if, they need it. The concept has taken off as consumer awareness has grown and developers have mastered the concept. Private companies such as Classic Residence by Hyatt and Erickson Retirement Communities have helped up the amenities ante, making it even more appealing. Today there are 1,800 CCRCs nationwide, and they've been growing at a rate faster than nursing homes and assisted-living facilities combined.

Discharge Planner
A social worker or other health care professional who assists hospital patients and their families in transitioning from the hospital to another level of care such as rehabilitation in a skilled nursing facility, home health care in the patient's home, or long-term care in a nursing home.

Home Care
Refers to any type of care (medical or non-medical) that is provided to the patient in their home. In recent years, however, there has been a slight shift in using the terminology to emphasize non-medical care such as companionship/homemaking services or personal care services.

Home Health Care
Typically refers to the provision of skilled nursing care and speech, physical or occupational therapy in the home environment.

Homemaker Services
Household services done by someone other than yourself because you are unable to do them. These services can include shopping, laundry, light cleaning, meal preparation and transportation assistance. Homemakers cannot provide hands-on care in most states.

Hybrid Medical Concierge Business Model
Unlike full concierge care, in which, physicians care for only a limited number of patients who pay an annual fee, the hybrid model enables practitioners to offer concierge care as an option to their patients. Patients can continue to see their doctor the way they always have or they can pay an annual membership fee -- typically between $1500 and $3000 -- and receive Senior Concierge Services. Senior Concierge Services include same- or next-day appointments, extended office consultations, comprehensive annual screening physical examinations, and often direct access to the physician via cell phone and e-mail.

Instrumental Activities of Daily Living (IADLs)
Those activities which are less basic than the traditional Activities of Daily Living (ADLs). IADLs need to be performed, but scheduling may not be as critical. IADLs include such activities as shopping, paying bills, cleaning, doing the laundry and meal preparation. Many seniors require assistance with IADLs rather than with ADLs. Senior concierge services offers an array of companionship and homemaking services to assist clients with the IADLs.

Organizer Concierges
Help clients to get organized to improve their productivity and/or reduce wasted space.

Personal Concierge Services
Personal services include concierge shopping, cleaning services, relocation assistance planning, dry cleaning pick up, house sitting, reminder services, appointment making services, grocery shopping and many others. Personal Concierges market their services directly to clients who pay them for running errands, buying gifts, making travel arrangements, etc.

Referral Fees
Payments from various companies given to concierges for directing business their way.

Residential Care Facility
A generic term for a group home, specialized apartment complex or other institution that provides care services where individuals live. The term is used to refer to a range of residential care options including assisted living facilities, board and care homes and skilled nursing facilities

Retailer Concierges
Employed by retail stores to help shoppers solve problems that are both related to the stores and not related to the store. They can make appointments with personal shoppers, arrange private shopping parties, request monogramming, preorder items from the high-end Collection line, order from the online catalog, etc. Concierges will also hold coats, packages and umbrellas, provide directions and make restaurant reservations.

Self-Serve Concierge
Microsoft Surface enables a do-it-yourself concierge concept, where up to four hotel guests can sit around an interactive flat screen surface built into a table and look through city maps, get restaurant and bar recommendations, find 24-hour pharmacies and get directions to nearby destinations.

Senior Center
Community-based programs that provide a variety of services that can include social activities, nutrition, and educational and recreational opportunities for older adults.

"Villages"
The membership concierge services that help people manage their homes, transportation and even personal care as they age. These grassroots "Villages" are emerging in communities across the U.S. to make continued living in their homes comfortable for thousands of older Americans. The "Village" name comes from Beacon Hill Village, the original neighborhood membership concierge service founded by a group of homeowners in the Beacon Hill area of Boston.

Virtual Assistance Service
Provide clients with an employee to perform the duties of a secretary or personal assistant.

Virtual Concierge Service
Works with clients via computer, fax and phone. May perform some duties in person depending on the types of services offered.

Resources:
www.aging-parents-and-elder-care.com/Pages/LTC_Glossary/LTC_GlossaryA.html

5.6 Industry Leaders

We plan to study the best practices of industry leaders and adapt certain selected practices to our business model concept. Best practices are those methods or techniques resulting in increased customer satisfaction when incorporated into the operation.

Brookdale Senior Living Inc.
Together with its subsidiaries, owns and operates senior living communities in the United States. The company operates retirement centers, assisted living and dementia-care communities, and continuing care retirement communities (CCRCs). Its retirement centers offer basic services, such as meal service, 24-hour emergency response, housekeeping, concierge services, transportation, and recreational activities; supplemental care services, including medication reminders, check-in services, and escort and companion services; and various education, wellness, therapy, home health, and other ancillary services. The company's assisted living communities provide housing and 24-hour assistance with activities of daily living to mid-acuity frail and elderly residents. These communities also offer health assessments, meals and snacks, coordination of special diets planned by a registered dietitian, assistance with coordination of physician care, social and recreational activities, housekeeping, and personal laundry services. In addition, these communities provide exercise programs and programs designed to address issues associated with early stages of Alzheimer's and other forms of dementia. Its CCRC offer living arrangements and services to accommodate various levels of physical ability and health; and ancillary services, including therapy, home health, and other services.

Comfort Keepers   www.comfortkeepers.com
They are an international franchise that provides in-home care to seniors. The company began in 1997 when an RN in home healthcare saw many of her patients prematurely enter long term care facilities because they needed just a little more care. Comfort Keepers is in 560 US markets and serves seniors in 4 international locations. This organization offers cutting edge technology as part of their service packages, such as:

- Home Alert system, with a 24-hour based monitoring system that will alert the call center of any needs such as a fall, illness or just the need for someone to check on them.
- Fall safety programs such as pressure pad mats that go beside a bed and fall alert devices that will go straight to the call-center.
- A GPS tracking system for those seniors prone to wandering or at risk of leaving the home.
- Home Security such as door and window alarms and smoke and carbon monoxide detectors.

Comfort Keepers only use carefully screened and trained care givers who undergo rigorous background checks. Each care giver is insured and bonded and covered by Worker's Compensation Insurance. Primary services include light housekeeping, transportation, bill paying, medication reminders, meal preparation, and assistance with personal hygiene. The cost for services is based upon what type of assistance is needed and how often. The services provided are not covered by most private insurances or Medicare/Medicaid but usually these costs are much cheaper than placement in a facility.

Visiting Angels www.visitingangels.com

A franchise business and was founded by a Social Services Director in a long-term care facility. He and 3 other directors founded this company in 1998 and was a nationwide provider by 2002. Concierge Employees are carefully screened, bonded and insured. They are licensed in states that have regulations that require it. They are also monitored both on-site and through their paperwork that they provide to show services were provided. The caregiver's supervisor will also follow up with the client and the contact person to ensure that all services were completed as requested. Services include companion services, social transportation as well as medical transportation. They can provide light housekeeping, meal services and medication monitoring. Personal care such as assisting with bathing and hygiene are also available services. These care givers are truly the "concierge," whatever services the client needs they will provide or find someone who can. Costs are hourly based or based upon the services requested.

Home Instead Senior Care www.homeinstead.com

A family owned network of locally owned franchises. The company started in 1995 in Omaha, NE by a family caring for an aging grandmother. By the year 2000 they had grown to international locations and employ nearly 65,000 trained staff members. There are now over 900 Home Instead franchise offices worldwide. They offer services in the United States, Canada, Ireland and 13 other countries. Home Instead providers web based technology to facilitate support groups for family care givers, as well as provide tips and tools for providing care for your loved one. They also provide help with technology in the home, such as assisting the senior with accessing the internet to use these tools.

Concierge Employees are carefully trained and have thorough background checks. They are all bonded and insured and closely followed by their supervisor through on-site visits, telephone visits with the client and satisfaction surveys conducted by JD Power and Associates to ascertain the satisfaction of the client and their families. Services provided are as limited or as extensive as the client needs them to be, regardless of if it's a couple of hours a day or 24-hour care, they are available. They offer all of the standard services as well as specialized Alzheimer's and Dementia Care. Pricing is hourly in this case as well and cost varies based upon the market of they are serving. The cost for services is roughly 1/3 of what it would cost for home health care and 1/5 of the cost of a nursing home. Although, insurance doesn't cover these services, they will work out a cost structure that is affordable.

ConciergeCare, Inc. www.conciergecareinc.com

Provides services ranging from case management and advocacy in residential or healthcare environments, to companionship via daily or weekly phone chats or home visits with a friendly concierge, to classic concierge services sourcing and arranging a variety of other goods and services that allow the individual or couple to continue living independently in the home they know best. After a full assessment of needs and wants, their concierge service takes over with a personalized care plan focused on the comfort and safety of the client consumer and taking an uncomfortable burden off the shoulders of the family who often do not know where to turn or what to do. They are providers of personalized services to ensure that seniors can continue to have amazing lives in their own homes, as well as essential services that secure this ability. They also assist those seniors who reside in nursing and assisted living facilities, so they can continue to have the quality experience they deserve.

Easy Living   www.easylivingfl.com

They established their affordable home care agency in response to their clients' demands for more personalized service, flexible scheduling and reliable, expert caregivers.
Resource:
www.easylivingfl.com/services/services-concierge/services-concierge-overview/

Senior Concierge Service   www.seniorconciergeservice.com

Independent Living Concierge   http://independentlivingconcierge.com/

Envoy   www.helloenvoy.com/

This company uses convenient web and smartphone apps to make managing visits, viewing updates, and family collaboration easy. It also offers preferred access to nationwide partner services like handyman, home maintenance, lawn mowing, tech help, etc. They have developed apps that make it easy to access services and membership benefits on the client's computer, tablet, or smartphone. Clients can schedule and manage upcoming visits, rides and services, and make shopping and to-do lists. They can also add family members to collaborate around care and communicate with their Envoy. There are also apps to receive photos and receipts documenting every visit, and automatic reminders before upcoming visits and services. Clients can also rate visits to praise their Envoy or help them to improve. They have received funding from Softech VC, which led the last round, with Lowercase Capital, Vayner/RSE and others participating.
Source:
https://techcrunch.com/2015/09/16/envoy-a-part-time-concierge-service-for-seniors-raises-3m/

Elder Concierge Services   www.elderconciergeservices.com/

This concierge service provides a full range of personalized care to older adults in the Denver metro area. Their services are completely customizable and vary from client to client. There is no minimum or maximum amount of time they provide care. They can begin work as soon as they are needed, and work with families, trustees, guardians, and care facilities to make sure they meet the clients' non-medical needs. They also help to develop senior care management plans and are active in the field of senior transitional services. They help with admission or discharge procedures, pack up belongings and transport clients between their home and hospital/care facility. They also send scheduled reports to client families or representatives after each visit.

5.7 Industry News

Lyft has partnered with healthcare information tech solutions company Allscripts to develop a healthcare platform that will enable doctors and hospitals to offer non-emergency transportation to patients.
Source:
www.healthcaredive.com/news/lyft-allscripts-partner-healthcare-platform/518396/

Pharmaceutical Product Development, LLC (PPD), a global contract research organization, and Acurian, the leading full-service provider of global patient enrollment and retention solutions and a subsidiary of PPD, today announced a new patient concierge service designed to make it easier for patients and their caregivers to participate in clinical trials and to help pharmaceutical and biotechnology clients retain patients. he patient concierge serves as a single point of contact to proactively guide a patient through trial participation and manage trial logistics. Concierges are assigned to patients for the duration of a study and check in with them regularly. That ongoing interaction helps to build a one-to-one relationship, enabling a concierge to better assess and address patient motivation, satisfaction and other non-medical issues, while facilitating services aimed at retaining the patient in the trial. Some of the specific amenities the patient concierge provides include: appointment reminders and follow-ups; trial experience feedback; trial information; device training and assistance; transportation and reimbursement support; and medication reminders.
Source:
www.businesswire.com/news/home/20180228005825/en/PPD-Acurian-Introduce-Innovative-Patient-Concierge-Service

Tending https://www.starttending.com/
Headquartered in the San Francisco Bay Area. Hardesty and Meghan Tartel co-founded this online care coordination platform and concierge service for caregivers. Tending partners with hospitals, physician groups and insurers to offer care coordination; its average customer's age: 85. Tending is testing the product in southern California and its cost to consumers is $100 a month. Revenue also comes from charging hospitals, medical groups and insurers (in the hope of minimizing readmissions). Customers can use Tending's Care Concierges to assign tasks, such as scheduling and arranging appointments and finding home care providers. It is a convenient, easy to use, one stop shop for family caregivers, supporting and caring for loved ones, whether they live in the next room or across the country.

6.0 Strategy and Implementation Summary

_____ (company name) will focus geographically on _____ County, in the state of _____ (state), particularly in the _____ (city/town) of _____.

_____ (company name) will aggressively target seniors through a comprehensive community involvement program. We will reach targeted market segments directly through emotional based direct response marketing, and indirectly through our strategic marketing alliance partners. We will also attract individual clients through our website and charitable involvements.

6.1 Promotional Strategy

Grand Opening Event:	Personal invitations to family and friends. Invitations to retirement communities and commercial establishments within 5 miles radius.
Advertisements:	Newspaper and other publication press releases. Yellow page ads in phone book and online.
Public Relations:	Series of the health awareness seminars on the stress reduction benefits of errand services.
Networking:	Participation in local civic and support groups.

The company's plan is to gain market share with niche positioning, high quality services, package deals for corporate accounts, fast turnaround, outstanding customer service and a unique client experience.

We will offer sales promotions on certain errand services as part of our grand opening campaign, to encourage the adding of new customers to our database. We will advertise this promotion in local newspapers and shopper magazines.

Promotion Expenses Table:

Type of Media	2018	2019	2020
Yellow Pages			
Business Magazine Ad			
Newspaper Ad			
Direct Mail			
Grand Opening Event			
Totals:			

6.1.1 Grand Opening

Our Grand Opening celebration will be a very important promotion opportunity to create word-of-mouth advertising results. We will advertise the date of our grand opening in local newspapers and on local radio.

We will do the following things to make the open house a successful event:
1. Enlist local business support to contribute a large number of door prizes.
2. Use a sign-in sheet to create an email/mailing list.
3. Sponsor a _____ competition.
4. Schedule appearance by local senior celebrities.
5. Create a festive atmosphere with balloons, beverages and music.
6. Get the local radio station to broadcast live from the event and handout fun gifts.
7. Offer an application/registration fee waiver.
8. Giveaway our logo imprinted T-shirts as a contest prize.
9. Allow potential customers to view your facility and ask questions.
10. Print promotional flyers and pay a few kids to distribute them locally.
11. Arrange for storytelling, physical exams, and snacks for everyone.
12. Arrange for local politician to do the official opening ceremony so all the local newspapers came to take pictures and do a feature story.
13. Arrange that people can tour our facility on the open day in order to see our facilities, collect sales brochures and find out more about our concierge services.
14. Allocate staff members to perform specific duties, handout business cards and sales brochures and instruct them to deal with any questions or queries.
16. Organize a drawing with everyone writing their name and phone numbers on the back of business cards and give a voucher as a prize to start a marketing list.
17. Hand out free samples of mini-products and consultation coupons.

6.1.2 Value Proposition

Our value proposition will summarize why a consumer should use our Senior Concierge Services. We will enable quick access to our broad line of quality and innovative personalized services, out of our conveniently located offices in the _____ (city) area. Our value proposition will convince prospects that our services will add more value and better solve their need for a convenient, one-stop, focused senior concierge service. We will use this value proposition statement to target customers who will benefit most from using our services. These are seniors looking for assistance with time-consuming and physically challenging errands.

Our value proposition will be concise and appeal to the customer's strongest decision-making drivers, which are convenience, 24/7 support, unusual request fulfillment and quality of personal relationships. Our Senior Concierge Service proposition will be fundamentally aligned with the principles of one-to-one marketing, that is building learning relationships with seniors, maintaining a dialogue, differentiating the proposition and ultimately anticipating their needs.

The focus of our Senior Concierge Service will be to provide a convenient and supportive service combined with a warm and friendly attitude. It will be a "a friendly service" where customers call to arrange for trusted completion of chores and to relieve their mind from the burden of anxiety and stress. Our senior concierge service will be designed to ensure all is well for older adults living at home. Trustworthy and flexible, our personal concierge service providers will offer professional, personal assistance, while caring relatives can rest assured that their loved ones have all the support they need. Our concierges will be able to handle it all, from weekly grocery shopping, refilling prescriptions, supervising contractors at the home, and rearranging the home to make it more convenient and accessible. ____ (company name) will be s a unique combination of personal concierge services and senior care services customized to the unique needs of seniors. In addition to customized personal concierge services, our members will also enjoy services specifically designed for senior clientele. An experienced member of our team will always be a phone call away, around the clock, to assist seniors with whatever they need.

Recap of Our Value Proposition:
Trust – We are known as a trusted business partner with strong customer and vendor endorsements. We have earned a reputation for quality, integrity, and delivery of successful senior concierge solutions.
Quality – We offer _____ experience and extensive professional backgrounds in _____ at competitive salary rates.
Experience – Our ability to bring people with ___ (#) years of _____ experience with deep technical knowledge of _____ is at the core of our success.
True Vendor Partnerships – Our true vendor partnerships enable us to offer the resources of much larger organizations with greater flexibility.
Customer Satisfaction and Commitment to Success – Through partnering with our customers and delivering quality solutions, we have been able to achieve an impressive degree of repeat and referral business. Since ____ (year), more than ____% of our business activity is generated by existing customers. Our philosophy is that "our customer's satisfaction is our success." Our success will be measured in terms of our customer's satisfaction survey scores and testimonials.

6.1.3 Positioning Statement

We will create a positioning statement for our company that describes what distinguishes our business from the competition. We will keep it simple, memorable and snappy. We will test our positioning statement to make certain that it appeals to our senior target audience. We will continue to refine it until it speaks directly to our targeted customer wants, support needs and lifestyle aspirations. We will use our positioning statement in every written communication to customers. This will ensure that our message is consistent and comes across loud and clear. We will create quality image marketing materials that communicate our positioning. We want to create the image of seniors being in the care of the 'good hands people'. We will offer one-on-one customized services to accommodate our clients' needs and schedule, and strive to deliver the highest level of customer service, every time

Our positioning strategy will be the result of conducting in-depth consumer market research to find out what benefits seniors want and how our Senior Concierge Services can meet those needs. Due to the increase in two-income families, many service-oriented professions are leaning toward differentiating themselves on the basis of convenience. This is also what we intend to do. For instance, we plan to have extended, "people" hours on various days of the week and offer the 24/7 availability of our senior concierge services, for those clients who desire that level of support.

We also plan to develop specialized services that will enable us to pursue a niche focus on specific interest-based programs, such as providing dining and entertainment recommendations based on assembled client profiles and transitional services for seniors who are either downsizing or relocating. These objectives will position us at the ___(mid-level/high-end) of the market and will allow the company to realize a healthy profit margin in relation to its low-end, discount rivals, and achieve long-term growth.

Market Positioning Recap
Price: The strategy is to offer competitive prices that are lower that the market leader, yet set to indicate value and worth. .
Quality: The senior concierge service quality will have to be very good as the finished service results will be showcased in highly visible situations.
Service: Highly individualized and customized service will be the key to success in this type of business. Personal attention to the customers will result in higher sales and word of mouth advertising.

6.1.4 Unique Selling Proposition (USP)

Our unique selling proposition will answer the question why a customer should choose to do business with our company versus any and every other option available to them in the marketplace. Our USP will be a description of a unique important benefit that our senior concierge service offers to customers, so that price is no longer the key to our sales.

Our USP will include the following:
Who our target audience is: _____
What we will do for them: _____
What qualities, skills, talents, traits do we possess that others do not: _____
What are the benefits we provide that no one else offers: _____
Why that is different from what others are offering: _____
Why that solution matters to our target audience: _____

6.1.5 Distribution Strategy

Customers can contact the _____ (company name) by telephone, fax, internet and by dropping in. Our nearest competitors are ___ (#) miles away in either direction.

Our customers will have the following access points:
1. **Order by Phone**
   Customers can contact us 24 hours a day, 7days a week at _____.
   Our Customer Service Representatives will be available to assist customers Monday through Friday from ___ a.m. to ___ p.m. EST.
2. **Order by Fax**
   Customers may fax their orders to _____ anytime.
   They must provide: Account number, Billing and shipping address, Purchase order number, if applicable, Name and telephone number, Product number/description, Unit of measure and quantity ordered and Applicable sales promotion source codes.
3. **Order Online**
   Customers can order online at www._____.com. Once the account is activated, customers will be able to place orders, browse the catalog, check stock availability and pricing, check order status and view both order and transaction history.
4. **In-person**
   All customers can be serviced in person at our facilities Monday through Friday from ___ a.m. to ___ p.m. EST.

We plan to pursue the following distribution channels: (select)
1. Our own retail outlets _____
2. Independent retail outlets _____
3. Chain store retail outlets _____
4. Wholesale outlets _____
5. Independent distributors _____
6. Independent commissioned sales reps _____
7. In-house sales reps _____
8. Direct mail using own catalog or flyers _____
9. Catalog broker agreement _____
10. In-house telemarketing _____
11. Contracted telemarketing call center _____
12. Cybermarketing via own website _____
13. Online sales via amazon, eBay, etc. _____
14. TV and Cable Direct Marketing _____
15. TV Home Shopping Channels _____

Sales Rep Plan

We plan to use sales reps to market our senior concierge services to corporations, and senior organizations and retirement communities.

1. In-house or Independent
2. Salaried or Commissioned
3. Salary or Commission Rate
4. Salary Plus Commission Rate
5. Special Performance Incentives
6. Negotiating Parameters   Price Breaks/Added Services/

7. Performance Evaluation Criteria   No. of New Customers/Sales Volume/

8. Number of Reps
9. Sales Territory Determinants   Geography/Demographics/

10. Sales Territories Covered
11. Training Program Overview
12. Training Program Cost
13. Sales Kit Contents

Rep Name   Compensation Plan   Assigned Territory

___

6.2   Competitive Advantages

A **competitive advantage** is the thing that differentiates a business from its competitors. It is what separates our business from everyone else. It answers the questions: "Why do customers buy from us versus a competitor?" and "What do we offer customers that is unique?". We will make certain to include our key competitive advantages into our marketing materials. We will use the following competitive advantages to set us apart from our competitors. The distinctive competitive advantages which _____ (company name) brings to the marketplace are as follows:
(Note: Select only those you can support)

1. With a diverse and experienced team of men and women on staff, we can act quickly, offer flexibility and advise on how to best enhance the life of an elder loved one.
2. We will develop an extensive training program to provide our employees with the tools necessary to maintain a high level of customer service.
3. Caregivers will be matched with family members' needs.
4. We will conduct a free onsite consultation where a customized care plan is developed with the client and family members.
5. We will offer 24/7 care when needed.

6. Supervisors will closely monitor the caregiver/client relationship with ongoing assessments and recommendations as needs change over time.
7. We will provide regular written assessments of the clients' progress and well-being.
8. A large variety of Senior Concierge Services will be offered.
9. A well-trained staff focused on the offering of great customer service.
10. Membership club plan discounts and benefits.
11. Building a customer database to track customer preferences, contact information and other important information.
12. Adopting proactive customer service policies, such as calling to confirm appointments and satisfaction.
13. Computer software to improve productivity, bookkeeping, communications, transaction processing, supplies ordering, etc.
14. The flexibility to respond to Senior Concierge Service trend changes.
15. We are constantly looking for and screening new vendors, and building our database of pre-approved businesses, all of whom provide first class service.
16. We maintain high standards for customer satisfaction, and offer impressive levels of quality, courtesy and professionalism.
17. We provide the right people, resources and information through an intelligent network that enforces adherences to our operating policies.
18. We offer flexible deployment options, with solutions that can be deployed on the client's premises or on-demand.
19. Employees and customers have immediate access to company experts via our website's chat function.

6.2.1 Branding Strategy

Our branding strategy involves what we do to shape what the customer immediately thinks our business offers and stands for. The purpose of our branding strategy is to reduce customer perceived purchase risk and improve our profit margins by allowing use to charge a premium for our Senior Concierge Services.

We will invest $____ every year in maintaining our brand name image, which will differentiate our senior concierge service business from other companies. The amount of money spent on creating and maintaining a brand name will not convey any specific information about our products, but it will convey, indirectly, that we are in this market for the long haul, that we have a reputation to protect, and that we will interact repeatedly with our customers. In this sense, the amount of money spent on maintaining our brand name will signal to consumers that we will provide products and services of consistent quality.

We will use the following ways to build trust and establish our personal brand:
1. Build a consistently published blog and e-newsletter with informational content.
2. Create comprehensive social media profiles.

3. Contribute articles to related online publications.
4. Earn career certifications

Resources:
https://www.abetterlemonadestand.com/branding-guide/

Our key to marketing success will be to effectively manage the building of our brand platform in the market place, which will consist of the following elements:

- **Brand Vision** - our envisioned future of the brand is to be the national source for senior concierge solutions to manage the complications of immobility for the elderly.
- **Brand Attributes** - Partners, problem solvers, responsive, integrity, flexible and easy to work with.
- **Brand Essence** - the shared soul of the brand, the spark of which is present in every experience a customer has with our services, will be "Problem Solving" and "Compassionate." This will be the core of our organization, driving the type of people we hire and the type of behavior we expect.
- **Brand Image** - the outside world's overall perception of our organization will be that we are senior concierge pros who are alleviating the complications of an aging population.
- **Brand Promise** - our concise statement of what we do, why we do it, and why customers should do business with us will be, "To prevent future senior lifestyle complications"

We will use the following methodologies to implement our branding strategy:
1. Develop processes, systems and quality assurance procedures to assure the consistent adherence to our quality standards and mission statement objectives.
2. Develop business processes to consistently deliver upon our value proposition.
3. Develop training programs to assure the consistent professionalism and responsiveness of our employees.
4. Develop marketing communications with consistent, reinforcing message content.
5. Incorporate testimonials into our marketing materials that support our promises.
6. Develop marketing communications with a consistent presentation style. (Logo design, company colors, slogan, labels, packaging, stationery, etc.)
7. Exceed our brand promises to achieve consistent customer loyalty.
8. Use surveys, focus groups and interviews to consistently monitor what our brand means to our customers.
9. Consistently match our brand values or performance benchmarks to our customer requirements.
10. Focus on the maintenance of a consistent number of key brand values that are tied to our company strengths.
11. Continuously research industry trends in our markets to stay relevant to customer needs and wants.
12. Attach a logo-imprinted product label and business card to all products, marketing communications and invoices.
13. Develop a memorable and meaningful tagline that captures the essence of our

brand.
14. Prepare a one-page company overview and make it a key component of our sales presentation folder.
15. Hire and train employees to put the interests of customers first.
16. Develop a professional website that is updated with fresh content on a regular basis.
17. Use our blog to circulate content that establishes our niche expertise and opens a two-way dialogue with our customers.
18. Attractive and tasteful uniforms will also help our staff's morale. The branding will become complete with the addition of our corporate logo, or other trim or accessories which echo the style and theme of our establishment.
19. Create an effective slogan with the following attributes:
    a. Appeals to customers' emotions.
    b. Shows off how our service benefits customers by highlighting our customer service or care.
    c. Has 8 words or less and is memorable
    d. Can be grasped quickly by our audience.
    e. Reflects our business' personality and character.
    f. Shows sign of originality.
20. Create a Proof Book that contains before and after photos, testimonial letters, our mission statement, copies of industry certifications and our code of ethics.
21. Make effective use of trade show exhibitions and email newsletters to help brand our image.

The communications strategy we will use to build our brand platform will include the following items:

Website - featuring product line information, research, testimonials, cost benefit analysis, frequently asked questions, and pricing information. This website will be used as a tool for both our sales team and our clients.

Presentations, brochures and mailers geared to the family decision maker, explaining the benefits of our service as part of a comprehensive senior support plan.

Presentations and brochures geared to the decision maker explaining the benefits of our program in terms of positive outcomes, reduced costs from complications, and reduced risk of negative survey events.

A presentation and recruiting brochure geared to prospective sales people that emphasizes the benefits of joining our organization.

Training materials that help every employee deliver our brand message in a consistent manner.

6.2.2   Brand Positioning Statement

We will use the following brand positioning statement to summarize what our brand means to our targeted market:

To _____ (target market)

_____ (company name) is the brand of _____ (product/service frame of reference) that enables the customer to _____ (primary performance benefit) because ____ (company name) _____ (products/services) _____ (are made with/offer/provide) the best _____ (key attributes)

6.3 Business SWOT Analysis

Definition: SWOT Analysis is a powerful technique for understanding your Strengths and Weaknesses, and for looking at the Opportunities and Threats faced.

Strategy: We will use this SWOT Analysis to uncover exploitable opportunities and carve a sustainable niche in our market. And by understanding the weaknesses of our business, we can manage and eliminate threats that would otherwise catch us by surprise. By using the SWOT framework, we will be able to craft a strategy that distinguishes our business from our competitors, so that we can compete successfully in the market.

Strengths   (select)

What Senior Concierge Services are we best at providing?
What unique resources can we draw upon?

1. Our employee training program produces staff capable of delivering superior customer service.
2. Our software system is capable of tracking client preferences and offers a reminder service.
3. We have close trusted relationships with our clients and this has provided a greater behavioral understanding of our client needs.
4. We possess the ability to create innovative, value-added services.
5. Provide creative, informed problem-solving solutions in real-time.
6. Provides ongoing training seminars and educational symposia for concierges and all employees.
7. Third party service providers excel at the specialty services they provide to guarantee better quality services than an in-house employee would give.
8. Our staff is highly qualified, experienced, multilingual and multicultural.
9. We encourage innovative service ideas.
10. We offer straightforward pricing and multiple packaged options.
11. We value accountability to our staff, to each other and to the clients.
12. _____

Weaknesses

In what areas could we improve?
Where do we have fewer resources than others?

1. Problems arise when corporate employees have unrealistic expectations.
2. Must do a better job of building trust so that clients will share personal info.
3. Must take more of a lifetime value perspective with regard to clients and the

building of long-term loyalty.
4. We need a critical mass of customers and a critical mass of product and information vendors to deliver sizeable revenue from partnership sales.
5. Possible client over-subscription and retailer under-subscription are real dangers that require contingency plans.
6. The staff must be trained to deliver superb, personalized service upon every client episode.
7. Multi-skilled staff will be hard to find, particularly for the potentially average remuneration that Senior Concierge Services will provide in the start-up phase.
8. Management expertise gaps.
9. Inadequate monitoring of competitor strategies, responses and reviews.
10. _____

Opportunities

What opportunities are there for new and/or improved services?
What trends could we take advantage of?
1. Obtain revenues from nominal monthly subscription or membership fees.
2. Drive commissions from the brokered purchasing of products and services for clients from partnered organizations.
3. The bundling of relevant products and services to create up-sell opportunities.
4. Trade help with the consumer's decision making process for insights into the consumer's buying priorities.
5. Develop a deeper customer understanding by integrating Senior Concierge Service data, profiles and preferences, with transactional data.
6. Not enough people understood the concierge business and need to be educated as to the money and time-saving benefits of our services.
7. Every customer episode is an opportunity to deliver superb, tailored service and to grow the relationship with the client.
8. Improve customer retention economics for core products and services
9. Improve rates of new customer acquisition.
10. Pursue premium permission marketing income.
11. Conduct market research and make aggregated data sales.
12. Build winning new customer experiences.
13. Improve the relevance and performance of existing products, services, marketing and brands.
14. Create new forms of customer value and respond to changes in customer needs.
15. _____

Threats

What trends or competitor actions could hurt us?
What threats do our weaknesses expose us to?
1. Competitors do better job of using software to facilitate client/vendor interactions.
2. Tight labor market makes it harder to hire multi-skilled staff at reasonable rates.
3. Another Senior Concierge Service provider could open for business in the area.
4. Price differentiation is a significant competition factor.
5. We need to do a better job of assessing the strengths and weaknesses of all

of our competitors.
6. _____

Recap:
We will use the following strengths to capitalize on recognized opportunities:
1. _____
2. _____

We will take the following actions to turn our weaknesses into strengths and prepare to defend against known threats.
1. _____
2. _____

6.4 Marketing Strategy

Overall Marketing Strategy:
___ (company name) will rely on the recommendations of satisfied customers as a means of attracting customers away from the competition. Past experience has also proven that many customers come on the recommendations of others. Although word-of-mouth is an effective way of increasing market share, it is also extremely slow. To accelerate the process of expanding the customer base, the business will maintain an advertising budget of $___ for the first year, which is a full percentage point above the industry average. The bulk of this budget will be spent on listings in the ___ (city) yellow pages, advertisements in local newspapers and lifestyle magazines, and direct mailings to preferred customers. We will use direct response advertising with an emotional message. We will place small display ads in local daily, weekly and monthly newspapers and lifestyle magazines.
Our customer relationship management system will automatically send out, on a predetermined schedule, follow-up materials, such as reports, article reprints, seminar invitations, email messages, surveys and e-newsletters.

The purpose of the free reports will be to show our prospects that we understand their needs and concerns. This will lead them to the next step in the sales process, which is a free consultation. All free offers will have a one month expiration date, with follow-up reports and progressively appealing offers being sent on a fixed schedule. Any prospect that does not schedule within the first month will automatically receive our newsletter the following month.

We will offset some of our advertising costs by asking our suppliers to place ads in our newsletter, and to fund and participate in the seminars. Like most concierge businesses, we will market our services by putting fliers and coupons in local advertising leaflets or Welcome Wagon baskets. We will also place ads in the AARP Magazine (http://www.aarp.org/magazine/).

Marketing Budget

Our objective in setting a marketing budget has been to keep it between three and five percent of our estimated annual gross sales.

Marketing budget per quarter:

Newspaper Ads	$_____	Radio advertisement	$_____
Web Page	$_____	Customer contest	$_____
Direct Mail	$_____	Sales Brochure	$_____
Trade Shows	$_____	Seminars	$_____
Superpages	$_____	Google Adwords	$_____
Giveaways	$_____	Vehicle Signs	$_____
Business Cards	$_____	Flyers	$_____
Labels/Stickers	$_____	Videos/DVDs	$_____
Samples	$_____	Newsletter	$_____
Bandit Signs	$_____	Email Campaigns	$_____
Sales Reps Comm.	$_____	Restaurant Placemats	$_____
Press Releases	$_____	Billboards	$_____
Movie Theater Ads	$_____	Fund Raisers	$_____
Infomercials	$_____	Speeches	$_____
Postcards	$_____	Proof Books	$_____
Social Networking	$_____	Charitable Donations	$_____
Magazine Ads	$_____	Other	$_____

Total: $_____

The following represent examples of our marketing programs:
- Promotion expenses
- Printed materials (sales brochures, pamphlets, fliers, postcards)
- Media advertisements (radio, newspapers, magazines, outdoor billboards)
- Bartering (exchanging our products for ad placement)
- Product donations (door prizes, building promotions, charities)
- Referral Program Brochure
- Website Development

Networking with Lead Exchange Groups

1. We will form a LeTip Chapter to exchange business leads.
2. We will join the local BNI.com referral exchange group.
3. We will join the Chamber of Commerce to further corporate relationships.
4. We will become a member of a local Concierge Association, such as Les Clefs d'Or USA, Ltd.

Local Marketing

By exploiting information gathered in our sales figures, we will identify our problems, take advantage of opportunities, and develop marketing objectives and strategies.

We plan to hire a marketing and community outreach assistant. The function of this newly created position will be to help educate the community about the benefits of our senior concierge services. The position requires experience in event planning, seminar presentations, fundraising and public relations.

Marketing Mix

Clients will primarily come from word-of-mouth and our referral program. The overall market approach involves creating brand awareness through targeted advertising, public relations, co-marketing efforts, direct mail, email campaigns (with constantcontact.com), trade show events, seminars and a website.

The Company plans to advertise through circulars which are inserted in newspapers or mailed directly to consumers' residences, and advertise in local newspapers and lifestyle magazines, and on the radio. We will also advertise directly to local employers by placing fliers with their company receptionist.

Video Marketing

We will link to our website a series of YouTube.com based video clips that talk about our range of Senior Concierge Services and demonstrate our expertise with certain types of emergency errand services. We will create business marketing videos that are both entertaining and informational, and significantly improve our search engine rankings.

The video will include:
- **Client testimonials** - We will let our best customers become our instant sales force because people will believe what others say about us more readily than what we say about ourselves.
- **Product Demonstrations** - We will train and pre-sell our potential clients on our most popular Senior Concierge Services by talking about and showing them. Often, our potential clients don't know the full range and depth of our products and services because we haven't taken the adequate time to show and tell them.
- **Include Business Website Address**
- **Interview with Owner.**
- **Frequently Asked Questions** - We will answer questions that we often get and anticipate objections we might get and give great reasons to convince potential clients that we are the Senior Concierge Service provider in the area.
- **Include a Call to Action** - We have the experience and the know-how to service your complete office support needs. So call us, right now, and let's get started.
- **Seminar** - Include a portion of a seminar on how families can remotely care for seniors and grandparents using senior concierge services.
- **Comment on industry trends and product news** - We will appear more in-tune and knowledgeable in our market if we can talk about what's happening in our industry and marketplace.

Resources: www.businessvideomarketing.tv
www.hotpluto.com
www.hubspot.com/video-marketing-kit
www.youtube.com/user/mybusinessstory

Analytics Report
http://support.google.com/youtube/bin/static.py?hl=en&topic=1728599&guide=1714169&page=guide.cs

Note: Refer to Video Marketing Tips in rear marketing worksheets section.

Example: http://www.youtube.com/watch?v=gqERbA5NU5M&feature=related

Top 11 places where we will share our videos online:

YouTube   www.youtube.com

This very popular website allows you to log-in and leave comments and ratings on the videos. You can also save your favorite videos and allows you to tag posted videos. This makes it easier for your videos to come up in search engines.

Google Video   http://video.google.com/

A video hosting site. Google Video is not just focused on sharing videos online, but this is also a market place where you can buy the videos you find on this site using Google search engine.

Yahoo! Video   http://video.yahoo.com/

Uploading and sharing videos is possible with Yahoo Video!. You can find several types of videos on their site and you can also post comments and ratings for the videos.

Revver   http://www.revver.com/

This website lets you earn money through ads on your videos and you will have a 50/50 profit split with the website. Another great deal with Revver is that your fans who posted your videos on their site can also earn money.

Blip.tv   http://blip.tv/

Allows viewers to stream and download the videos posted on their website. You can also use Creative Commons licenses on your videos posted on the website. This allows you to decide if your videos should be attributed, restricted for commercial use and be used under specific terms.

Vimeo   http://www.vimeo.com/

This website is family safe and focuses on sharing private videos. The interface of the website is similar to some social networking sites that allow you to customize your profile page with photos from Flickr and embeddable player. This site allows users to socialize through their videos.

Metacafe   http://www.metacafe.com/

This video sharing site is community based. You can upload short-form videos and share it to the other users of the website. Metacafe has its own system called VideoRank that ranks videos according to the viewer reactions and features the most popular among the viewers.

ClipShack   http://www.clipshack.com/

Like most video sharing websites, you can post comments on the videos and even tag some as your favorite. You can also share the videos on other websites through the html code from ClipShack and even sending it through your email.

Veoh   http://www.veoh.com/

You can rent or sell your videos and keep the 70% of the sales price. You can upload a range of different video formats on Veoh and there is no limit on the size and length of the file. However, when your video is over 45 minutes it has to be downloaded before the viewer can watch it.

Jumpcut   http://download.cnet.com/JumpCut/3000-18515_4-10546353.html

Jumpcut allows its users to upload videos using their mobile phones. You will have to attach the video captured from your mobile phone to an email. It has its own movie making wizard that helps you familiarize with the interface of the site.

DailyMotion   www.dailymotion.com

As one of the leading sites for sharing videos, Dailymotion attracts over 114 million unique monthly visitors (source: comScore, May 2015) 1.2 billion videos views worldwide (source: internal). Offers the best content from users, independent content creators and premium partners. Using the most advanced technology for both users and content creators, provides high-quality and HD video in a fast, easy-to-use online service that also automatically filters infringing material as notified by content owners.
Offering 32 localized versions, their mission is to provide the best possible entertainment experience for users and the best marketing opportunities for advertisers, while respecting content protection.

Business Cards

Our business card will include our company logo, complete contact information, name and title, association logos, slogan or markets serviced, licenses and certifications. The center of our bi-fold card will contain a listing of the Senior Concierge Services we offer. We will give out multiple business cards to friends, family members, and to each customer, upon the completion of the service. We will also distribute business cards in the following ways:
1.   Attached to invoices, surveys, flyers and door hangers.
2.   Included in customer errand packages.
3.   We will leave a stack of business cards in a Lucite holder with the local Chamber of Commerce and any other businesses offering free counter placement.

We will use fold-over cards because they will enable us to list all of our services and complete contact instructions on the inside of the card. We will also give magnetic business cards to new clients for posting on the refrigerator door.

We will place the following referral discount message on the back of our business cards:
> - Our business is very dependent upon referrals. If you have associates who could benefit from our quality products, please write your name at the bottom of this card and give it to them. When your friend presents this card upon their first visit, he or she will be entitled to 10% off discount. And, on your next invoice, you will also get a 10% discount as a thank you for your referral.

Resource: www.vistaprint.com

Direct Mail Package

To build name recognition and to announce the opening of our Senior Concierge Service company, we will create a mail package consisting of a tri-fold brochure containing a discount coupon to welcome our new customers. We plan to make a mailing to local subscribers of business magazines. From those identified local customers, we shall ask them to complete a survey and describe any specific Senior Concierge Services they would like to see added. Those customers returning completed surveys would receive a premium (giveaway) gift.
Resource: www.melissadata.com

Trade Shows

We will exhibit at as many local trade shows per year as possible. These include Home and Garden Shows, County Fairs, Business Expos, open exhibits in shopping malls, business spot-lights with our local Chamber of Commerce, and more. The objective is to get our company name and service out to as many people as possible. When exhibiting at a trade show, we will put our best foot forward and represent ourselves as professionals. We will be open, enthusiastic, informative and courteous. We will exhibit our Senior Concierge Services with sales brochures, logo-imprinted giveaways, a photo book for people to browse through and a computer to run our video presentation through. We will use a 'free drawing' for a concierge basket prize and a sign-in sheet to collect names and email addresses. We will also develop a questionnaire or survey that helps us to assemble an ideal customer profile and qualify the leads we receive. We will train our booth attendants to answer all type of questions and to handle objections. We will also seek to present educational seminars at the show to gain increased publicity, and name and expertise recognition. Most importantly, we will develop and implement a follow-up program to stay-in-touch with prospects.

Resources:
- www.tsnn.com
- www.acshomeshow.com/
- www.Biztradeshows.com
- www.newpa.com
- www.expoworld.net
- www.eventseye.com
- www.fita.org
- www.expocentral.com
- www.EventsInAmerica.com
- www.commerce.gov
- www.sba.gov/international
- www.biztradeshows.gov
- www.trade-show-advisor.com
- www.tscentral.com

New Homeowners / Movers

We will reach out to new movers in our immediate neighborhood. Marketing to new movers will help bring in more long-term customers. And, because new movers are five times more likely to become loyal, this marketing program, will generate new, fresh customers who are likely to turn in to the regular customers. The value of a new loyal customer will be significant, as a new loyal customer who comes in ___ (#) times a month can be worth up to $_____ a year for standard services. Furthermore, many studies suggest that new movers typically stay in their new homes for an average of 5.6 years. We will also participate in local Welcome Wagon activities for new residents, and assemble a mailing list to distribute sales literature from county courthouse records and Realtor supplied information. We will use a postcard mailing to promote a special get-acquainted offer to new residents.

We will adhere the following routine when marketing to new local homeowners:
1. Send out a friendly welcome letter / flyer / brochure welcoming each new family to the community along with information on our pest control services.
2. Include a gift certificate or a new client discount coupon / certificate to entice the new family to try our service, risk free with no obligation.
3. Send out a new client discount or offer an initial free evaluation.
4. Send out a postcard with a discount or coupon.

Resources:
Welcome Wagon   www.WelcomeWagon.com

Welcome Mat Services   www.WelcomeMatServices.com
Welcomemat Services uses specialized, patent-pending technology to store and log customer demographics for use by the local companies it supports.

Bench Ads
These ads will provide us with an affordable way to improve our visibility.
Resource: www.BenchAds.net

Networking
Networking will be a key to success because referrals and alliances formed can help to improve our community image and keep our business growing. We will strive to build long-term mutually beneficial relationships with our networking contacts and join the following types of organizations:
1. We will form a LeTip Chapter to exchange business leads.
2. We will join the local BNI.com referral exchange group.
3. We will join the Chamber of Commerce to further corporate relationships.
4. We will join the Rotary Club, Lions Club, Kiwanis Club, Church Groups, etc.
5. We will do volunteer work for American Heart Assoc. and Habitat for Humanity.
6. We will become an affiliated member of the local board of Realtors and the Women's Council of Realtors.
7. We will join local garden and women's clubs.
8. We will join the American Seniors Association (http://www.americanseniors.org/) and AARP.org.
9. We will join the Association for Senior Citizens (www.associationforseniorcitizens.com/) and other senior citizen clubs.

We will use our metropolitan _____ (city) Chamber of Commerce to target businesses that target seniors. We will mail letters to each member describing our senior concierge services. We will follow-up with phone calls and offer to give an educational presentation on the benefits of Senior Concierge Services at one of their meetings.

We will pursue speaking engagements at the following venues:
1. Senior Civic and Social Groups
3. Professional Service Provider Trade Associations
5. Chamber of Commerce

We will join and participate, as an official event coordinator, in any organization that promotes stress reduction and the importance of time management.

Newsletter
We will develop a one-page newsletter to be handed out to customers to take home. We will also create an email version, which will be sent to our in-house built email database. No other communication method will give our Senior Concierge Service a more cost-effective way to keep customers up-to-date on important news, events, services, and

"preferred customer" programs. The monthly newsletter will also be used to build our brand and update clients on special promotions and new services. The newsletter will be produced in-house and for the cost of paper and computer time. We will include the following types of information:
1. Our involvement with charitable events.
2. New Concierge Service Introductions
3. Featured employee/customer of the month.
4. New concierge industry technologies and trends.
5. Customer endorsements/testimonials.
6. Classified ads from local sponsors and suppliers.
7. Announcements / Upcoming events schedule.
8. Customer Questions and Answers

Resources: Microsoft Publisher   www.aweber.com

We will adhere to the following newsletter writing guidelines:
1. We will provide content that is of real value to our subscribers.
2. We will provide solutions to our subscriber's problems or questions.
3. We will communicate regularly on a weekly basis.
4. We will create HTML Messages that look professional and allow us to track how many people click on our links and/or open our emails.
5. We will not pitch our business opportunity in our Ezine very often.
6. We will focus our marketing dollars on building our Ezine subscriber list.
7. We will focus on relationship building and not the conveying of a sales message.
8. We will vary our message format with videos, articles, checklists, quotes, pictures and charts.
9. We will recommend occasionally affiliate products in some of our messages to help cover our marketing costs.
10. We will consistently follow the above steps to build a database of qualified prospects and customers.

Resources:
http://oi.vresp.com/?fid=3f0fbb1380
www.mailchimp.com
www.constantcontact.com/email-templates/newsletter-templates
http://lmssuccess.com/10-reasons-online-business-send-regular-newsletter-customers/
www.smallbusinessmiracles.com/how/newsletters/
www.fuelingnewbusiness.com/2010/06/01/combine-email-marketing-and-social-media-for-ad-agency-new-business/

Vehicle Signs

We will place magnetic and vinyl signs on our vehicles and include our company name, phone number, company slogan and website address, if possible. We will create a cost-effective moving billboard with high-quality, high-resolution vehicle wraps. We will wrap a portion of the vehicle or van to deliver excellent marketing exposure.
Resource: http://www.fastsigns.com/

Design Tips:
1. Avoid mixing letter styles and too many different letter sizes.
2. Use the easiest to recognize form of your logo.
3. The standard background is white.
4. Do not use a background color that is the same as or close to your vehicle color.
5. Choose colors that complement your logo colors.
6. Avoid the use too many colors.
7. Use dark letter colors on a light background or the reverse.
8. Use easy to read block letters in caps and lower case.
9. Limit content to your business name, slogan, logo, phone number and website-address.
10. Include your license number if required by law.
11. Magnetic signs are ideal for door panels (material comes on 24" wide rolls).
12. Graphic vehicle window wraps allow the driver to still see out.
13. Keep your message short so people driving by can read it at a glance.
14. Do not use all capital letters.
15. Be sure to include your business name, phone number, slogan and web address.

Vehicle Wraps

Vehicle wrapping will be one of our preferred marketing methods. According to company research, wrapped vehicles have more impact than billboards, create a positive image for the company and prompt the public to remember the words and images featured in the company's branding. Vehicle wrapping is also an inexpensive marketing strategy. A typical truck wrap costs about $2,500 and is a one-time payment for an ad that spans the life of a truck's lease.

Advertising Wearables

We will give all preferred club members an eye-catching T-shirt or sweatshirt with our company name and logo printed across the garment to wear about town. We will also give them away as a thank you for customer referral activities. We will ask all employees to wear our logo-imprinted shirts.

Sales Brochures

The sales brochure will enable us to make a solid first impression when pursing business from commercial accounts and high-end clients. Our sales brochure will include the following contents and become a key part of our sales presentation folder and direct mail package:

- Contact Information
- Customer Testimonials
- Competitive Advantages
- Trial Coupon
- Business Hours

- Business Description
- List of Services/Benefits
- Owner Resume/Bio
- Map of Service Area

Sales Brochure Design
1. Speak in Terms of Our Prospects Wants and Interests.
2. Focus on all the Benefits, not Just Features.

3. Put the company logo and Unique Selling Proposition together to reinforce the fact that your company is different and better than the competition.
4. Include a special offer, such as a discount, a free report, a sample, or a free trial to increase the chances that the brochure will generate sales.

We will incorporate the following Brochure Design Guidelines:
1. Design the brochure to achieve a focused set of objectives (marketing of programs) with a target market segment (residential vs. commercial).
2. Tie the brochure design to our other marketing materials with colors, logo, fonts and formatting.
3. List capabilities and how they benefit clients.
4. Demonstrate what we do and how we do it differently.
5. Define the value proposition of our engineering installing services
6. Use a design template that reflects your market positioning strategy.
7. Identify your key message (unique selling proposition)
8. List our competitive advantages.
9. Express our understanding of client needs and wants.
10. Use easy to read (scan) headlines, subheadings, bullet points, pictures, etc.
11. Use a logo to create a visual branded identity.
12. The most common and accepted format for a brochure is a folded A3 (= 2 x A4), which gives 4 pages of information.
13. Use a quality of paper that reflects the image we want to project.
14. Consistently stick to the colors of our corporate style.
15. Consider that colors have associations, such as green colors are associated with the environment and enhance an environmental image.
16. Illustrations will be appropriate and of top quality and directly visualize the product assortment, product application and production facility.
17. The front page will contain the company name, logo, the main application of your product or service and positioning message or Unique Selling Proposition.
18. The back page will be used for testimonials or references, and contact details.

Sales Presentation Folder Contents

1.	Resumes	2.	Patient Photos
3.	Contract/Application	4.	Frequently Asked Questions
5.	Sales Brochure	6.	Business Cards
7.	Testimonials/References	8.	Program Descriptions
9.	Informative Articles	10.	Referral Program
11.	Company Overview	12.	Operating Policies
13.	Article Reprints	14.	Press Releases

Employee Personal Marketing

We will develop a training program and business cards to help employees to market themselves as sales agents and get new people interested in our retail business. Employee personal marketing is the ability to showcase employee talents and present them in a fashion that our customers and prospects will recognize them. We will need to be able to back up and actually do what we say we can do. This type of marketing will also be very important for the customers we already have. We will develop an employee certification program to make sure our customers are aware of all the ways our products and services can benefit them, and that every customer gets served properly.

Coupons

We will use coupons with limited time expirations to get prospects to try our products and service programs. We will also accept the coupons of our competitors to help establish new client relationships. We will run ads directing people to our Web site for a $___ coupon certificate. This will help to draw in new clients and collect e-mail addresses for the distribution of a monthly newsletter. Research indicates that we can use our coupons to spark online searches of our website and drive sales. This will help to draw in new clients and collect e-mail addresses for the distribution of a monthly newsletter. We will include a coupon with each sale or send them by mail to our mailing list.

Examples:
http://www.localsaver.com/henderson-nv/professional-services/personal-assistants/senior-concierge-services-llc-coupon?dsc=MYDS&bizid=52027922&cpnid=3840934

https://my.datasphere.com/biz/after_all_these_years_senior_concierge_services-health_beauty_senior_care_services-suffern_ny-52033511-4303814

We will leverage bargain-hunting services like FatWallet, RetailMeNot, and DealsPl.us to reach our most price-sensitive buyers.

Resources:
http://www.businessknowhow.com/marketing/couponing.htm
https://www.constantcontact.com/features/coupons

We will use coupons selectively to accomplish the following:
1. To introduce a new product or service.
2. To attract loyal customers away from the competition
3. To prevent customer defection to a new competitor.
4. To help celebrate a special event.
5. To thank repeat customers for their steady business.

Types of Coupons include:
1. Courtesy Coupons   Rewards for repeat business
2. Cross-Marketing Coupons   Incentive to try other products/services.
3. Companion Coupon   Bring a friend incentive.

Websites like Groupon, LivingSocial, Eversave, and BuyWithMe sell discount vouchers for services ranging from custom framing to museum visits. Best known is Chicago-based Groupon. To consumers, discount vouchers promise substantial savings — often 50% or more. To merchants, discount vouchers offer possible opportunities for price discrimination, exposure to new customers, online marketing, and "buzz." Vouchers are more likely to be profitable for merchants with low marginal costs, who can better accommodate a large discount and for patient merchants, who place higher value on consumers' possible future return visits.

Yipit.com
Gathers over 30,000 offers per month from 809 daily deal sites like Groupon, LivingSocial, Gilt City, Google Offers and filters them based on where subscribers are located and what types of deals they want to be notified of. Yipit is a simple way to access them all - via web, a personalized email or iPhone - in 118 cities in North America.

Cross-Promotions
We will develop and maintain partnerships with local businesses that cater to the needs of our customers, such as beauty salons, fitness clubs, event planners and senior daycare centers, and conduct cross-promotional marketing campaigns. These cross-promotions will require the exchanging of customer mailing lists and endorsements.

Premium Giveaways
We will distribute logo-imprinted promotional products at events, also known as giveaway premiums, to foster top-of-mind awareness (www.promoideas.org). These items include logo-imprinted T-shirts, business cards with magnetic backs, mugs with contact phone number, and calendars that feature important celebration/holiday date reminders.

Newspaper Ads
We will design advertisements that focus on a particular client problem or pain, such as limited mobility. We will maximize the potential of each advertisement by eliminating the unnecessary information and appealing as strongly as possible to the needs of our senior target audience.

Our newspaper ads will utilize the following design tips:
1. We will start by getting a media kit from the publisher to analyze their demographic information as well as their reach and distribution.
2. Don't let the newspaper people have total control of our ad design, as we know how we want our company portrayed to the market.
3. Make sure to have 1st class graphics since this will be the only visual distinction we can provide the reader about our business.
4. Buy the biggest ad we can afford, with full-page ads being the best.
5. Go with color if affordable, because consumers pick color ads over black 82% of the time.
6. Ask the paper if they have specific days that more of our type of buyer reads their paper.
7. If we have a hit ad on our hands, we will make it into a circular or door-hanger to extend the life of the offer.
8. Don't change an ad because we are getting tired of looking at it.
9. We will start our headline by telling our story to pull the reader into the ad.

10. We will use "Act Now" to convey a sense of urgency to the reader.
11. We will use our headline to tell the reader what to do.
12. The headline is a great place to announce a free offer.
13. We will write our headline as if we were speaking to one person and make it personal.
14. We will use our headline to either relay a benefit or intrigue the reader into wanting more information.
15. Use coupons giving a dollar amount off, not a percentage, as people hate doing the math.

Local Publications

We will place low-cost classified ads in neighborhood publications to advertise our organic wines. We will also submit public relations and informative articles to improve our visibility and establish our expertise and trustworthiness. These publications include the following:

1. Neighborhood Newsletters and Church Bulletins
2. Local Restaurant Association Newsletter
3. Local Chamber of Commerce Newsletter
4. Realtor Magazines
5. Homeowner Association Newsletters

Resource:
Hometown News   www.hometownnews.com
Pennysaver   www.pennysaverusa.com

Publication Type	Ad Size	Timing	Circulation	Section	Fee

Yellow Page Ads

Research indicates that the use of the traditional Yellow Page Book is declining, but that new residents or people who don't have many personal acquaintances will look to the Yellow Pages to establish a list of potential businesses to call upon. Even a small 2" x 2" boxed ad can create awareness and attract the desired target client, above and beyond the ability of a simple listing. We will use the following design concepts:

1. We will use a headline to sell people on the unique time-saving benefits of our Senior Concierge Services.
2. We will include a service guarantee to improve our credibility.
3. We will include a coupon offer for a free first time use of our service and a tracking code to monitor the response rate.
4. We will choose an ad size equal to that of our competitors and evaluate the response rate for future insertion commitments.
5. We will include our hours of operation, motto or slogan and logo.
6. We will include our competitive advantages.
7. We will list under the same categories as our competitors.
8. We will use some bold lettering to make our ad standout.

9.   We will utilize yellow books that also offer an online dimension.
Resource: www.superpages.com   www.yellowpages.com
Examples:
https://www.yellowpages.com/charlotte-nc/senior-concierge-services

Ad Information:
    Book Title: _____   Coverage Area: _____
    Yearly Fee: $_____   Ad Size: _____ page
    Renewal date: _____   Contact: _____

Doorhangers

Our doorhangers will feature a calendar of 'Free Concierge Promo Events'. The doorhanger will include a list of all our Senior Concierge Service categories and info about our transitional programs. We will also attach our business card to the doorhanger and distribute the doorhangers multiple times to the same subdivision.

Article Submissions

We will pitch articles to consumer magazines, local newspapers, business magazines and internet articles directories to help establish our specialized expertise in senior care and improve our visibility. Hyperlinks will be placed within written articles and can be clicked on to take the customer to another webpage within our website or to a totally different website. These clickable links or hyperlinks will be keywords or relevant words that have meaning to our Senior Concierge Service. In fact, we will create a position whose primary function is to link our company with opportunities to be published in local publications.

Publishing requires an understanding of the following publisher needs:
1. Review of good work.   2. Editor story needs.
3. Article submission process rules   4. Quality photo portfolio
5. Exclusivity requirements.   6. Target market interests

Our Article Submission Package will include the following:
1. Well-written materials   2. Good Drawings
3. High-quality Photographs   4. Well-organized outline.

Examples of General Publishing Opportunities:
1. Document a new solution to old problem   2. Publish a research study
3. Mistake prevention advice   4. Present a different viewpoint
5. Introduce a local angle on a hot topic.   6. Reveal a new trend.
7. Share specialty niche expertise.   8. Share concierge health benefits

Examples of Specific Article Titles:
1. "Everything You Ever Wanted to Know About Gift Giving Etiquette"
2. "How to Evaluate and Compare Senior Concierge Service Companies"
3. "How to Maximize the Benefits from a Senior Concierge Service"
4. " How to Devote More Free Time to Fun Recreational Activities"
5. "How to Use Senior Concierge Services as a Family Survival Tool"

6. "How Concierge Companies Research Vendors Before Making Trade Recommendations"
7. "How to Care for Seniors on Hot Summer days"

Sample Articles: http://parentyourparents.com/articles/
http://parentyourparents.com/resources-for-aging-parents/

Write Articles with a Closing Author Resource Box or Byline
1. Author Name with credential titles.
2. Explanation of area of expertise.
3. Mention of a special offer.
4. A specific call to action
5. A Call to Action Motivator
6. All possible contact information
7. Helpful Links
8. Link to Firm Website.

Article Objectives:

Article Topic	Target Audience	Target Date

Article Tracking Form

Subject	Publication	Target Audience	Business Development	Resources Needed	Target Date

Possible Magazines to submit articles include:
1. AARP The Magazine
2. In-Style Magazine
3. Senior Times Magazine
4. Fifty-Plus News
5. Grand Times
6. Senior Citizens Magazine
7. Senior Living
8. Senior News
9. Senior Times
10. Senior Voice
11. Today's Senior

Resource:
http://www.world-newspapers.com/seniors.html

Resources:
Writer's Market   www.writersmarket.com
Directory of Trade Magazines   www.techexpo.com/tech_mag.html

Internet article directories include:
http://ezinearticles.com/   http://www.mommyshelpercommunity.com
http://www.wahm-articles.com   http://www.ladypens.com/
http://www.articlecity.com   http://www.amazines.com
http://www.articledashboard.com   http://www.submityourarticle.com/articles
http://www.webarticles.com   http://www.articlecube.com
http://www.article-buzz.com   http://www.free-articles-zone.com
www.articletogo.com   http://www.content-articles.com
http://article-niche.com   http://superpublisher.com

www.internethomebusinessarticles.com
http://www.articlenexus.com
http://www.articlefinders.com
http://www.articlewarehouse.com
http://www.easyarticles.com
http://ideamarketers.com/
http://clearviewpublications.com/
http://www.goarticles.com/
http://www.webmasterslibrary.com/
http://www.connectionteam.com
http://www.MarketingArticleLibrary.com
http://www.dime-co.com
http://www.allwomencentral.com
http://www.reprintarticles.com
http://www.articlestreet.com
http://www.articlepeak.com
http://www.simplysearch4it.com
http://www.zongoo.com
http://www.mainstreetmom.com
http://www.valuablecontent.com
http://www.article99.com

http://www.site-reference.com
www.articlebin.com
www.articlesfactory.com
www.buzzle.com
www.isnare.com
//groups.yahoo.com/group/article_announce
www.ebusiness-articles.com
www.authorconnection.com/
www.businesstoolchest.com
www.digital-women.com/submitarticle.htm
www.searchwarp.com
www.articleshaven.com
www.marketing-seek.com
www.articles411.com
www.articleshelf.com
www.articlesbase.com
www.articlealley.com
www.selfgrowth.com
www.LinkGeneral.com
www.articleavenue.com
www.virtual-professionals.com

Online Classified Ad Placement Opportunities

The following free classified ad sites, will enable our Senior Concierge Service to thoroughly describe the benefits of our using our services:

1. **Craigslist.org**
2. Ebay Classifieds
3. Classifieds.myspace.com
4. KIJIJI.com
5. //Lycos.oodle.com
6. Webclassifieds.us
7. USFreeAds.com
8. www.oodle.com
9. Backpage.com
10. stumblehere.com
11. Classifiedads.com
12. gumtree.com
13. Inetgiant.com
14. www.sell.com
15. Freeadvertisingforum.com
16. Classifiedsforfree.com
17. www.olx.com
18. www.isell.com
19. Base.google.com
20. www.epage.com
21. Chooseyouritem.com
22. www.adpost.com
23. Adjingo.com
24. Kugli.com

Sample Classified Ad#1:
Are you too busy to properly care for your aging parents? Do you have parents who would prefer to age in place, rather than transition to a old age home? For these concerns and other senior care possibilities, visit our website at _____ for details on our Senior Concierge Services in _____ (city). If you are interested in learning more about our Senior Concierge Services, please email _____ or visit the website. We have been serving the _____ area since _____ (year). Give us a call at _____, or visit us at _____ (Website) for our senior seminar schedule.

Sample Classified Ad#2:
_____ (senior concierge company name) is independently and locally owned in the city of _____. It was formed to provide a dependable, compassionate, and professional service to assist seniors in living the most productive and independent lifestyle possible. We are a unique, personal non-medical concierge service that strives to meet the individual and changing lifestyle needs of our clients. Our goal is to assist in organizing, enhancing, and streamlining the lives of seniors. By creating memorable experiences, we hope to form long-lasting, one-on-one relationships with both the active senior and their family so that we can be there to assist for many years. Visit Us at
www._____.com

Two-Step Direct Response Classified Advertising
We will use 'two-step direct response advertising' to motivate readers to take a step or action that signals that we have their permission to begin marketing to them in step two. Our objective is to build a trusting relationship with our prospects by offering a free unbiased, educational report in exchange for permission to continue the marketing process. This method of advertising has the following benefits:

1. Shorter sales cycle.
2. Eliminates need for cold calling.
3. Establishes expert reputation.
4. Better qualifies prospects
5. Process is very trackable.
6. Able to run smaller ads.

Sample Two Step Lead Generating Classified Ad:
FREE Report Reveals "The Secrets to Happily Aging in Place"
Or….. "How to Best Utilize a Senior Concierge Service".
Call 24 hour recorded message and leave your name and address.
Your report will be sent out immediately.
Note: The respondent has shown they have an interest in our service specialty.
We will also include a section in the report on our other services and our complete contact information, along with a time limited discount coupon.

Post ads on Craigslist every three days:
Post an ad about your business on the website www.craigslist.com , under the appropriate section in the city or town where you live. Ads are placed chronologically and when too many ads are above yours, you get fewer calls. You will get the best results if you delete and repost your ad every three days.

Stage External Events
We will stage external events to become known in our community. This is essential to attracting referrals. We will schedule regular external events, such as trade fairs, and seminar talks on retirement living strategies. We will use event registration forms, our website and an event sign-in sheet to collect the names and email addresses of all attendees. This database will be used to feed our automatic customer relationship follow-up program and newsletter service.
Resource: wwweventbrite.com

Seminars

Seminars present the following marketing and bonding opportunities:
1. Signage and branding as a presenting sponsor.
2. Opportunity to provide logo imprinted handouts.
3. Media exposure through advertising and public relations.
4. The opportunity for one-on-one interaction with a targeted group of consumers to demonstrate an understanding of their needs and our matching expert solutions.
5. Use of sign-in sheet to collect names and email addresses for database build.

Possible seminar funding sources:
1. Small registration fee to cover the cost of hand-outs and refreshments.
2. Get sponsorship funding from partner/networking organizations.
3. Sponsorship classified ads in the program guide or handouts.

We will establish our expertise and trustworthiness by offering free seminars on the following types of topics:
1. Considerations in Choosing a Senior Concierge Service
2. How to Improve Senior Lifestyle Options
3. How to Use Senior Concierge Services to Reduce Family Stress and Improve the Mental Health of Aging Loved Ones.
4. How Senior Concierge Service Providers Pre-screen Vendor Partners.

Seminar target groups include the following:
1. Physicians
2. Senior Organizations
3. Assisted Living Managers
4. Realtors
5. Women's Clubs
6. Health Clubs

Seminar marketing approaches include:
1. Posting to website and enabling online registrations.
2. Email blast using www.constantcontact.com
3. Include seminar schedule in newsletter.
4. Classified ads using craigslist.org

Seminar Objectives:

Seminar Topic	Target Audience	Handout	Target Date

Note: Refer to Seminar Worksheet in appendix.

Cable Television Advertising

Cable television will offer us more ability to target certain market niches or demographics with specialty programming. We will use our marketing research survey to determine which cable TV channels our customers are watching. It is expected that many watch the Home & Garden TV channel, and that people with surplus money watch the Golf Channel and the Food Network. Our plan is to choose the audience we want, and to hit them often enough to entice them to take action. We will also take advantage of the fact that we will be able to pick the specific areas we want our commercial to air. Ad pricing will be dependent upon the number of households the network reaches, the ratings the particular show has earned, contract length and the supply and demand for a particular network.

Resource:
Spot Runner	www.spotrunner.com
Television Advertising	http://televisionadvertising.com/faq.htm

Ad Information:

Length of ad "spot": ___ seconds	Development costs: $____ (onetime fee)
Length of campaign: __ (#) mos.	Runs per month: Three times per day
Cost per month.: $_____	Total campaign cost: $_____.

Press Release Overview

We will use market research surveys to determine the media outlets that our demographic customers read and then target them with press releases. We will draft a cover letter for our media kit that explains that we would like to have the newspaper print a story about the start-up of our new local business or a milestone that we have accomplished. And, because news releases may be delivered by feeds or on news services and various websites, we will create links from our news releases to content on our website. These links which will point to more information or a special offer, will drive our clients into the sales process. They will also increase search engine ranking on our site. We will follow-up each faxed package to the media outlet with a phone call to the lifestyle section editor.

Media Kit
We will compile a media kit with the following items:
1. A pitch letter introducing our Senior Concierge Service.
2. A press release with news story facts.
3. Biographical fact sheet or sketches of key personnel.
4. Listing of service features and benefits to customers.
5. Photos and Testimonials.

Public Relations Opportunities
Travel magazines often include articles featuring interviews with concierges.
The following represents a partial list of some of the reasons for issuing a free press release on a regular basis:
1. Announce the availability of services.
2. Certifications Received/Designation Requirements
3. Open of a new business
4. Addition of New Services
5. Announce Business Relocation/Move
6. Announce Open House Event
7. Support for a Non-Profit Cause
8. Involvement with a local school or sporting event.
9. Presentation of a free seminar on aging in place.
10. Publish accumulated Survey Results

11. Publication of an article or book on senior care options.
12. Addition of a new staff member.
13. Notable Client Successes/Case Studies/Success Stories
14. Other Milestone Accomplishments

Examples:
www.pr.com/press-release/514236
www.prnewswire.com/news-releases/cutv-news-welcomes-h-frances-reaves-of-parent-your-parents-300607969.html

We will use the following techniques to get our press releases into print:
1. Find the right contact editor at a publication, that is, the editor who specializes in travel, health and wellness issues.
2. Understand the target publication's format, flavor and style and learn to think like its readers to better tailor our pitch.
3. Ask up front if the journalist is on deadline.
4. Request a copy of the editorial calendar--a listing of targeted articles or subjects broken down by month or issue date, to determine the issue best suited for the content of our news release or article.
5. Make certain the press release appeals to a large audience by reading a couple of back issues of the publication we are targeting to familiarize ourselves with its various sections and departments.
6. Customize the PR story to meet the magazine's particular style.
7. Avoid creating releases that look like advertising or self-promotion.
8. Make certain the release contains all the pertinent and accurate information the journalist will need to write the article and accurately answer the questions "who, what, when, why and where".
9. Include a contact name and telephone number for the reporter to call for more information.

PR Distribution Checklist
We will send copies of our press releases to the following entities:
1. Send it to clients to show accomplishments.
2. Send to prospects to help prospects better know who you are and what you do.
3. Send it to vendors to strengthen the relationship and to influence referrals.
4. Send it to strategic partners to strengthen and enhance the commitment and support to our firm.
5. Send it to employees to keep them in the loop.
6. Send it to Employees' contacts to increase the firm's visibility exponentially.
7. Send it to elected officials who often provide direction for their constituents.
8. Send it to trade associations for maximum exposure.
9. Put copies in the lobby and waiting areas.
10. Put it on our Web site, to enable visitors to find out who we are and what our firm is doing, with the appropriate links to more detailed information.
11. Register the Web page with search engines to increase search engine optimization.

12. Put it in our press kit to provide members of the media background information about our firm.
13. Include it in our newsletter to enable easy access to details about company activities.
14. Include it in our brochure to provide information that compels the reader to contact our firm when in need of legal counsel.
15. Hand it out at trade shows and job fairs to share news with attendees and establish credibility.

Media List

Journalist	Interests	Organization	Contact Info

Distribution:
- www.1888PressRelease.com
- www.prweb.com
- www.PR.com
- www.24-7PressRelease.com
- www.PRnewswire.com
- www.PRLog.org
- www.businesswire.com
- www.primezone.com
- www.xpresspress.com/
- www.Mediapost.com
- www.ecomwire.com
- www.WiredPRnews.com
- www.eReleases.com
- www.NewsWireToday.com
- www.onlinePRnews.com
- www.marketwire.com
- www.primewswire.com
- www.ereleases.com/index.html

Journalist Lists:
- www.mastheads.org
- www.helpareporter.com
- www.easymedialist.com

Media Directories
- Bacon's – www.bacons.com/   AScribe – www.ascribe.org/
- Newspapers – www.newspapers.com/   Gebbie Press – www.gebbieinc.com/

Support Services
- PR Web - http://www.prweb.com
- Yahoo News – http://news.yahoo.com/
- Google News – http://news.google.com/

Media Resource Expert

We will send email and mail to local media outlets, like our local TV news stations, Local Newspapers, and News Radio Stations, to advise them that we are a readily available resource for senior concierge related new stories. We will include our areas of specialty, and how we can contribute to media stories about _____ and home tasting and cocktail parties in general. We will also indicate our willingness to share our knowledge on how the public can prevent from being scammed by unethical _____. We will always be on the look-out for opportunities to interview with local and national reporters. We will sign up for the following services that notify companies of reporters looking for interviews:

Reporter Connection   http://reporterconnection.com/
ProfNet Connection   http://www.profnetconnect.com/

Muck Rack						https://muckrack.com/benefits
News Wise						www.newswise.com/
Pitch Rate						http://pitchrate.com/
Experts							www.experts.com
News Basis						http://newsbasis.com/

Help A Reporter Out			www.helpareporter.com/
An online platform that provides journalists with a robust database of sources for upcoming stories. It also provides business owners and marketers with opportunities to serve as sources and secure valuable media coverage.

Resources:
http://www.thebuzzfactoree.com/journalists-seeking-sources/
http://ijnet.org/en/blog/5-ways-find-sources-online

Sample Letter Template:
http://locksmithprofits.com/locksmith-guest-expert-marketing/

Radio Advertising

We will use non-event based radio advertising. This style of campaign is best suited for non-retail businesses, such as our senior concierge service. We will utilize a much smaller schedule of ads on a consistent long-range basis (48 to 52 weeks a year) with the objective of continuously maintaining top-of-mind-awareness. This will mean maintaining a sufficient level of awareness to be either the number one or number two choice when a triggering-event, such as a senior aging problem moves the consumer into the market for services and forces "a consumer choice" about which company in the consumer's perception might help them the most. This consistent approach will utilize only one ad each week day (260 days per year) and allow our company to cost-effectively keep our message in front of consumers once every week day. The ad copy for this non-event campaign, called a positioning message, will not be time-sensitive. It will define and differentiate our business' "unique market position" and will be repeated for a year. Note: On the average, listeners spend over 3.5 hours per day with radio.

Radio will give us the ability to target our audience, based on radio formats, such as news-talk, classic rock and the oldies. Radio will also be a good way to get repetition into our message, as listeners tend to be loyal to stations and parts of the day.
1.	We will use radio advertising to direct prospects to our Web site, advertise a limited time promotion or call for an informational brochure.
2.	We will try to barter our services for radio ad spots.
3.	We will use a limited-time offer to entice first-time customers to try our senior concierge services.
4.	We will explore the use of on-air community bulletin boards to play our public announcements about community sponsored events.
5.	We will also make the radio station aware of our expertise in the concierge

industry and our availability for interviews.
6. Our choice of stations will be driven by the market research information we collect via our surveys.
7. We will capitalize on the fact that many stations now stream their programming on the internet and reach additional local and even national audiences, and if online listeners like what they hear in our streaming radio spot, they can click over to our website.
8. Our radio ads will use humor, sounds, compelling music or unusual voices to grab attention.
9. Our spots will tell stories or present situations our target audience can relate to.
10. We will make our call to action, a website address or vanity phone number, easy to remember and tie it in with our company name or message.
11. We will focus on the time and money savings benefits of our services to both corporations and individuals.
12. We will approach radio stations about buying their unsold advertising space for deep discounts. (Commonly known at radio stations' as "Run of Station")
On radio, this might mean very early in the morning or late at night. We will talk to our advertising representatives and see what discounts they can offer when one of those empty spaces comes open.

Examples: http://www.sheridancare.com/
Resources: Radio Advertising Bureau   www.RAB.com
           Radio Locator   www.radio-locator.com
           Radio Directory   www.radiodirectory.com

Ad Information:
Length of ad "spot": ___ seconds   Development costs: $____ (onetime fee)
Length of campaign: __ (#) mos.   Runs per month: Three times per day
Cost per month.: $_____   Total campaign cost: $_____.

Script Resources:
www.voices.com/documents/secure/voices.com-commercial-scripts-for-radio-and-
    television-ads.pdf
http://smallbusiness.chron.com/say-30second-radio-advertising-spot-10065.html
https://voicebunny.com/blog/5-tips-make-radio-ads-grab-attention-sell/

Blog Talk Radio

National Public Radio (www.NPR.org) plays host to a radio program called _____. The program features _____ (type of experts) who talk and blog about senior concierge tips. This will help to establish our _____ expertise and build the trust factor with potential clients. Even if we can't get our own nationally syndicated talk show, we will try to make guest appearances and try our hand with podcasting by using apps like Spreaker or joining podcasting communities like BlogTalkRadio.

Resources:
National Public Radio   www.npr.org
Spreaker   http://www.spreaker.com/
Blog Talk Radio   http://www.blogtalkradio.com/

With BlogTalkRadio, people can either host their own live talk radio show with any phone and a computer or listen to thousands of new shows created daily.

Resource:
CUTV News Radio (http://www.blogtalkradio.com/cutvnewsradio) with veteran broadcast TV and radio hosts/media personalities Jim Masters and Doug Llewelyn is an informative, entertaining, thought-provoking and empowering broadcast series featuring several LIVE episodes daily and is a service of the Telly-award winning CUTV News, a full-service media company that provides entrepreneurs, business owners and extraordinary people a platform to share their story worldwide. Features fascinating guests from every walk of life, including entertainment, music, publishing, art, travel, health & wellness, self-help, sports, business, finance, science and much more. With shows 7 days a week, it offers the opportunity to hear amazing stories from amazing guests and from around the globe. Their Facebook Fan Page is: www.facebook.com/cutvnewsradio.
Example:
http://parentyourparents.com/news/cutv-news-radio-interview/
https://www.youtube.com/watch?v=yV1QIEyr-to

Postcards
1. We will use postcards to communicate the value of our services and target our known client demographic.
2. Postcards will offer cheaper mailing rates, staying power and attention-grabbing graphics, but require repetition, like most other advertising methods.
3. We will develop an in-house list of potential clients for routine communications from events, seminar registrations, direct response ads, etc.
4. We will use postcards to encourage prospects to visit our website to see a comprehensive list of our Senior Concierge Services, join the membership club, take advantage of a special offer and/or schedule an appointment.
5. We will grab attention and communicate a single-focus message in just a few words.
6. The visual elements of our postcard (color, picture, symbol) will be strong to help get attention and be directly supportive of the message.
7. We will facilitate a call to immediate action by prominently displaying our phone number and website address.
8. We will include a clear deadline, expiration date, limited quantity, or consequence of inaction that is connected to the offer to communicate immediacy and increase response.

Resource: www.postcardmania.com

Direct Mail
1. We will send a sales letter to senior organization members and advise the benefits of our targeted concierge services.
2. We will build a mailing list of target market prospects, such as dual income families and successful business people, and offer a one-month free trial membership in our senior concierge club.

3. We will build our in-house mailing list by scanning the local newspaper for likely prospect names, collecting business cards at networking events, and using a sign-in registration form at staged events.

Flyers
1. We will seek permission to post flyers on the bulletin boards in local businesses, community centers, party supply stores and local colleges.
2. We will use our flyers as part of a handout package at open house events.
3. The flyers will feature a discount coupon.
4. The flyers will contain a listing of our Senior Concierge Service categories and service benefits.
5. We will use flyers to promote upcoming seminars events on grandparent care options.
6. We will also insert flyers into our direct mailings and invoice/statement mailings.
7. We will use our flyers as part of a handout package at seminars and open house events.

Resources: www.uprinting.com   www.retailmenot.com

Customer Reward Program
As a means of building business by word-of-mouth, customers will be encouraged and rewarded as repeat customers. This will be accomplished by offering a discounted concierge coupon to those customers who sign-up for our frequent buyer card and purchase $___ of Senior Concierge Services within a ___ (#) month period.

Resources:
http://www.refinery29.com/best-store-loyalty-programs
https://thrivehive.com/customer-retention-and-loyalty-programs/
http://blog.fivestars.com/5-companies-loyalty-programs/
www.americanexpress.com/us/small-business/openforum/articles/10-cool-mobile-apps-that-increase-customer-loyalty/
https://squareup.com/loyalty
www.consumerreports.org/cro/news/2013/10/retailer-loyalty-rewards-programs/index.htm

Frequent Buyer Program Types:
1. Punch Cards   Receive something for free after? Purchases.
2. Dollar-for-point Systems Accrue points toward a free product.
3. Percentage of Purchase   Accrue points toward future purchases.

Sample: Loyalty Program
_____ (company name) LOYALTY PROGRAM
ACCRUE YOUR POINTS WITH THE FOLLOWING:
    Sign-up Bonus receive 1,000 points
    Pre-book your next visit receive 1,000 points

Refer a Friend receive 2,500 points
Retail Purchase receive 1 point/dollar spent
Service Purchase receive 1 point/dollar spent
REDEEMING POINT VALUE 100 POINTS = $1
Ex: For a $100 purchase, you will redeem 10,000 points

Referral Program
1. We will give a premium reward based simply on people supplying referral names.
2. Send an endorsed testimonial letter from a loyal client to the referred prospect.
3. Include a separate referral form as a direct response device.
4. Provide a space on the response form for leaving positive comments that can be used to build a testimonial letter, that will be sent to each referral.
5. Start the sales letter with an intriguing, benefit-laden opening headline that grabs the reader's attention.
6. Include a photo of the provider in the headline to build recognition and trust.
7. Use the letter to immediately launch into a "value-building" story, as stories build credibility, and get the reader deeply involved.
8. Use the sub-headlines to force the reader to read the offer paragraph.
9. Use the offer paragraph to set a response time limit and to build upon the fear of scarcity, which prompts people to take action.
10. Offer a free month of service for every three referral names supplied or for any referral name that actually becomes a client.
11. Give the referred prospect a 50% discount off of their first concierge service.
12. Require the average new client to sign up for a minimum of 4 months to cover the reward cost of the referral.

Sample Referral Program Guidelines:
_____ (company name) referral program provides one free hour of service added to an existing account or to a future purchase (within 6 months) of a service package for every new client referred that purchased a service package. The free hour will be granted to the referrer after the person referred has completed payment for service. The referral program does not apply to a la carte services.

Sample Referral Program
We want to show our appreciation to established customers and business network partners for their kind referrals to our business. ____ (company name) wants to reward our valued and loyal customers who support our _____ Programs by implementing a new referral program. Ask any of our team members for referral cards to share with your family and friends to begin saving towards your next ____ (product/service) purchase. We will credit your account $___ (?) for each new customer you refer to us as well as give them 10% off their first visit. When they come for their first visit, they should present the card upon arrival. We will automatically set you up a referral account.

The Referral Details Are As Follows:
1. You will receive a $__ (?) credit for every customer that you refer for _____

(products/services). Credit will be applied to your referral account on their initial visit.
2. We will keep track of your accumulated reward dollars and at any time we can let you know the amount you have available for use in your reward account.
3. Each time you visit _____ (company name), you can use your referral dollars to pay up to 50% of your total charge that day
4. Referral dollars are not applicable towards the purchase of _____ services.
5. All referral rewards are for _____ services and cannot be used towards _____ services.

Examples:
https://my.datasphere.com/biz/coles_concierge_services-health_beauty_senior_care_services-houston_tx-52019414-3116883

Resources:
http://brightsmack.com/marketing-strategies/37-referral-ideas-to-grow-your-business/
http://www.nisacards.com/Business-Referral-Marketing-Cards.aspx
https://www.referralsaasquatch.com/resources/
https://www.referralcandy.com/blog/47-referral-programs/
www.consultingsuccess.com/10-referral-strategies-to-grow-your-consulting-business

Resources:
Referral Program Software Packages
    www.invitebox.com
    www.referralsaasquatch.com/
    www.referralcandy.com/
    www.getambassador.com/

Statistics that support referral programs include:
92% of consumers trust peer recommendations, 40% trust advertising in search results, 36% trust online video ads, 36% trust sponsored ads on social networking sites and 33% trust online banner ads.

The average value of a referred customer is at least 16% higher than that of a non-referred customer with similar demographics and time of acquisition.

Referral Coupon Template
Company Name: _____
Address: _____
Phone: _____ Website: _____
Print and present this coupon with your first order and the existing customer who referred you will receive a credit for $_____ .

Current customer   **Referred customer**
Name: _____   Name: _____
Address: _____   Address: _____

Phone: _____   Phone: _____
Email: _____   Email: _____
Date referred:

Office use only
Credit memo number: _____
Credit issued date: _____   Credit applied by: _____

Invite-A-Friend
We will setup an aggressive invite-a-friend referral program. We will encourage new members or newsletter subscribers, during their initial registration process, to upload and send an invitation to multiple contacts in their email address books. We will encourage them by providing an added incentive, such as a free _____.

Testimonial Marketing
We will either always ask for testimonials immediately after a completed project or contact our clients once a quarter for them. We will also have something prepared that we would like the client to say that is specific to a service we offer, or anything relevant to advertising claims that we have put together. For the convenience of the client we will assemble a testimonial letter that they can either modify or just sign off on. Additionally, testimonials can also be in the form of audio or video and put on our website or mailed to potential clients in the form of a DVD or Audio CD. A picture with a testimonial is also excellent. We will put testimonials directly on a magazine ad, slick sheet, brochure, or website, or assemble a complete page of testimonials for our sales presentation folder.

Examples:
http://happyathomellc.com/testimonials/

We will collect customer testimonials in the following ways:
1. Our website – A page dedicated to testimonials (written and/or video).
2. Social media accounts – Facebook fan pages offer a review tab, which makes it easy to receive and display customer testimonials.
3. Google+ also offers a similar feature with Google+ Local.
4. Local search directories – Ask customers to post more reviews on Yelp and Yahoo Local.
5. Customer Satisfaction Survey Forms

We will pose the following questions to our customers to help them frame their testimonials:
1. What was the obstacle that would have prevented you from buying this product?
2. "What was your main concern about buying this product?"
3. What did you find as a result of buying this product?
4. What specific feature did you like most about this product?
5. What would be three other benefits about this product?
6. Would you recommend this product? If so, why?
7. Is there anything you'd like to add?

Resource:
https://smallbiztrends.com/2016/06/use-customer-testimonials.html
https://seniorservicebusiness.com/the-power-of-testimonials-for-your-senior-service-business/

Reminder Service

We will use our reminder service to help customers remember important birthdays and other occasions. A form will ask for the concierge recipient's name, relationship, occasion, date, and suitable product type. We will e-mail registrants a month before the occasion with a reminder and concierge suggestion, followed up with a reminder a few days before the occasion. We will instruct the program to send out a customized e-mail reminder to each shopper on the days specified. We will use a four-tier reminder system in the following sequence: email, postcard, letter, phone call. We will stress the importance of staying in touch in our messages and keeping the customer's profile updated with their activities. We will also try to determine the reason for the non-response or inactivity and what can be done to reactivate the client. The reminder service will also work to the benefit of regular clients, that want to be reminded of an agreed upon special date or coming event.

Business Logo

Our logo will graphically represent who we are and what we do, and it will serve to help brand our image. It will also convey a sense of uniqueness and professionalism. The logo will represent our company image and the message we are trying to convey. Our business logo will reflect the philosophy and objectives of our Senior Concierge Service business. Our logo will incorporate the following design guidelines:

1. It will relate to our industry, our name, a defining characteristic of our company or a competitive advantage we offer.
2. It will be a simple logo that can be recognized faster.
3. It will contain strong lines and letters which show up better than thin ones.
4. It will feature something unexpected or unique without being overdrawn.
5. It will work well in black and white (one-color printing).
6. It will be scalable and look pleasing in both small and large sizes.
7. It will be artistically balanced and make effective use of color, line density and shape.
8. It will be unique when compared to competitors.
9. It will use original, professionally rendered artwork.
10. It can be replicated across any media mix without losing quality.
11. It appeals to our target audience.
12. It will be easily recognizable from a distance if utilized in outdoor advertising.

Examples: https://www.48hourslogo.com/project.php?id=20517
Resources: www.freelogoservices.com/   www.hatchwise.com
www.logosnap.com   www.99designs.com
www.fiverr.com   www.freelancer.com

www.upwork.com

Logo Design Guide:
www.bestfreewebresources.com/logo-design-professional-guide
www.creativebloq.com/graphic-design/pro-guide-logo-design-21221

Fundraisers

Community outreach programs involving charitable fundraising and showing a strong interest in the local school system will serve to elevate our status in the community as a "good corporate citizen" while simultaneously increasing our lead generation. We will execute a successful fundraising program for our Senior Concierge Service business and build goodwill in the community, by adhering to the following guidelines:

1. Keep It Local
   When looking for a worthy cause, we will make sure it is local so the whole neighborhood will support it.
2. Plan It
   We will make sure that we are organized and outline everything we want to accomplish before planning the fundraiser.
3. Contact Local Media
   We will contact the suburban newspapers to do stories on the event and send out press releases to the local TV and radio stations.
4. Contact Area Businesses
   We will contact other businesses and have them put up posters in their stores and pass out flyers to promote the event.
5. Get Recipient Support
   We will make sure the recipients of the fundraiser are really willing to participate and get out in the neighborhood to invite everyone into our store for the event, plus help pass out flyers and getting other businesses to put up the posters.
6. Give Out Bounce Backs
   We will give a "bounce-back" coupon that allows for both a discount and an additional donation in exchange for customer next purchase. (It will have an expiration date of two weeks to give a sense of urgency.)
7. Be Ready with plenty of product and labor on hand for the event.

Fundraiser Action Plan Checklist:
1. Choose a good local cause for your fundraiser.
2. Calculate donations as a percentage for normal sales.
3. Require the group to promote and support the event.
4. Contact local media to get exposure before and after the event.
5. Ask area businesses to put up flyers and donate printing of materials.
6. Use a bounce-back coupon to get new customers back.
7. Be prepared with sufficient labor and product.

Resource:
www.thefundraisingauthority.com/fundraising-basics/fundraising-event/

Online Directory Listings

The following directory listings use proprietary technology to match customers with industry professionals in their geographical area. The local search capabilities for specific niche markets offer an invaluable tool for the customer. These directories help member businesses connect with purchase-ready buyers, convert leads to sales, and maximize the value of customer relationships. Their online and offline communities provide a quick and easy low or no-cost solution for customers to find a Senior Concierge Service quickly. We intend to sign-up with all no cost directories and evaluate the ones that charge a fee.

Concierge Directory   www.concierge-directory.com
Directory   www.conciergedirectory.org
E On Demand Concierge   www.eondemandconcierge.com/
Association Directory   http://iclma.org/member_directory
Got Task   http://www.gottask.com/#
Eldercare Link   http://info.eldercarelink.com

Care   www.care.com

We will sign up with Care.com to be matched with families looking for an in-home care provider.

Other General Directories Include:

Listings.local.yahoo.com	Switchboard Super Pages
YellowPages.com	MerchantCircle.com
Bing.com/businessportal	Local.com
Yelp.com	BrownBook.com
InfoUSA.com	iBegin.com
Localeze.com	Bestoftheweb.com
YellowBot.com	HotFrog.com
InsiderPages.com	MatchPoint.com
CitySearch.com	YellowUSA.com
Profiles.google.com/me	Manta.com
Jigsaw.com	LinkedIn.com
Whitepages.com	PowerProfiles.com
Judysbook.com	Company.com
Google.com	Yahoo.com
SuperPages.com	TrueLocal.com
ExpressUpdate.com	Citysquares.com
MojoPages.com	DMOZ
BOTW	Business.com

Get Listed   http://getlisted.org/enhanced-business-listings.aspx
Universal Business Listing   https://www.ubl.org/index.aspx
                                    www.UniversalBusinessListing.org

Universal Business Listing (UBL) is a local search industry service dedicated to acting as a central collection and distribution point for business information online. UBL provides business owners and their marketing representatives with a one-stop location for broad distribution of complete, accurate, and detailed listing information.

Billboards

We will use billboard advertising to create brand awareness and strong name recognition. We will design Billboards that are eye-catching and informative. We will include our business name, location, a graphic, and no more than eight words. In designing the billboard, we will consider the fact that the eye typically moves from the upper left corner to the lower right corner of a billboard. We will use colors and pictures to contrast with the sky and other surroundings. We will keep the layout uncluttered and the message simple, and include a direct call to action. Depending on the billboards size and location, the cost will range from $1,000 to $5,000 per month. We will try to negotiate a discount on a long-term contract.

Ex: Looking for a Senior Concierge Service that Can Anticipate Your Needs?

Resources:
Outdoor Advertising Association of America   www.oaaa.org
EMC Outdoor, Inc.   www.emcoutdoor.com

Theater Advertising

Theater advertising is the method of promoting our business through in-theatre promotions. The objective of theater advertising is to expose the movie patron to our advertising message in various ways throughout the theater. Benefits include; an engaged audience that can't change the channel, an audience that is in a quiet environment, an audience that is in a good mood and receptive, advertising that is targeted to our local geographic area, full color video advertising on a 40 foot screen, and a moving and interactive ad with music and voiceover.

Resources:
Velocity Cinema Advertising   www.movieadvertising.com/index.html
NCM   www.nationalcinemedia.com/intheatreadvertising/

Mobile Marketing

In a texting component, customers will be able to text "____" to _____ (#) and receive mobile coupons for Senior Concierge Services. The second part of the message asks customers if they would like to register their e-mail addresses to receive weekly communications from _____ (company name). The first mobile coupon will reward customers with $___ off as an introductory trial offer. Customers will continue to receive additional offers, including special offers on holiday services. This will purely an opt in campaign, and will let us create an ongoing conversation with our customers.

We will use the following to leverage our mobile marketing program:
1.   We will offer customers the opportunity to join a mobile loyalty club and receive special rewards and offers for mobile club members only.
2.   We will encourage customers to sign up for the mobile program at the reception counter, on the website and on social media platforms.

3. We will develop compelling up-sell and cross-sell mobile coupon offers, such as a discount on a product when purchasing a service, or up-selling through offering service packages.
4. We will use mobile loyalty programs to stay top of mind with existing customers and drive repeat sales.
5. Our mobile messages will include mobile coupons as well as announcements about new employees or new available services and treatments.
6. We will use mobile messaging on special occasions, such as Mother's Day, and to drive traffic during the slower season.

Resource:
Mobile Marketing Association	www.mmaglobal.com
BxP Marketing visit	www.bxpmarketing.com.

E-mail Marketing

We will use the following email marketing tips to improve communications, boost senior customer loyalty and attract new and repeat business.

1. Define our objectives as the most effective email strategies are those that offer value to our subscribers: either in the form of educational content or promotions. To drive sales, a promotional campaign is the best format. To create brand recognition and reinforce our expertise in our industry we will use educational newsletters.
2. A quality, permission-based email list will be a vital component of our email marketing campaign. We will ask customers and prospects for permission to add them to our list at every touch-point.
3. We will listen to our customers by using easy-to-use online surveys to ask specific questions about customers' preferences, interests and satisfaction.
4. We will send only relevant and targeted communications.
5. We will reinforce our brand to ensure recognition of our brand by using a recognizable name in the "from" line of our emails and including our company name, logo and a consistent design and color scheme in every email.

Resources:
https://cbtnews.com/8-tips-drive-successful-email-marketing-campaign/
https://www.inman.com/2017/06/05/4-tips-for-effective-email-marketing/
https://due.com/blog/ways-take-good-care-email-list/

Every ___ (five?) to ____ (six?) weeks, we will send graphically-rich, permission-based, personalized, email marketing messages to our list of customers who registered on our website. The emails will alert customers in a ____ (50?)-mile radius to sales and promotions as well as other local events sponsored by our company. This service will be provided by VerticalResponse.com, ExactTarget.com or ConstantContact.com. The email will announce a special event and contain a short sales letter. The message will invite recipients to click on a link to the club website to checkout more information about the event, then print out the page and bring it with them to the event. The software offered by these companies will automatically personalize each email with the customer's name. The software also provides detailed click-through behavior reports that will enable us to evaluate the success of each message. The software will also allow our business to dramatically scale back its direct mail efforts and associated costs. We will send a promotional e-mail about a promotion that the customer indicated was important to them in their preferred membership application. Each identified market segment will get notified of new products, specials and offers based on past buying patterns and what they've clicked on in our previous e-newsletters or indicated on their surveys. The objective is to tap the right customer's need at the right time, with a targeted subject line and targeted content. Our general e-newsletter may appeal to most customers, but targeted mailings that reach out to our various audience segments will build even deeper relationships and drive higher sales.

Resources:
www.constantcontact.com/pricing/email-marketing.jsp
http://www.verticalresponse.com/blog/10-retail-marketing-ideas-to-boost-sales/

Google Reviews
We will use our email marketing campaign to ask people for reviews. We will ask people what they thought of our business or senior concierge services and encourage them to write a Google Review if they were impressed. We will incorporate a call to action (CTA) on our email auto signature with a link to our Google My Review page.

Source:
https://superb.digital/how-to-ask-your-clients-for-google-reviews/

Resources:
https://support.google.com/business/answer/3474122?hl=en
https://support.google.com/maps/answer/6230175?co=GENIE.Platform
    %3DDesktop&hl=en
www.patientgain.com/how-to-get-positive-google-reviews

Example:
We will tell our customers to:
1. Go to https://www.google.com/maps
2. Type in your business name, select the listing
3. There's a "card" (sidebar) on the left-hand side. At the bottom, they can click 'Be the First to Write a Review' **or** 'Write a Review' if you already have one review.

Source:
https://www.reviewjump.com/blog/how-do-i-get-google-reviews/

Voice Broadcasting
A web-based voice broadcast system will provide a powerful platform to generate thousands of calls to clients and customers or create customizable messages to be delivered to specific individuals. Voice broadcasting and voice mail broadcast will allow our company to instantly send interactive phone calls with ease while managing the entire process right from the Web. We will instantly send alerts, notifications, reminders, GOTV - messages, and interactive surveys with ease right from the Web. The free VoiceShot account will guide us through the process of recording and storing our

messages, managing our call lists, scheduling delivery as well as viewing and downloading real-time call and caller key press results. The voice broadcasting interface will guide us through the entire process with a Campaign Checklist as well as tips from the Campaign Expert. Other advanced features include recipient targeting, call monitoring, scheduling, controlling the rate of call delivery and customized text to speech (TTS).

Resource:
http://www.voiceshot.com/public/outboundcalls.asp

Facebook.com

We will use Facebook to move our businesses forward and stay connected to our customers in this fast-paced world. Content will be the key to staying in touch with our customers and keeping them informed. The content will be a rich mix of information, before and after photos, interactive questions, current trends and events, industry facts, education, promotions and specials, humor and fun. We will use the following step system to get customers from Facebook.com:

1. We will open a free Facebook account at Facebook.com.
2. We will begin by adding Facebook friends. The fastest way to do this is to allow Facebook to import our email addresses and send an invite out to all our customers.
3. We will post a video to get our customers involved with our Facebook page. We will post a video called "How to Plan for Proper Senior Care." The video will be first uploaded to YouTube.com and then simply be linked to our Facebook page. Video will be a great way to get people active and involved with our Facebook page.
4. We will send an email to our customers base that encourages them to check out the new video and to post their feedback about it on our Facebook page. Then we will provide a link driving customers to our Facebook page.
5. We will respond quickly to feedback, engage in the dialogue and add links to our response that direct the author to a structured mini-survey.
6. We will optimize our Facebook profile with our business keyword to make it an invaluable marketing tool and become the "go-to" expert in our industry
7. On a monthly basis, we will send out a message to all Facebook fans with a special offer, as Fan pages are the best way to interact with customers and potential customers on Facebook,
8. We will use Facebook as a tool for sharing success stories and relate the ways in which we have helped our customers.
9. We will use Facebook Connect to integrate our Facebook efforts with our regular website to share our Facebook Page activity. This will also give us statistics about our website visitors, and add social interaction to our site.

Examples:
www.facebook.com/pages/Nature-and-Nurture-Senior-Concierge-Ltd/70429283920
https://www.facebook.com/ElderConciergeServices/

Resources:

http://www.facebook.com/advertising/
http://www.wordstream.com/blog/ws/2015/01/28/facebook-ad-targeting
www.socialmediaexaminer.com/how-to-set-up-a-facebook-page-for-business/
www.socialmediaexaminer.com/how-to-build-a-better-target-audience-for-your-facebook-ads/
http://smallbizsurvival.com/2009/11/6-big-facebook-tips-for-small-business.html

Facebook Profiles represent individual users and are held under a person's name. Each profile should only be controlled by that person. Each user has a wall, information tab, likes, interests, photos, videos and each individual can create events.

Facebook Groups are pretty similar to Fan Pages but are usually created for a group of people with a similar interest and they are wanting to keep their discussions private. The members are not usually looking to find out more about a business - they want to discuss a certain topic.

Facebook Fan Pages are the most viral of your three options. When someone becomes a fan of your page or comments on one of your posts, photos or videos, that is spread to all of their personal friends. This can be a great way to get your information out to lots of people...and quickly! In addition, one of the most valuable features of a business page is that you can send "updates" about new products and content to fans and your home building brand becomes more visible.

Facebook Live lets people, public figures and Pages share live video with their followers and friends on Facebook.
Source:
https://live.fb.com/about/
Resource:
http://smartphones.wonderhowto.com/news/facebook-is-going-all-live-video-streaming-your-phone-0170132/

Small Business Promotions
This group allows members to post about their products and services and is a public group designated as a Buy and Sell Facebook group.
Source: https://www.facebook.com/groups/smallbusinesspronotions/
Resource:
https://www.facebook.com/business/a/local-business-promotion-ads
https://www.facebook.com/business/learn/facebook-create-ad-local-awareness
www.socialmediaexaminer.com/how-to-use-facebook-local-awareness-ads-to-target-customers/

Facebook Ad Builder
https://waymark.com/signup/db869ac4-7202-4e3b-93c3-80acc5988df9/?partner=fitsmallbusiness

Facebook Lead Ads   www.facebook.com/business/a/lead-ads

A type of sponsored ad that appears in your audience's timeline just like other Facebook ads. However, the goal with lead ads is literally to capture the lead's info without them leaving Facebook. These ads don't link to a website landing page, creating an additional step.

Best social media marketing practices:
1. Assign daily responsibility for Facebook to a single person on your staff with an affinity for dialoguing.
2. Set expectations for how often they should post new content and how quickly they should respond to comments – usually within a couple hours.
3. Follow and like your followers when they seem to have a genuine interest in your area of health and wellness expertise.
4. Post on the walls of not only your own Facebook site, but also on your most active, influential posters with the largest networks.
5. Periodically post a request for your followers to "like" your page.
6. Monitor Facebook posts to your wall and respond every two hours throughout your business day.

We will use Facebook in the following ways to market our Senior Concierge Service:
1. Promote our blog posts on our Facebook page
2. Post a video of our service people in action.
3. Make time-sensitive offers during slow periods
4. Create a special landing page for coupons or promotional giveaways
5. Create a Welcome tab to display a video message from our owner.
   Resource: Pagemodo.
6. Support a local charity by posting a link to their website.
7. Thank our customers while promoting their businesses at the same time.
8. Describe milestone accomplishments and thank customers for their role.
9. Give thanks to corporate accounts.
10. Ask customers to contribute stories about _____ occurrences.
11. Use the built-in Facebook polling application to solicit feedback.
12. Use the Facebook reviews page to feature positive comments from customers, and to respond to negative reviews.
13. Introduce customers to our staff with resume and video profiles.
14. Create a photo gallery of unusual requests to showcase our expertise.

We will also explore location-based platforms like the following:
- FourSquare   - GoWalla
- Facebook Places   - Google Latitude

As a senior concierge service serving a local community, we will appreciate the potential for hyper-local platforms like these. Location-based applications are increasingly attracting young, urban influencers with disposable income, which is precisely the audience we are trying to attract. People connect to geo-location apps primarily to "get informed" about local happenings.

Foursquare.com

A web and mobile application that allows registered users to post their location at a venue ("check-in") and connect with friends. Check-in requires active user selection and points are awarded at check-in. Users can choose to have their check-ins posted on their accounts on Twitter, Facebook, or both. In version 1.3 of their iPhone application, foursquare enabled push-notification of friend updates, which they call "Pings". Users can also earn badges by checking in at locations with certain tags, for check-in frequency, or for other patterns such as time of check-in.]

Resource:
https://foursquare.com/business/

Examples:
https://foursquare.com/v/on-the-go-concierge-services/4ed670480cd6b3fd

Instagram

Instagram.com is an online photo-sharing, video-sharing and social networking service that enables its users to take pictures and videos, apply digital filters to them, and share them on a variety of social networking services, such as
Facebook, Twitter, Tumblr and Flickr. A distinctive feature is that it confines photos to a square shape, similar to Kodak Instamatic and Polaroid images, in contrast to the
16:9 aspect ratio now typically used by mobile device cameras. Users are also able to record and share short videos lasting for up to 15 seconds.

Resources:
http://www.wordstream.com/blog/ws/2015/01/06/instagram-marketing

We will use Instagram in the following ways to help amplify the story of our brand, get people to engage with our content when not at our store, and get people to visit our store or site:

1. Let our customers and fans know about specific product availability.
2. Tie into trends, events or holidays to drive awareness.
3. Let people know we are open and our client base is spectacular.
4. Run a monthly contest and pick the winning hashtagged photograph to activate our customer base and increase our exposure.
5. Encourage the posting and collection of happy onsite or offsite customer photos.

Examples:
https://www.instagram.com/305elite/?hl=en

Note: Commonly found in tweets, a hashtag is a word or connected phrase (no spaces) that begins with a hash symbol (#). They're so popular that other social media platforms including Facebook, Instagram and Google+ now support them. Using a hashtag turns a word or phrase into a clickable link that displays a feed (list) of other posts with that same hashtag. For example, if you click on #_____ in a tweet, or enter #_____ in the search box, you'll see a list of tweets all about _____.

MySpace Advertising

MySpace.com offers a self-service, graphical "display" advertising platform that will enable our company to target our marketing message to our audience by demographic characteristics. With the new MySpace service, we will be able to upload our own ads or make them quickly with an online tool, and set a budget of $25 to $10,000 for the campaigns. We can choose to target a specific gender, age group and geographic area. We will then pay MySpace each time someone clicks on our ad. Ads can link to other MySpace pages, or external websites. MyAds will let us target our ads to specific groups of people using the public data on MySpace users' profiles, blogs and comments. MySpace will enable our company to target potential customers with similar interests to our existing customer base, as revealed via our marketing research surveys. Also the bulletin function on MySpace will allow us to update customers on company milestone achievements and coming events. We will also post a short video to our home page and encourage the sharing of the video with other MySpace users.

LinkedIn.com

Linkedin provides options that will allow our detailed profile to be indexed by search engines, like Google. We will make use of these options, so our business will achieve greater visibility on the Web. We will use widgets to integrate other tools, such as importing your blog entries or Twitter stream into your profile, and go market research and gain knowledge with Polls. We will answer questions in Questions and Answers to show our expertise, and ask questions in Questions and Answers to get a feel for what customers and prospects want or think. We will publish our LinkedIn URL on all our marketing collateral, including business cards, email signature, newsletters, and web site. We will grow our network by joining industry and alumni groups related to our business. We will update our status examples of recent work, and link our status updates with our other social media accounts. We will start and manage a group or fan page for our product, brand or business. We will share useful articles that will be of interest to concierge customers, and request LinkedIn recommendations from customers willing to provide testimonials. We will post our presentations on our profile using a presentation application. We will ask our first-level contacts for introductions to their contacts and interact with LinkedIn on a regular basis to reach those who may not see us on other social media sites. We will link to articles posted elsewhere, with a summary of why it's valuable to add to our credibility and list our newsletter subscription information and archives. We will post discounts and package deals. We will buy a LinkedIn direct ad that our target market will see. We will find vendors and contractors through connections.
Examples:
www.linkedin.com/company/beyond-expectations-senior-concierge-service
www.linkedin.com/company/senior-concierge-providers

Podcasting

Podcasting is a way of publishing audio broadcasts via the internet through MP3 files, which users can listen to using PCs and i-Pods. Our podcasts will provide both information and advertising. Our podcasts will allow us to pull in a lot of customers. Our monthly podcasts will be heard by ___ (#) eventual subscribers. Podcasts can now be downloaded for mobile devices, such as an iPod. Podcasts will give our company a new way to provide information and an additional way to advertise. Podcasting will give our business another connection point with customers. We will use this medium to communicate on important issues, what is going on with a planned event, and other things of interest to our health-conscious customers. The programs will last about 10 minutes and can be downloaded for free on iTunes. The purpose is not to be a mass medium. It is directed at a niche market with an above-average educational background and very special interests. It will provide a very direct and a reasonably inexpensive way of reaching our targeted audience with relevant information about our alcoholic beverages, products and services. The key ingredients to create a podcast are:

1. Garage Band for Macs
2. Audacity for PC's
3. Microphone
4. Editing Ability
5. Intro & Exit Music
6. Pictures
7. RSS Feed Creator!
8. Podcatchers e.g, iTunes
9. An Internet connection

Our podcasts will provide both information and advertising. Our podcasts will allow us to pull in a lot of customers. Our monthly podcasts will be heard by ___ (#) eventual subscribers. Podcasts can now be downloaded for mobile devices, such as an iPod. Podcasts will give our company a new way to provide information and an additional way to advertise. Podcasting will give our business another connection point with customers. We will use this medium to communicate on important issues, what is going on with a planned event, and other things of interest to our health-conscious customers. The programs will last about 10 minutes and can be downloaded for free on iTunes. The purpose is not to be a mass medium. It is directed at a niche market with an above-average educational background and very special interests. It will provide a very direct and a reasonably inexpensive way of reaching our targeted audience with relevant information about our alcoholic beverages, products and services.

Resources:
www.apple.com/itunes/download/.
www.cbc.ca/podcasting/gettingstarted.html
Examples:
www.sheridancare.com/video-library/30-how-in-home-agencies-should-measure-success-of-caregivers

Blogging

We will use our blog to keep customers and prospects informed about products, events and services that relate to our Senior Concierge Service business, new releases, contests, and specials. Our blog will show readers that we are a good source of expert information that they can count on. With our blog, we can quickly update our customers anytime our company releases a new product, the holding of a contest or are placing items on special pricing. We will use our blog to share customer testimonials and meaningful success stories. We will use the blog to supply advice on creative use of senior concierge services. Our visitors will be able to subscribe to our RSS feeds and be instantly updated without any spam filters interfering. We will also use the blog to solicit service usage recommendations and future service addition suggestions. Additionally, blogs are free and allow for constant ease of updating.

Our blog will give our company the following benefits:
1. An cost-effective marketing tool.
2. An expanded network.
3. A promotional platform for new senior concierge services.
4. An introduction to people with similar interests.
5. Builds credibility and expertise recognition.

We will use our blog for the following purposes:
1. To share customer testimonials, experiences and meaningful success stories.
2. Update our clients anytime our company releases a new service.
3. Supply advice on _____ options.
4. Discuss research findings.
5. To publish helpful content.
6, To welcome feedback in multiple formats.
7. Link together other social networking sites, including Twitter.
8. To improve Google rankings.
9. Make use of automatic RSS feeds.

We will adhere to the following blog writing guidelines:
1. We will blog at least 2 or 3 times per week to maintain interest.
2. We will integrate our blog into the design of our website.
3. We will use our blog to convey useful information and not our advertisements.
4. We will make the content easy to understand.
5. We will focus our content on the needs of our targeted audience.

Our blog will feature the following on a regular basis:
1. Useful articles and assessment coupons.
2. Give away of a helpful free report in exchange for email addresses
3. Helpful information for our professional referral sources, as well as clients, and online and offline community members.
5. Use of a few social media outposts to educate, inform, engage and drive people back to our blog for more information and our free report.

To get visitors to our blog to take the next action step and contact our firm we will do the following:
1. Put a contact form on the upper-left hand corner of our blog, right below the header.
2. Put our complete contact information in the header itself.
3. Add a page to our blog and title it, "Become My Client.", giving the reader somewhere to go for the next sign-up steps.
4. At the end of each blog post, we will clearly tell the reader what to do next; such as subscribe to our RSS feed, or to sign up for our newsletter mailing list.

Resources:
www.blogger.com
www.blogspot.com
www.wordpress.com
Example:
http://seniorconciergeny.com/blog/
http://www.elderconciergeservices.com/blog

Twitter

We will use 'Twitter.com' as a way to produce new business from existing clients and generate prospective clients online. Twitter is a free social networking and micro-blogging service that allows its users to send and read other users' updates (otherwise known as tweets), which are text-based posts of up to 140 characters in length.
Updates are displayed on the user's profile page and delivered to other users
who have signed up to receive them. The sender can restrict delivery to those in his or her circle of friends, with delivery to everyone being the default. Users can receive updates via the Twitter website, SMS text messaging, RSS feeds, or email. We will use our Twitter account to respond directly to questions, distribute news, solve problems, post updates, hold contests and offer special discounts on our Senior Concierge Services.

We will provide the following instructions to register as a 'Follower' of _____ (company name) on Twitter:
1. In your Twitter account, click on 'Find People' in the top right navigation bar, which will redirect to a new page.
2. Click on 'Find on Twitter' which will open a search box that says 'Who are you looking for?'
3. Type '_____ (company name) / _____ (owner name)' and click 'search'. This will bring up the results page.
4. Click the blue '_____' name to read the bio or select the 'Follow' button.

Example:
http://twitter.com/#!/seniorconcierg1

Membership Club

We also plan to establish a Membership Club with the following member benefits:
1. The earning of points, equal to dollars, to be applied to future purchases.
2. Exclusive discounts and product/service offerings.
3. Early previews on new product/service introductions.
4. Special bonus point earning opportunities.

We plan to develop a survey that will be used to follow up with customers who stopped using our services, to see if there are quality/service issues that need to be addressed.

Google Maps
We will first make certain that our business is listed in Google Maps. We will do a search for our business in Google Maps. If we don't see our business listed, then we will add our business to Google Maps. Even if our business is listed in Google Maps, we will create a Local Business Center account and take control of our listing, by adding more relevant information. Consumers generally go to Google Maps for two reasons: Driving Directions And to Find a Business.
Resource:
http://maps.google.com/

Bing Maps   www.bingplaces.com/
This will make it easy for customers to find our business.

Apple Maps
A web mapping service developed by Apple Inc. It is the default map system of iOS, macOS, and watchOS. It provides directions and estimated times of arrival for automobile, pedestrian, and public transportation navigation.
Resources:
  http://www.stallcupgroup.com/2012/09/19/three-ways-to-make-your-pawn-business-
       more-profitable-and-sellable/
http://www.apple.com/ios/maps/
https://en.wikipedia.org/wiki/Apple_Maps

Google Places
Google Places helps people make more informed decisions about where to go, from senior concierge services to wine shops. Place Pages connect people to information from the best sources across the web, displaying photos, reviews and essential facts, as well as real-time updates and offers from business owners. We will make sure that our Google Places listing is up to date to increase our online visibility. Google Places is linked to our Google Maps listing, and will help to get on the first page of Google search page results when people search for a senior concierge service in our area.
Resource:
www.google/com/places

Yelp.com
We will use Yelp.com to help people find our local senior concierge business. Visitors to Yelp write local reviews, over 85% of them rating a business 3 stars or higher In addition to reviews, visitors can use Yelp to find events, special offers, lists and to talk with other Yelpers. As business owners, we will setup a free account to post offers, photos and message our customers. We will also buy ads on Yelp, which will be clearly labeled "Sponsored Results". We will also use the Weekly Yelp, which is available in 42 city editions to bring news about the latest business openings and other happenings.
Examples:
http://www.yelp.com/biz/the-senior-concierge-west-hollywood

Manta.com
Manta is the largest free source of information on small companies, with profiles of more than 64 million businesses and organizations. Business owners and sales professionals use Manta's vast database and custom search capabilities to quickly find companies, easily connect with prospective customers and promote their own services. Manta.com, founded in 2005, is based in Columbus, Ohio.
Examples:
http://www.manta.com/c/mrlczbb/senior-concierge-providers-inc

Pay-Per-Click Advertising
Google AdWords, Yahoo! Search Marketing, and Microsoft adCenter are the three largest network operators, and all three operate under a bid-based model. Cost per click (CPC) varies depending on the search engine and the level of competition for a particular keyword. Google AdWords are small text ads that appear next to the search results on Google. In addition, these ads appear on many partner web sites, including NYTimes.com (The New York Times), Business.com, Weather.com, About.com, and many more. Google's text advertisements are short, consisting of one title line and two content text lines. Image ads can be one of several different Interactive Advertising Bureau (IAB) standard sizes. Through Google AdWords, we plan to buy placements (ads) for specific search terms through this "Pay-Per-Click" advertising program. This PPC advertising campaign will allow our ad to appear when someone searches for a keyword related to our business, organization, or subject matter. More importantly, we will only pay when a potential customer clicks on our ad to visit our website. For instance, since we operate a Senior Concierge Service in ___ (city), _____ (state), we will target people using search terms such as "Senior Concierge Service, errand service, gift buying service, aging in place, assisted living, in ____ (city), ____ (state)". With an effective PPC campaign our ads will only be displayed when a user searches for one of these keywords. In short, PPC advertising will be the most cost-effective and measurable form of advertising for our Senior Concierge Service
Resources:
http://adwords.google.com/support/aw/?hl=en
www.wordtracker.com

Yahoo Local Listings
We will create our own local listing on Yahoo. To create our free listing, we will use our web browser and navigate to http://local.yahoo.com. We will first register for free with Yahoo, and create a member ID and password to list our business. Once we have accessed http://local.yahoo.com, we will scroll down to the bottom and click on "Add/Edit a Business" to get onto the Yahoo Search Marketing Local Listings page. In the lower right of the screen we will see "Local Basic Listings FREE". We will click on the Get Started button and log in again with our new Yahoo ID and password. The form for our local business listing will now be displayed. When filling it out, we will be sure to include our full web address (http://www.companyname.com). We will include a description of our Senior Concierge Services in the description section, but avoid hype or blatant advertising, to get the listing to pass Yahoo's editorial review. We will also be

sure to select the appropriate business category and sub categories.
Examples
https://search.yahoo.com/local/s?p=Concierge+Services&addr=Roseville,+CA&fr=
   local_lyc_lsyc_rd

Advertorials

An advertorial is an advertisement written in the form of an objective article, and presented in a printed publication—usually designed to look like a legitimate and independent news story. We will use quotes as testimonials to back up certain claims throughout our copy and break-up copy with subheadings to make the material more reader-friendly. We will include the "call to action" and contact information with a 24/7 voicemail number and a discount coupon. The advertorial will have a short intro about a client's experience with our senior concierge services and include quotes, facts, and statistics. We will present helpful information about the importance of senior companion services.

Affiliate Marketing

We will create an affiliate marketing program to broaden our reach. We will first devise a commission structure, so affiliates have a reason to promote our business. We will give them ___ (10) % of whatever sales they generate. We will go after senior care bloggers or webmasters who get a lot of web traffic for our keywords. These companies would then promote our products/services, and they would earn commissions for the sales they generated. We will work with the following services to handle the technical aspects of our program.

ConnectCommerce	https://www.connectcommerce.com/
Commission Junction	https://members.cj.com
ShareASale	http://www.shareasale.com/
Share Results	
LinkShare	

Resources:
https://www.affilorama.com/
www.godaddy.com/garage/smallbusiness/market/share-love-create-affiliate-program/
  www.google.com/affiliatenetwork/ntn.html?advid=223777

Gift with Purchase (GWP)

A GWP is an item that is presented to our client when he or she spends above a specified amount on products or services. The Gift with purchase or free item could be anything from recipe booklets, company voucher, journals, product samples, etc. We will attach our marketing logo and business card to the gift and use it as means to thank the customer for their patronage. We will also explore the dramatic impact of a surprise gift with purchase, because an unexpected bonus item is often very appreciated and remembered.

HotFrog.com

HotFrog is a fast-growing free online business directory listing over 6.6 million US

businesses. HotFrog now has local versions in 34 countries worldwide.
Anyone can list their business in HotFrog for free, along with contact details, and products and services. Listing in HotFrog will direct sales leads and enquiries to our business. Businesses are encouraged to add any latest news and information about their products and services to their listing. HotFrog is indexed by Google and other search engines, meaning that customers can find your HotFrog listing when they use Google, Yahoo! or other search engines.
Resource:
http://www.hotfrog.com/AddYourBusiness.aspx

Local.com
Local.com owns and operates a leading local search site and network in the United States. Its mission is to be the leader at enabling local businesses and consumers to find each other and connect. To do so, the company uses patented and proprietary technologies to provide over 20 million consumers each month with relevant search results for local businesses, products and services on Local.com and more than 1,000 partner sites. Local.com powers more than 100,000 local websites. Tens of thousands of small business customers use Local.com products and services to reach consumers using a variety of subscription, performance and display advertising and website products.
Resource:
http://corporate.local.com/mk/get/advertising-opportunities

Autoresponder
An autoresponder is an online tool that will automatically manage our mailing list and send out emails to our customers at preset intervals. We will write a short article that is helpful to potential senior concierge service buyers. We will load this article into our autoresponder. We will let people know of the availability of our article by posting to newsgroups, forums, social networking sites etc. We will list our autoresponder email address at the end of the posting, so they can send a blank email to our autoresponder to receive our article and be added to our mailing list. We will then email them at the interval of our choosing with special offers. We will load the messages into our autoresponder and set a time interval for the messages to be mailed out.
Resource:
www.aweber.com

Corporate Incentive/Employee Rewards Program
Our Employee Rewards Program will motivate and reward the key resources of local corporations – the people who make their business a success. We will use independent sales reps to market these programs to local corporations. It will be a versatile program, allowing the corporate client to customize it to best suit the following goals:
1. Welcome New Hires
2. Introduce an Employee Discount Program for our senior concierge services.
3. Reward increases in sales or productivity with an Employee Incentive Program
4. Thank Retirees for their service to the company
5. Initiate a Loyalty Rewards Program geared towards the customers of our

corporate clients or their employees.

Database Marketing

Database marketing is a form of direct marketing using databases of customers or prospects to generate personalized communications in order to promote a product or service for marketing purposes. The method of communication can be any addressable medium, as in direct marketing. With database marketing tools, we will be able to implement customer nurturing, which is a tactic that attempts to communicate with each customer or prospect at the right time, using the right information to meet that customer's need to progress through the process of identifying a problem, learning options available to resolve it, selecting the right solution, and making the purchasing decision. We will use our databases to learn more about customers, select target markets for specific campaigns, through customer segmentation, compare customers' value to the company, and provide more specialized offerings for customers based on their transaction histories, demographic profile and surveyed needs and wants. This database will gives us the capability to automate regular promotional mailings, to semi-automate the telephone outreach process, and to prioritize prospects as to interests, timing, and other notable delineators. The objective is to arrange for first meetings, which are meant to be informal introductions, and valuable fact-finding and needs-assessment events.

We will use sign-in sheets, coupons, surveys and newsletter subscriptions to collect the following information from our clients:
1. Name
2. Telephone Number
3. Email Address
4. Home Address
5. Birth Date
6. Other Relevant Dates

We will utilize the following types of contact management software to generate leads and stay in touch with customers to produce repeat business and referrals:
1. Act   www.act.com
2. Front Range Solutions   www.frontrange.com
3. The Turning Point   www.turningpoint.com
4. Acxiom   www.acxiom.com/products_and_services/
5. Microsoft Access

We will utilize contact management software, such as ACT and Goldmine, to track the following:
1. Dates for follow-ups.
2. Documentation of prospect concerns, objections or comments.
3. Referral source.
4. Marketing Materials sent.
5. Log of contact dates and methods of contact.
6. Ultimate disposition.

Cause Marketing

Cause marketing or cause-related marketing refers to a type of marketing involving the

cooperative efforts of a "for profit" business and a non-profit organization for mutual benefit. The possible benefits of cause marketing for business include positive public relations, improved customer relations, and additional marketing opportunities.
Cause marketing sponsorship by American businesses is rising at a dramatic rate, because customers, employees and stakeholders prefer to be associated with a company that is considered socially responsible. Our business objective will be to generate highly cost-effective public relations and media coverage for the launch of a marketing campaign focused on _____ (type of cause), with the help of the _____ (non-profit organization name) organization.
Resources:
www.causemarketingforum.com/
www.cancer.org/AboutUs/HowWeHelpYou/acs-cause-marketing

Courtesy Advertising

We will engage in courtesy advertising, which refers to a company or corporation "buying" an advertisement in a nonprofit dinner program, event brochure, and the like. Our company will gain visibility this way while the nonprofit organization may treat the advertisement revenue as a donation. We will specifically advertise in the following non-profit programs, newsletters, bulletins and event brochures: _____
_____

Speaking Engagements

We will consider a "problem/solution" format where we describe a challenge and tell how our expertise achieved an exceptional solution. We will use speaking engagements as an opportunity to expose our areas of expertise to prospective clients. By speaking at conferences and forums put together by professional and industry trade groups, we will increase our firm's visibility, and consequently, its prospects for attracting new business. Public speaking will give us a special status, and make it easier for our speakers to meet prospects. Attendees expect speakers to reach out to the audience, which gives speakers respect and credibility. We will identify speaking opportunities that will let us reach our targeted audience. We will designate a person who is responsible for developing relationships with event and industry associations, submitting proposals and, most importantly, staying in touch with contacts. We will tailor our proposals to the event organizers' preferences.

Speaking Proposal Package:
1. Speech Topic/Agenda/Synopsis
2. Target Audience: Community and Civic Groups
3. Speaker Biography
4. List of previous speaking engagements
5. Previous engagement evaluations

Possible Targets:
1. AARP Groups
2. Churches
3. YMCAs
4. JCC's

5. Support Groups
6. Corporations
7. Event Planners

Possible Speech Topics:
1. How to Make the Most of a Senior Concierge Service
2. Senior Concierge Service Trends

Speech Tracking Form

Group/Class	Subject/Topic	Business Development Potential	Resources Needed	Target Date

We will use the following techniques to leverage the business development impact of our speaking engagements:
1. Send out press releases to local papers announcing the upcoming speech. We will get great free publicity by sending the topic and highlights of the talk to the newspaper.
2. Produce a flyer with our picture on it, and distribute it to our network.
3. Send publicity materials to our prospects inviting them to attend our presentation.
4. Whenever possible, get a list of attendees before the event. Contact them and introduce yourself before the talk to build rapport with your audience. Arrive early and don't leave immediately after your presentation.
5. Always give out handouts and a business card. Include marketing materials and something of value to the recipient, so that it will be retained and not just tossed away. You might include tips or secrets you share in your talk.
6. Give out an evaluation form to all participants. This form should request names and contact information. Offer a free consultation if it's appropriate. Follow up within 72 hours with any members of the audience who could become ideal clients.
7. Have a place on the form where participants can list other groups that might need speakers, along with the name of the program chairperson or other contact person.
8. Offer a door prize as incentive for handing in the evaluation. When you have collected all of the evaluations, you can select a winner of the prize.
9. Meet with audience members, answer their questions and listen to their concerns. Stay after your talk and mingle with the audience. Answer any questions that come up and offer follow-up conversations for additional support.
10. Request a free ad in the group's newsletter in exchange for your speech.
11. Send a thank-you note to the person who invited you to speak. Include copies of some of the evaluations to show how useful it was.

Speaking Engagement Package
1. Video or DVD of prior presentation.
2. Session Description
3. Learning Objectives
4. Takeaway Message
5. Speaking experience
6. Letters of recommendation

7. General Biography 8. Introduction Biography
Resource:
www.toastmasters.com

Meet-up Group
We will form a meet-up group to encourage people to participate in our wine tasting programs.
Resource:
http://www.meetup.com/create/
Example:
http://concierge.meetup.com/cities/us/fl/naples/

Marketing Associations/Groups
We will set up a marketing association comprised of complementary businesses. We will market our senior concierge service as a member of a group of complementary companies. Our marketing group will include a caterer, an event planner, and a party supply store. Any business that provides event services will be a likely candidate for being a member of our marketing group. The group will joint advertise, distribute joint promotional materials, exchange mailing lists, and develop a group website. The obvious benefit is that we will increase our marketing effectiveness by extending our reach.

BBB Accreditation
We will apply for BBB Accreditation to improve our perceived trustworthiness. BBB determines that a company meets BBB accreditation standards, which include a commitment to make a good faith effort to resolve any consumer complaints. BBB Accredited Businesses pay a fee for accreditation review/monitoring and for support of BBB services to the public. BBB accreditation does not mean that the business' products or services have been evaluated or endorsed by BBB, or that BBB has made a determination as to the business' product quality or competency in performing services. We will place the BBB Accreditation Logo in all of our ads.
Examples:
www.bbb.org/sandiego/business-reviews/senior-citizens-service-
    organization/five-star-concierge-in-san-diego-ca-26000702/

Sponsor Events
The sponsoring of events, such as golf tournaments, will allow our company to engage in what is known as experiential marketing, which is the idea that the best way to deepen the emotional bond between a company and its customers is by creating a memorable and interactive experience. We will ask for the opportunity to prominently display our company signage and the set-up of a booth from which to handout sample products and sales literature. We will also seek to capitalize on networking, speech giving and

workshop presenting opportunities.

Sponsorships
We will sponsor a local team, such as our child's little league baseball team, the local soccer club or a senior community bowling group. We will then place our company name on the uniforms or shirts in exchange for providing the equipment and/or uniforms.

Patch.com
A community-specific news and information platform dedicated to providing comprehensive and trusted local coverage for individual towns and communities. Patch makes it easy to: Keep up with news and events, Look at photos and videos from around town, Learn about local businesses, Participate in discussions and Submit announcements, photos, and reviews.
Examples:
  http://oldnortheast.patch.com/articles/the-doctor-is-always-in-with-concierge-medicine

MerchantCircle.com
The largest online network of local business owners, combining social networking features with customizable web listings that allow local merchants to attract new customers. A growing company dedicated to connecting neighbors and merchants online to help build real relationships between local business owners and their customers. To date, well over 1,600,000 local businesses have joined MerchantCircle to get their business more exposure on the Internet, simply and inexpensively.

Mobile iPhone Apps
We will use new distribution tools like the iPhone App Store to give us unprecedented direct access to consumers, without the need to necessarily buy actual mobile *ads* to reach people. Thanks to Apple's iPhone and the App Store, we will be able to make cool mobile apps that may generate as much goodwill and purchase intent as a banner ad. We will research Mobile Application Development, which is the process by which application software is developed for small low-power handheld devices, such as personal digital assistants, enterprise digital assistants or mobile phones. These applications are either pre-installed on phones during manufacture, or downloaded by customers from various mobile software distribution platforms. iPhone apps make good marketing tools. The bottom line is iPhones and smartphones sales are continually growing, and people are going to their phones for information. Apps will definitely be a lead generation tool because it gives potential clients easy access to our contact and business information and the ability to call for more information while they are still "hot". Our apps will contain: directory of staffers, publications on relevant issues, office location, videos, etc.

We will especially focus on the development of apps that can accomplish the following:

1. **Mobile Reservations:** Customers can use this app to access mobile reservations linked directly to your in-house calendar. They can browse open slots and book appointments easily, while on the go.
2. **Appointment Reminders:** You can send current customers reminders of regular or special appointments through your mobile app to increase your yearly revenue per customer.
3. **Style Libraries**
   Offer a style library in your app to help customers to pick out a _____ style. Using a simple photo gallery, you can collect photos of various styles, and have customers browse and select specific _____.
4. **Customer Photos**
   Your app can also have a feature that lets customers take photos and email them to you. This is great for creating a database of customer photos for testimonial purposes, advertising, or just easy reference.
5. **Special Offers**
   Push notifications allow you to drive activity on special promotions, deals, events, and offers. If you ever need to generate revenue during a down time, push notifications allow you to generate interest easily and proactively.
6. **Loyalty Programs**
   A mobile app allows you to offer a mobile loyalty program (buy ten ___, get one free, etc.). You won't need to print up cards or track anything manually – it's all done simply through users' mobile devices.
7. **Referrals**
   A mobile app can make referrals easy. With a single click, a user can post to a social media account on Facebook or Twitter about their experience with your business. This allows you to earn new business organically through the networks of existing customers.
8. **Product Sales**
   We can sell ____ products through our mobile app. Customers can browse products, submit orders, and make payments easily, helping you open up a new revenue stream.

Resources: http://www.apple.com/iphone/apps-for-iphone/
http://iphoneapplicationlist.com/apps/business/

Software Development: http://www.mutualmobile.com/
http://www.avenuesocial.com/mob-app.php#
http://www.biznessapps.com/

Examples:
http://snappy.appypie.com/marketplace/iphone-android/senior-concierge-service

Quick Response Codes

QR Codes are a type of matrix barcode (or two-dimensional code) that is designed to be read by smartphones. The code consists of black modules arranged in a square pattern on a white background. The information encoded may be text, a URL, or other data. Many Android, Nokia, and Blackberry handsets come with QR code readers installed. QR reader software is available for most mobile platforms. QR codes storing addresses and

Uniform Resource Locators (URLs) may appear in magazines, on signs, buses, business cards, or almost any object about which users might need information. Users with a camera phone equipped with the correct reader application can scan the image of the QR code to display text, contact information, connect to a wireless network, or open a web page in the telephone's browser. This act of linking from physical world objects is termed hardlinking or object hyperlinking. Sectors of the general public are still getting acquainted with the practice of scanning the codes that appear with increasing frequency in advertisements, and thus consider an educational step or simple line of adjacent text to encourage a scan. The bar codes digitally store a lot of content in a small space, enabling smartphone code readers to connect the user with a website page, maps, phone numbers, email or other QR capability. Among the benefits to marketing and advertising is that the use of QR codes typically occurs at the moment when the reader is most interested in the subject matter and likely to act. In many applications, the objective is to provide an easy means for the reader to act now. A comScore survey data says QR code users are more likely to be male (60.5%), between the ages of 18 to 34 (53.4%) and have a household income in excess of $100,000 (36.1%). Magazines and newspapers are the preferred vehicle for scanning QR codes (49.4%), followed by product packaging (34.3%).

Transit Ads

According to the Metropolitan Transportation Authority, MTA subways, buses and railroads provide billions of trips each year to residents. Marketing our senior concierge service in subway cars and on the walls of subway stations will be a great way to advertise our business to a large, captive audience.

Restroom billboard advertising (Bathroom Advertising)

We will target a captive audience by placing restroom billboard advertising in select high-traffic venues with targeted demographics. A simple, framed ad on the inside of a bathroom stall door or above a urinal gets at least a minute of viewing, according to several studies. The stall door ads are a good choice for venues with shorter waiting times, such as small businesses, while large wall posters are well-suited to airports or movie theatres where people are more likely to be standing in line near the entrance or exit. Many new restroom based ad agencies that's specialize in restroom advertisement have also come about, such as; Zoom Media, BillBoardZ , Flush Media , Jonny Advertising, Insite Advertising, Inc, Wall AG USA, ADpower, NextMedia, and Alive Promo (American Restroom Association, 9/24/2009).
Resources:
http://www.indooradvertising.org/
http://www.stallmall.com/
http://www.zoommedia.com/

Tumblr.com

Tumblr will allow us to effortlessly share anything. We will be able to post text, photos, quotes, links, music, and videos, from our browser, phone, desktop, email, or wherever we happen to be. We will be able to customize everything, from colors, to our theme's HTML.

Gift Certificates

We will offer for sale Gift Certificates via our website. This will provide an excellent way to be introduced to new clients and improve our cash flow position. An e-commerce platform for small businesses. BoomTime protects info with 256-bit SSL encryption when transmitting certain kinds of information, such as financial services information or payment information. An icon resembling a padlock is displayed on the bottom of most browser windows during SSL transactions, which you can also verify by looking at the address bar, which will start with "https://" instead of just "http://". The information you provide will be stored securely on BoomTime servers.

Resources:

- Boom Time — https://ps1419.boomtime.com/lgift
- Gift Cards — www.giftcards.com
- Gift Card Café — www.TheGiftCardCafe.com
  Allows companies to create their own special deals and discount services, and send it to just the contacts in their client database.

Examples:
http://www.theurbaneconcierge.com/gift_certificates.html

thumbtack.com

A directory for finding and booking trustworthy local services, which is free to consumers.

Resource:
www.thumbtack.com/postservice

Citysearch.com

Citysearch.com is a local guide for living bigger, better and smarter in the selected city. Covering more than 75,000 locations nationwide, Citysearch.com combines in-the-know editorial recommendations, candid user comments and expert advice from local businesses. Citysearch.com keeps users connected to the most popular and undiscovered places wherever they are.

Publish e-Book

Ebooks are electronic books which can be downloaded from any website or FTP site on the Internet. Ebooks are made using special software and can include a wide variety of media such as HTML, graphics, Flash animation and video. We will publish an e-book to establish our senior concierge expertise, and reach people who are searching for ebooks on how to make better use our products and/or services. Included in our ebook will be links back to our website, product or affiliate program. Because users will have permanent access to it, they will use our ebook again and again, constantly seeing a link or banner which directs them to our site. The real power behind ebook marketing will be the viral aspect of it and the free traffic it helps to build for our website. ebook directories include:

- www.e-booksdirectory.com/
- www.ebookfreeway.com/p-ebook-directory-list.html
- www.quantumseolabs.com/blog/seolinkbuilding/top-5-free-ebook-directories-

subscribers/
Resource: www.free-ebooks.net/

e-books are available from the following sites:
    Amazon.com
    Createspace.com
    Lulu.com
    Kobobooks.com
    BarnesandNoble.com
    Scribd.com
    AuthorHouse.com
Resource:
www.smartpassiveincome.com/ebooks-the-smart-way/

Business Card Exchanges
We will join our Chamber of Commerce or local retail merchants' association and volunteer to host a mixer or business card exchange. We will take the opportunity to invite social and business groups to our store to enjoy wine tastings, and market to local businesses that will be looking for employee benefits. We will also build our email database by collecting the business cards of all attendees.

Storefront Banner Advertising
We will use banners as an affordable way to draw attention to our business. We will place one on the side or front of our building, or on a prominent building and have it point to ours. We will use colorful storefront banners with catchy phrases to grab the attention of local foot and vehicle traffic.
Resource:
http://www.fastsigns.com/
Ex: "Free Senior Care Classes"

Hubpages.com
HubPages has easy-to-use publishing tools, a vibrant author community and underlying revenue-maximizing infrastructure. Hubbers (HubPages authors) earn money by publishing their Hubs (content-rich Internet pages) on topics they know and love, and earn recognition among fellow Hubbers through the community-wide HubScore ranking system. The HubPages ecosystem provides a search-friendly infrastructure which drives traffic to Hubs from search engines such as Google and Yahoo, and enables Hubbers to earn revenue from industry-standard advertising vehicles such as Google AdSense and the eBay and Amazon Affiliates program. All of this is provided free to Hubbers in an open online community.
Resources:
http://hubpages.crabbysbeach.com/blogs/
http://hubpages.com/learningcenter/contents
Examples:
http://toobusytothink.hubpages.com/
http://l-l-woodard.hubpages.com/hub/Facing-Difficult-Choices-in-Senior-Care

Pinterest.com

The goal of this website is to connect everyone in the world through the 'things' they find interesting. They think that a favorite book, toy, or recipe can reveal a common link between two people. With millions of new pins added every week, Pinterest is connecting people all over the world based on shared tastes and interests. What's special about Pinterest is that the boards are all visual, which is a very important marketing plus. When users enter a URL, they select a picture from the site to pin to their board. People spend hours pinning their own content, and then finding content on other people's boards to "re-pin" to their own boards. We will use Pinterest for remote personal shopping appointments. When we have a customer with specific needs, we will create a board just for them with items we sell that would meet their needs, along with links to other tips and content. We will invite our customer to check out the board on Pinterest, and let them know we created it just for them.

Examples:

http://lifesavorconcierge.com/

1. Conduct market research by showing photos of potential products or test launches, asking the customer base for feedback.
2. Personalize the brand by showcasing style and what makes the brand different, highlighting new and exciting things through the use of imagery.
3. Add links from Pinterest photos to the company webstore, putting price banners on each photo and providing a link where users can buy the products directly.
4. Share high-quality pictures or property images and put links back to our blog/website.
5. Make Boards interesting with home décor photos.
6. Showcase beautiful pictures of seniors serviced and include a link back to our website or blog.
7. Focus on educating followers and sharing what they would like to see, like images from a adult community service websites.
8. Ask happy clients to pin pictures of themselves in their new houses.
9. We will create a video and add a Call to Action in the description or use annotations, such as check my YouTube article, for the viewers to Pin videos or follow our Pins on Pinterest.
10. Encourage followers' engagement with a call to action, because 'likes', home décor questions, comments and 'repins' will help our pins get more authority and visibility.
11. Optimize descriptions with keywords that people might be looking for when searching Pinterest, as we can add as many hashtags as we want.
12. Be consistent by pinning regularly.
13. Let people know we are on Pinterest by adding "Pin it" and "follow" buttons to our blog and/or website.

Resources:

www.copyblogger.com/pinterest-marketing/

www.shopify.com/infographics/pinterest

www.pinterest.com/entmagazine/retail-business/

www.pinterest.com/brettcarneiro/ecommerce/
www.pinterest.com/denniswortham/infographics-retail-online-shopping/
www.cio.com/article/3018852/e-commerce/how-to-use-pinterest-to-grow-your-business.html

Topix.com
Topix is the world's largest community news website. Users can read, talk about and edit the news on over 360,000 of our news pages. Topix is also a place for users to post their own news stories, as well as comment about stories they have seen on the Topix site. Each story and every Topix page comes with the ability to add your voice to the conversation.

Survey Marketing
We will conduct a door-to-door survey in our target area to illicit opinions to our proposed business. This will provide valuable feedback, lead to prospective clients and serve to introduce our senior concierge business, before we begin actual operations.

'Green' Marketing
We will target environmentally friendly customers to introduce new customers to our business and help spread the word about going "green". We will use the following 'green' marketing strategies to form an emotional bond with our customers:
1. We will use clearly labeled 'Recycled Paper' and Sustainable Packaging, such as receipts and storage containers.
2. We will use "green", non-toxic cleaning supplies.
3. We will install 'green' lighting and heating systems to be more eco-friendly.
4. We will use web-based Electronic Mail and Social Media instead of using paper advertisements.
5. We will find local suppliers to minimize the carbon footprint that it takes for deliveries.
6. We will use products that are made with organic ingredients and supplies.
7. We will document our 'Green' Programs in our sales brochure and website.
8. We will be a Certified Energy Star Partner.
9. We will install new LED warehouse lighting, exit signs, and emergency signs.
10. We will install motion detectors in low-traffic areas both inside and outside of warehouses.
11. We will implement new electricity regulators on HVAC units and compressors to lower energy consumption.
12. We will mount highly supervised and highly respected recycling campaigns.
13. We will start a program for waste product to be converted into sustainable energy sources.
14. We will start new company-wide document shredding programs.
15. We will use of water-based paints during the finishing process to reduce V.O.C.'s to virtually zero.
16. Use of solar panels for non-critical sections and facilities in the complex.

17. Use of only hybrid or electric vehicles.

Sticker Marketing

Low-cost sticker, label and decal marketing will provide a cost-effective way to convey information, build identity and promote our company in unique and influential ways. Stickers can be affixed to almost any surface, so they can go and stay affixed where other marketing materials can't; opening a world of avenues through which we can reach our target audience. Our stickers will be simple in design, and convey an impression quickly and clearly, with valuable information or coupon, printed optionally as part of its backcopy. Our stickers will handed-out at trade shows and special events, mailed as a postcard, packaged with product and/or included as part of a mailing package. We will insert the stickers inside our product or hand them out along with other marketing tools such as flyers or brochures. Research has found that the strongest stickers are usually less than 16 square inches, are printed on white vinyl, and are often die cut. Utilizing a strong design, in a versatile size, and with an eye-catching shape, that is, relevant to our business, will add to the perceived value of our promotional stickers.

We will adhere to the following sticker design tips:
1. We will strengthen our brand by placing our logo on the stickers and using company colors and font styles.
2. We will include our phone number, address, and/or website along with our logo to provide customers with a call to action.
3. We will write compelling copy that solicits an emotional reaction.
4. We will use die-cut stickers using unusual and business relevant shapes to help draw attention to our business.
5. We will consider that size matters and that will be determined by where they will be applied and the degree of desired visibility to be realized.
6. We will be aware of using color on our stickers as color can help create contrast in our design, which enables the directing of prospect eyes to images or actionable items on the stickers.
7. We will encourage customers to post our stickers near their phones, on yellow page book covers, on event invitations, on notepads, on book covers, on gift boxes and product packaging, etc.
8. We will place our stickers on all the products we sell.

USPS Every Door Direct Mail Program

Every Door Direct Mail from the U.S. Postal Service® is designed to reach every home, every address, every time at a very affordable delivery rate. Every business and resident living in the _____ zip code will receive an over-sized post card and coupon announcing the _____ (company name) grand opening 7-days before the grand opening:

Price – USPS Marketing Mail™ Flats up to 3.3 oz
EDDM Retail® USPS Marketing Flats $0.177 per piece
EDDM BMEU USPS Marketing Mail at $0.156 per piece

Resource:

https://www.usps.com/business/every-door-direct-mail.htm
https://eddm.usps.com/eddm/customer/routeSearch.action

Google Calendar   www.google.com/calendar
We will use Google Calendar to organize our mobile senior concierge service schedule and share events with friends.

ZoomInfo.com
Their vision is to be the sole provider of constantly verified information about companies and their employees, making our data indispensible — available anytime, anywhere and anyplace the customer needs it. Creates just-verified, detailed profiles of 65 million businesspeople and six million businesses. Makes data available through powerful tools for lead generation, prospecting and recruiting.

Zipslocal.com
Provides one of the most comprehensive ZIP Code-based local search services, allowing visitors to access information through our online business directories that cover all ZIP Codes in the United States. Interactive local yellow pages show listings and display relevant advertising through the medium of the Internet, making it easy for everyone to find local business information

Hold Biggest Fan Contest
Do you love _____ (company name)? Do you have a great story about how the team at ____ (company Name) helped you "get there" to achieve your goals? Well, then ____ (company name) wants to hear from you! _____ (company name) has launched the "Biggest Fan Contest" on its Facebook Page at the beginning of ____ (month), inviting current and former customers to share why they are _____'s (company name) "Biggest Fan." Participants are eligible to win a number of prizes including: _____.
To enter, visit www.facebook.com/_____ (company name), "like" the page, and click the "Biggest Fan Contest" tab on the righthand side. Participants are then asked to write a short blurb or upload a photo sharing why they love _____ (company name). If you have a story to tell or photo to share, enter today. Contest ends _____ (date). See contest tab for full details.

BusinessVibes   www.businessvibes.com/about-businessvibes
A growing B2B networking platform for global trade professionals. BusinessVibes uses a social networking model for businesses to find and connect with international partner companies. With a network of over 5000+ trade associations, 20 million companies and 25,000+ business events across 100+ major industries and 175 countries, BusinessVibes is a decisive source to companies looking for international business partners, be they clients, suppliers, JV partners, or any other type of business contact.

Yext.com

Lets companies manage their digital presence in online maps, directories and apps. Over 400,000 businesses make millions of monthly updates across 85+ exclusive global partners, making Yext the global market leader. Digital presence is a fundamental need for all 50 million businesses in the world, and Yext's mission is perfect location information in every hand. Yext is based in the heart of New York City with 350 employees and was named to Forbes Most Promising Companies lists for 2014 and 2015, as well as the Fortune Best Places to Work 2014 list.

Google+

We will pay specific attention to Google+, which is already playing a more important role in Google's organic ranking algorithm. We will create a business page on Google+ to achieve improved local search visibility. Google+ will also be the best way to get access to Google Authorship, which will play a huge role in SEO.
Resources:
https://plus.google.com/pages/create
http://www.google.com/+/brands/
https://www.google.com/appserve/fb/forms/plusweekly/
https://plus.google.com/+GoogleBusiness/posts
http://marketingland.com/beyond-social-benefits-google-business-73460
Examples:
https://plus.google.com/+AlwaysBestCareSeniorServicesHobeSound

Inbound Marketing

Inbound marketing is about pulling people in by sharing relevant senior concierge information, creating useful content, and generally being helpful. It involves writing everything from buyer's guides to blogs and newsletters that deliver useful content. The objective will be to nurture customers through the buying process with unbiased educational materials that turn consumers into informed buyers.
Resource:
www.Hubspot.com

Google My Business Profile   www.google.com/business/befound.html

We will have a complete and active Google My Business profile to give our senior concierge company a tremendous advantage over the competition, and help potential customers easily find our firm and provide relevant information about our business.

Sampling Program

We will give each sample with a mini-survey to enable customers to rate the product or service and supply constructive feedback. We will also make certain to always trade free samples for the recipient's contact information. All samples will have a label with our complete contact information.

Reddit.com
An online community where users vote on stories. The hottest stories rise to the top, while the cooler stories sink. Comments can be posted on every story, including stories about startup hot sauce companies.

6.4.1 Strategic Alliances

We will form strategic alliances to accomplish the following objectives:
1. To share marketing expenses.
2. To realize bulk buying power on wholesale purchases.
3. To engage in barter arrangements.
4. To collaborate with industry experts.
5. To set-up mutual referral relationships.

_____ (company name) will seek out opportunities to establish viable strategic alliances. We will develop strategic alliances with the following service providers by conducting introductory 'cold calls' to their offices and making them aware of our capabilities by distributing our brochures and business cards:

1.	Financial Advisors	2.	Senior Daycare Centers
3.	Jewelry Stores	4.	Accountants
5.	Day Spas	6.	Physicians
7.	Health Clubs	8.	Beauty Salons
9.	Nail Salons	10.	Bankers
11.	Rehabilitation Clinics	12.	Event Planners
13.	Estate Planners	14.	Gift Basket Makers
15.	Restaurants	16.	Gift Stores

We will assemble and present a sales presentation package that includes sales brochures, business cards, and a DVD presentation of basic errand planning tips, and client testimonials. We will include coupons that offer a discount or other type of introductory deal. We will ask to set-up a take-one display for our sales brochures at the business registration counter.

We will promptly give the referring business any one or combination of the following agreed upon reward options:
1. Referral fees
2. Free services
3. Mutual referral exchanges

We will monitor referral sources to evaluate the mutual benefits of the alliance and make certain to clearly define and document our referral incentives prior to initiating our referral exchange program.

6.4.2 Monitoring Marketing Results

We will study the current marketing situation on a daily and monthly basis to analyze trends and identify sources of business growth. In order to justify and focus future marketing dollars, we will use the following tracking methodologies to monitor our marketing results:
    Coupons: ad-specific coupons that easily enable tracking
    Landing Pages: unique web landing pages for each advertisement
    800 Numbers: unique 1-800-# per advertisement
    Embedded codes in ad response copy.
    Email Service Provider: Instantly track email views, opens, and clicks

Our financial statements will offer excellent data to track all phases of sales. These are available for review on a daily basis. _____ (company name) will benchmark our objectives for sales promotion and advertising in order to evaluate our return on invested marketing dollars and determine where to concentrate our limited advertising dollars to realize the best return. We will also strive to stay within our marketing budget.

Key Marketing Metrics
We will use the following two marketing metrics to evaluate the cost-effectiveness of our marketing campaign:
1. The cost to acquire a new customer: The average dollar amount invested to get one new client. Example: If we invest $3,000 on marketing in a single month and end the month with 10 new customers, our cost of acquisition is $300 per new customer.
2. The lifetime value of the average active customer. The average dollar value of an average customer over the life of their business with you. To calculate this metric for a given period of time, we will take the total amount of revenue our business generated during the time period and divide it by the total number of customers we had from the beginning of the time period.
3. We will track the following set of statistics on a weekly basis to keep informed of the progress of our business:
    - A. Number of total referrals.
    - B. Percentage increase of total referrals (over baseline).
    - C. Number of new referral sources.
    - D. Number of new customers/month.
    - E. Number of Leads
    - F. Appointments

Key Marketing Metrics Table
We've listed some key metrics in the following table. We will need to keep a close eye on these, to see if we meet our own forecasted expectations. If our numbers are off in too many categories, we may, after proper analysis, have to make substantial changes to our marketing efforts.

Key Marketing Metrics	2018	2019	2020
Revenue			
Leads			
Leads Converted			
Avg. Transaction per Customer			
Avg. Dollars per Customer			
Number of Referrals			
Number of PR Appearances			
Number of Testimonials			
Number of New Club Members			
Number of Returns			
Number of BBB Complaints			
Number of Completed Surveys			
Number of Blog readers			
Number of Twitter followers			
Number of Facebook Fans			

Metric Definitions

1. Leads: Individuals who step into the store to consider a purchase.
2. Leads Converted: Percent of individuals who actually make a purchase.
3. Average Transactions Per Customer: Number of purchases per customer per month. Expected to rise significantly as customers return for more and more _____ items per month
4. Average $ Per Customer: Average dollar amount of each transaction. Expected to rise along with average transactions.
5. Referrals: Includes customer and business referrals
6. PR Appearances: Online or print mentions of the business that are not paid advertising. Expected to be high upon opening, then drop off and rise again until achieving a steady level.
7. Testimonials: Will be sought from the best and most loyal customers. Our objective is ___ (#) per month) and they will be added to the website. Some will be sought as video testimonials.
8. New Loyalty Club Members: This number will rise significantly as more customers see the value in repeated visits and the benefits of club membership.
9. Number of Returns/BBB Complaints: Our goal is zero.
10. Number of Completed Surveys: We will provide incentives for customers to complete customer satisfaction surveys.

6.4.3 Word-of-Mouth Marketing

We plan to make use of the following techniques to promote word-of-mouth advertising:
1. Repetitive Image Advertising
2. Provide exceptional customer service.

3. Make effective use of loss leaders.
2. Schedule in-store activities, such as demonstrations or special events.
3. Make trial easy with a coupon or introductory discount.
4. Initiate web and magazine article submissions
5. Utilize a sampling program
6. Add a forward email feature to our website.
7. Share relevant and believable testimonial letters
8. Publish staff bios.
9. Make product/service upgrade announcements
10. Hold contests or sweepstakes
12. Have involvement with community events.
13. Pay suggestion box rewards
14. Distribute a monthly newsletter
15. Share easy-to-understand information (via an article or seminar).
16. Make personalized marketing communications.
17. Structure our referral program.
18. Sharing of Community Commonalities
19. Invitations to join our community of shared interests.
20. Publish Uncensored Customer Reviews
21. Enable Information Exchange Forums
22. Provide meaningful comparisons with competitors.
23. Clearly state our user benefits.
24. Make and honor ironclad guarantees
25. Provide superior post-sale support
26. Provide support in the pre-sale decision making process.
27. Host Free Informational Seminars or Workshops
28. Get involved with local business organizations.
29. Issue Press Release coverage of charitable involvements.
30. Hold traveling company demonstrations/exhibitions/competitions.

6.4.4 Customer Satisfaction Survey

We will design a customer satisfaction survey to measure the "satisfaction quotient" of our Senior Concierge Service customers. By providing a detailed snapshot of our current customer base, we will be able to generate more repeat and referral business and enhance the profitability of our company.

Our Customer Satisfaction Survey will include the following basics:
1. How do our customers rate our senior concierge service business?
2. How do our customers rate our competition?
3. How well do our customers rate the value of our products or services?
4. What new customer needs and trends are emerging?
5. How loyal are our customers?
6. What can be done to improve customer loyalty and repeat business?
7. How strongly do our customers recommend our business?
8. What is the best way to market our business?

9. What new value-added services would best differentiate our business from that of our competitors?
10. How can we encourage more referral business?
11. How can our pricing strategy be improved?

Our customer satisfaction survey will help to answer these questions and more. From the need for continual new products and services to improved customer service, our satisfaction surveys will allow our company to quickly identify problematic and underperforming areas, while enhancing our overall customer satisfaction.

Examples:
https://www.surveymonkey.com/r/2ZJ859M
http://www.choicesinseniorcare.com/client-satisfaction-survey/
http://smallbiztrends.com/2007/06/the-small-biz-7-survey.html

Resources:
https://www.survata.com/
https://www.google.com/insights/consumersurveys/use_cases
www.surveymonkey.com
http://www.smetoolkit.org/smetoolkit/en/content/en/6708/Customer-Satisfaction-Survey-Template-
http://smallbusiness.chron.com/common-questions-customer-service-survey-1121.html

6.4.5 Marketing Training Program

Our Marketing Training Program will include both an initial orientation and training, as well as ongoing continuing education classes. Initial orientation will be run by the owner until an HR manager is hired. For one week, half of each day will be spent in training, and the other half shadowing the operations manager.

Training will include:
- Learning the entire selection of senior concierge services.
- Understanding our Mission Statement, Value Proposition, Position Statement and Unique Selling Proposition.
- Appreciating our competitive advantages.
- Understanding our core message and branding approach.
- Learning our store's policies; returns processing, complaint handling, etc.
- Learning our customer services standards of practice.
- Learning our customer and business referral programs.
- Learning our Membership Club procedures, rules and benefits.
- Becoming familiar with our company website, and online ordering options.
- Service procedures specific to the employee's role.

Ongoing workshops will be based on customer feedback and problem areas identified by mystery buyers, which will better train employees to educate customers. These ongoing workshops will be held _____ (once?) a month for _____ (three?) hours.

6.6 Sales Strategy

The development of our sales strategy will start by developing a better understanding of our customer needs. To accomplish this task, we will pursue the following research methods:
1. Join the senior associations that our target customers belong to.
2. Contact the membership director and establish a relationship to understand their member's needs, challenges and concerns.
3. Identify non-competitive suppliers who sell to our customer to learn their challenges and look for partnering solutions.
4. Work directly with our customer and ask them what their needs are and if our business may offer a possible solution.

Our sales strategy for individuals will be based on our website presence. Through all of our marketing materials and campaigns, we will be driving individuals to our website. Once on our website, people will see the wide range of services that we offer and can then contact us for a service request estimate. The website will be especially useful for out-of-town clients who are in need of a _____ (city) based Senior Concierge Service.

We will be accepting approved credit from the corporations. This is based on the premise that the corporations would find this option to be a major benefit. They would then only have to reconcile their account with us on a monthly basis, instead of every time a transaction occurred. We will hire a local independent commissioned sales rep to sell our services to local corporations.

Our basic sales strategy is to:
  Develop a website for e-commerce sales by _____ (date).
  Provide quality customer service.
  Accept all major credit cards.
  Establish approved open accounts with corporations.
  Survey our customers regarding services they would like to see added to our menu.
  Motivate employees with a pay-for-performance component to their straight salary compensation package, based on profits and customer satisfaction rates.
  Build long-term customer relationships by putting the interests of customers first.

Our Sales Presentation Folder Kit will contain the following items:
1. A Welcome Letter
2. Owner Biography/Resume
3. Listing of Services/Benefits
4. Membership Details
5. Client Application/Contract
6. Pricing/Rate Schedule (Subject to Change)

7. Business Cards
8. Company Sales Brochure
9. Sample Company Newsletter
10. Page of Testimonials
11. Article Reprints
12. Referral Program Details
13. Sample Customer Satisfaction Survey

Direct Sales

The company will develop a database of customer names, addresses, email addresses, key dates and personal preferences. This information will be used for email, account processing and direct mail efforts to build customer loyalty. The company will offer a 30-day contract cancellation policy to build trust with our customers and improve retention rates.

Indirect Sales

We will establish a referral program for customers and an affiliate program for strategic business alliance partners.

6.6.1 Channels of Distribution

_____ (company name) will utilize its network of independent contractors to provide its services. The owners have obtained a written agreement from each pre-screened service vendor to provide the various services and give _____ (company name) a ____ (10?) % commission on each sale, plus a onetime registration processing fee of $_____.

6.6.2 Sales Forecast

The development of our sales strategy will start by developing a better understanding of our customer needs. To accomplish this task, we will pursue the following research methods:
1. Join the associations that our target customers belong to.
2. Contact the membership director and establish a relationship to understand their member's needs, challenges and concerns.
3. Identify non-competitive suppliers who sell to our customer to learn their challenges and look for partnering solutions.
4. Work directly with our customer and ask them what their needs are and if our business may offer a possible solution.

The first month will be spent setting up the business, dealing with legal and accounting issues, and developing an employee training manual and an operations control manual.

The second month will witness some real sales activity. These clients will be served by the founder, as there will not be a need to bring on new employees.

We expect sales to steadily increase as our marketing program and contact management system are executed. By using advertising, especially discounted introductory coupons, as a catalyst for this prolonged process, _____ (company name) plans to attract more customers sooner.

After month five, we will bring on another employee to serve the clients, and the founder will begin to focus on administrative details from the office. At this point, we expect to receive at least six hours of jobs a day.

Month seven will see the addition of a second employee, and by month 12 we will plateau with three employees. Years two and three will be similar to the activity in month 12.

The average unit cost to acquire a new client is estimated to be $ _____ (150?). Year two reflects a conservative growth rate of _____ (10?) percent. Year three reflects a growth rate of ____ (10?) percent.

Table: Sales Forecast

Sales	Frequency	Annual Sales 2018	2019	2020
Seniors				
Families				
Businesses				
Other				
Total Sales Forecast				
Direct Cost of Sales:				
Seniors				
Families				
Businesses				
Other				
Subtotal Direct Cost of Sales				

Note: The per-unit price of inventory purchases, includes cost of shipping.

6.7 Pricing Strategy

In setting our pricing strategy, we will consider the following factors:
1. Our overhead or fixed expenses.
2. Percentage allocation for marketing.
3. Our daily desired labor rate.
4. Profit objective.

We will develop a pricing strategy that will reinforce the perception of value to the customer and manage profitability, especially in the face of rising inflation.

The underlying premise of our pricing strategy is based on the understanding that not all prices are equally important to our customers, and not all markets have the same competitive environment. To ensure our success, we will use periodic competitor analysis and customer-driven market research surveys to determine what people might consider paying for a service like ours.

Our non-medical concierge services will be billed by the hour, with a 1 hour minimum. Our fees are based upon a fixed, all-inclusive hourly rate that we guarantee will be the lowest in the industry. Rates will vary depending on the service needed and will be firmly quoted after a personal consultation. Because most services are customized and non-traditional, we will quote a firm price once we understand the details of the assignment. Additional time is billed in 15-minute increments. Billing rate begins at start of service and ends upon completion. Package Deals are also available. Rates do not include charges for any merchandise purchased to complete service requested.

Note: Most senior concierges charge an hourly rate instead of by the job. Rates are lower in rural areas and small towns, and higher in cities, where expenses and living costs are higher. According to a recent survey, rates range from $20 to $45 per hour, with a national average of $28 per hour. A normal 8-hour day brings in $224, or $1120 a week. That's over $56,000 a year for a simple service business. Most concierge service businesses also add a small per-mile charge to cover their extra vehicle costs.
Source:
https://seniorservicebusiness.com/how-to-make-224-a-day-with-a-senior-concierge-business/

Our Billing Process

1. We will start our business with an introductory rate of $___ (40?) an hour for the first year.
2. Third party services will be billed at the rate of the service quote.
3. We will bill twice monthly in advance of service.
4. Now Service payment is due at the time of service.
5. We will bill to the nearest half hour.
6. The minimum billed time is a half hour.
7. We will not bill for drive time unless the service requires a trip to the airport or requires leaving the ____ (city) Metro area.
8. We will charge for wait time if we have to wait for an item that needs to be picked up.
9. We will establish a discounted rate for Specific Need Care Contracts that are ___ (6?) months or more, based on Care Consultant evaluations.
10. We will establish rates and share them with clients before the start of the service.
11. If a client is a continual and ongoing client, we will set up the service to automatically bill the client's credit card twice monthly.

12. We will bill the client for any parking fees incurred while completing a service.
13. We will work with each client to determine how 3rd party vendors will be paid.
14. We will charge a management fee for 3rd party services and will ensure that customer satisfaction is met.
15. The client will be responsible for all taxes on any work performed by a third-party contractor.
16. We will only charge a ___ (5?) % processing fee on top of the regular hourly rate if we pay for items (groceries, prescriptions, etc.) at the time of pick up.
17. We will charge a late fee of $1 per day or 1% of bill due, depending on which is greater, for accounts that are 15 days past due.
18. We will charge a $___ (25?) fee for returned checks or credit card charges that are reversed.
19. We will welcome out of town clients who would like to set up accounts for their loved ones and automatically set up their account to reload with hours and charge their credit card based on the amount of time needed.

We will offer our clients a variety of concierge plans with distinct pricing strategies.
1. Charge membership fees based on how many requests are usually made per month.
2. Invoice on a monthly retainer.
3. Charge per service or per hour (A La Carte).
4. Flat fee plus cost of errands

We also expect to make money from ___ (10?) % commission fees from various vendors when we direct business to them. Companies that usually pay referral fees include caterers, event planners, florists, movers, etc.

Menu of Possible Concierge Plans

		Hours/Month	Days/week	Hrs/day	Cost
1.	Exclusive Monthly Plan	160	Sun - Sat.	24	_____
2.	Select Monthly Plan	40	Sun - Sat.	24	_____
3.	Premium Monthly Plan	8	Mon - Fri	7AM-10PM	_____
4.	Basic Monthly Plan	4	Mon-Fri.	7AM-6PM	_____
5.	Event Planning Plans				
6.	Employee Corporate Services Plans				
7.	Customer Loyalty Program Plans				

Example:
www.seniorconciergeproviders.com/library/documents/Promotion_Packages.pdf

Pricing Strategy
We will charge depending on:
– The services requested
– Experts retained
– How many services are used

We will offer a customized plan that fits the individual's needs and their budget.

Price List Comparison

Competitor	Service	Our Price	Competitor Price	B/(W) Competitor

We will adopt the following pricing guidelines:
1. We must insure that our price plus service equation is perceived to be an exceptional value proposition.
2. We must refrain from competing on price, but always be price competitive.
3. We must develop value-added services, and bundle those with our products to create offerings that cannot be easily price compared.
4. We must focus attention on our competitive advantages.
5. Development of a pricing strategy based on our market positioning strategy, which is ____ (mass market value leadership/exceptional premium niche value?)
6. Our pricing policy objective, which is to _____ (increase profit margins/ achieve revenue maximization to increase market share/lower unit costs).
7. We will use marketplace intelligence and gain insights from competitor pricing.
8. We will solicit pricing feedback from customers using surveys and interviews.
9. We will utilize limited time pricing incentives to penetrate niche markets
10. We will conduct experiments at prices above and below the current price to determine the price elasticity of demand. (Inelastic demand or demand that does not decrease with a price increase, indicates that price increases may be feasible.)
11. We will keep our offerings and prices simple to understand and competitive, based on market intelligence.
12. We will consider a price for volume strategy on certain items, and study the effects of price on volume and of volume on costs, as in a recession, trying to recover these costs through a price increase can be fatal.

6.8 Differentiation Strategies

We will use differentiation strategies to develop and market unique products for different customer segments. To differentiate ourselves from the competition, we will focus on the assets, creative ideas and competencies that we have that none of our competitors has. The goal of our differentiation strategies is to be able to charge a premium price for our unique Senior Concierge Services and/or to promote loyalty and assist in retaining our customers.

Differentiation in our senior concierge service will be achieved in the following types of ways, including:

Explanation

☐ Product features _____
☐ Complementary services _____
☐ Technology embodied in design _____
☐ Location _____
☐ Service innovations _____
☐ Superior service _____
☐ Creative advertising _____
☐ Better supplier relationships _____

Source: http://scholarship.sha.cornell.edu/cgi/viewcontent.cgi?article=1295&context=articles

Differentiating will mean defining who our perfect target market is and then catering to their needs, wants and interests better than everyone else. It will be about using surveys to determine what's most important to our targeted market and giving it to them consistently. It will not be about being "everything to everybody"; but rather, "the absolute best to our chosen targeted group".

In developing our differentiation strategy will we use the following form to help define our differences:

1. Targeted customer segments _____
2. Customer characteristics _____
3. Customer demographics _____
4. Customer behavior _____
5. Geographic focus _____
6. Ways of working _____
7. Service delivery approach _____
8. Customer problems/pain points _____
9. Complexity of customers' problems _____
10. Range of services _____

We will use the following approaches to differentiate our products and services from those of our competitors to stand apart from standardised offerings:

1. Superior quality
2. Unusual or unique product features
3. More responsive customer service
4. Rapid product or service innovation
5. Advanced technological features
6. Engineering design or styling
7. Additional product features
8. An image of prestige or status

Specific Differentiators will include the following:
1. Being a Specialist in one procedure
2. Utilizing advanced/uncommon technology

3. Possessing extensive experience
4. Building an exceptional facility
5. Consistently achieving superior results
6. Having a caring and empathetic personality
7. Giving customer s WOW experience, including a professional customer welcome package.
8. Enabling convenience and 24/7 online accessibility
9. Calling customers to express interest in their challenges.
10. Keeping to the appointment schedule.
11. Remembering customer names and details like they were family.
12. Assuring customer fears.
13. Building a visible reputation and recognition around our community
14. Acquiring special credentials or professional memberships
15. Providing added value services, such as taxi service, longer hours, financing plans, and post-sale services.

Primary Differentiation Strategies:
1. We will staff these services with service providers willing to work on a pay-for-performance basis, to reduce our fixed salary overhead expenses.
2. We will offer extended hours of service.
3. We will advertise our environmentally friendly policies.
4. We will guarantee our response timeliness.
5. We will provide a high-touch, face-to-face customer experience, backed by a high-tech operational software platform that includes a special event reminder service and a profile of client preferences.
6. We will offer _____ (#) Concierge Membership Plan Options that require only 60 days of advance notice to terminate.
7. We will provide clients with multiple communication channel options, including telephone, mail, mobile, email, fax, etc.
8. We will use the client data records that we build over time to switch from a reactive to a proactive service mode.
9. We plan to develop a web-based program that allows clients to place their service requests online.

6.9 Milestones

The Milestones Chart is a timeline that will guide our company in developing and growing our business. It will list chronologically the various critical actions and events that must occur to bring our business to life. We will make certain to assign real, attainable dates to each planned action or event.

_____ (company name) has identified several specific milestones which will function as goals for the company. The milestones will provide a target for achievement as well as a mechanism for tracking progress. The dates were chosen based on realistic delivery times and necessary construction times. All critical path milestones will be completed within their allotted time frames to ensure the success of contingent milestones. The following table will provide a timeframe for each milestone.

Table: Milestones

Milestones	**Start Date**	**End Date**	**Budget**	**Manager**
Business Plan Completion				
Secure Permits/Licenses				
Office Set-up				
Obtain Insurance				
Secure Additional Financing				
Establish Vendor Accounts				
Purchase Tools/Equipment				
Define Marketing Programs				
Install Equipment				
Set-up Accounting System				
Finalize Media Plan				
Create Facebook Business Page				
Open Twitter Account				
Conduct Blogger Outreach				
Develop Personnel Plan				
Hire sales associate				
Personnel Training Program				
Implement Marketing Plan				
Get Website Live				
Conduct SEO				
Form Strategic Alliances				
Purchase Supplies				
Press Release Announcements				
First Customer				
Full Time Work Threshold				
Kickoff Advertising Program				
Join Community Orgs./Network				
Conduct Satisfaction Surveys				
Devise Growth Strategy				
Monitor Social Media Networks				
Respond Positively to Reviews				
Measure Return on Marketing $$$				
Quarterly Training				
Revenues Exceed $_____				
Totals:				

7.0 Website Plan Summary

_____ (company name) is currently developing a website at the URL address www. (company name).com.

The website will be developed to offer customers a product catalog for online orders. The overriding design philosophy of the site will be ease of use. We want to make the process of placing an order as easy and fast as possible thereby encouraging increased sales. We will incorporate special features such as a section that is specific to each customer so the customer can easily make purchases of repeat items. Instead of going through the website every month and locating their monthly needs, the site will capture regularly ordered items for that specific customer, significantly speeding up the ordering process. This ease-of-use feature will help increase sales as customers become more and more familiar with the site and appreciate how easy it is to place an order.

We will also provide multiple incentives to sign-up for various benefits, such as our newsletters and promotional sale notices. This will help us to build an email database, which will supply our automated customer follow-up system. We will create a personalized drip marketing campaign to stay in touch with our customers and prospects.

We will develop our website to be a resource for web visitors who are seeking knowledge and information about brand comparisons, with a goal to service the knowledge needs of our customers and generate leads. Our home page will be designed to be a "welcome mat" that clearly presents our service offerings and provides links through which visitors can gain easy access to the information they seek. We will use our website to match the problems our customers face with the solutions we offer.

We will use the free tool, Google Analytics (http://www.google.com/analytics), to generate a history and measure our return on investment. Google Analytics is a free tool that can offer insight by allowing the user to monitor traffic to a single website. We will just add the Google Analytics code to our website and Google will give our firm a dashboard providing the number of unique visitors, repeat traffic, page views, etc.
This will help to stop wasting our company's money on inefficient marketing. Using an analytic program will show exactly which leads are paying off, and which ones to do without. We will find out what's bringing our site the most traffic and how to improve upon that.

To improve the readability of our website, we will organize our website content in the following ways.
1. Headlines
2. Bullet points
3. Callout text
4. Top of page summaries

To improve search engine optimization, we will maximize the utilization of the following;
1. Links
2. Headers
3. Bold text
4. Bullets

5. Keywords   6. Meta tags

This website will serve the following purposes:

Contact Us	Customer Service contact info
Frequently Asked Questions	FAQs
How to Get Started	How It Works
Newsletter Sign-up	Build email database
Our Services	Benefits Received
Testimonials	With client photos
Referral Program	Details
Helpful Articles	Establish expertise.
Print Complimentary Consultation Coupon	Plus free first-time usage
Gift Certificates/Card	Print
Customer Satisfaction Survey	Feedback
Seminar Schedule	Post dates and locations
Schedule an Appointment	Hours of operation
Executive Team	Resumes
Why Choose Us	Our Competitive Advantages
Media Center	Press Release Archive
Strategic Alliance Partners	Links
Policies and Procedures	Privacy Policy
	Terms and Conditions
Guarantees	Satisfaction Guarantee
About Us	Company History/Overview
Customer Inquiry Form	Start dialogue process.
Favorite Links	Professional Associations
Our Blog	Accept feedback comments
Email a Friend	Viral marketing
My Account	Check account balance/pay bill.
	Register Personal Preferences
	Register for Reminder Service
Customer Loyalty Program	Register for Frequent Client Club
Partnering Opportunities	Vendor Evaluation Process
Client Pricing Alternatives	A la carte/per hour/membership
Membership Plan Options	Deluxe to Basic Programs
Careers	Job Opportunities

7.1 Website Marketing Strategy

Our online marketing strategy will employ the following distinct mechanisms:

1. Search Engine Submission
    This will be most useful to people who are unfamiliar with _____(company name), but are looking for a local Senior Concierge Service. There will also be

searches from customers who may know about us, but who are seeking additional information.

Search Engine Optimization (SEO)
SEO is a very important digital marketing strategy because search engines are the primary method of finding information for most internet users. SEO is simply the practice of improving and promoting a website in order to increase the number of visitors a site receives from search engines. Basic SEO techniques will range from the naming of webpages to the way that other websites link to our website. We will also need to get our business listed on as many relevant online directories as possible, such as Google, Yelp, Kudzu and Yahoo Local, write a blog that solicit comments and be active on social media sites.
We will also try to incorporate local terms potential clients would use, such as "_____ (city) senior concierge service" or "_____ (city) elder concierge company." This will make it more likely that local customers will find us close to the top of their search.
Resource;
www.officerreports.com/blog/wp-content/uploads/2014/11/SEOmoz-The-Beginners-Guide-To-SEO-2012.pdf

2. Website Address (URL) on Marketing Materials
   Our URL will be printed on all marketing communications, business cards, letterheads, faxes, and invoices and product labels. This will encourage a visit to our website for additional information

3. Online Directories Listings
   We will make an effort to list our website on relevant, free and paid online directories and manufacturer website product locators.
   The good online directories possess the following features:
   Free or paid listings that do not expire and do not require monthly renewal.
   Ample space to get your advertising message across.
   Navigation buttons that are easy for visitors to use.
   Optimization for top placement in the search engines based on keywords that people typically use to find tanning salons.
   Direct links to your website, if available.
   An ongoing directory promotion campaign to maintain high traffic volumes to the directory site.
   Directory Examples:
Triangle Concierge   http://www.triangleconcierge.com/concierge_directory.htm
DMOZ Open Directory Project:
www.dmoz.org/Business/Business_Services/Office_Services/Concierge_Services/North_America/United_States/
Concierge Directory   //conciergedirectory.org/opportunity.html

4. Strategic Business Partners
   We will use a Business Partners page to cross-link to complementary companies and brand name suppliers who want to cross-link with our site. We will also insist

on cross-linking to businesses that accept our gift certificate donations as in-house run contest prize awards.

5. YouTube Posting

   We will produce a video of testimonials from several of our satisfied clients. Our research indicates that the YouTube video will also serve to significantly improve our ranking with the Google Search Engine.

6. Exchange of links with referral vendors.

7. E-Newsletter

   Use the newsletter sign-up as a reason to collect email addresses and limited profiles, and then use embedded links in the newsletter to return readers to your website.

8. Create an account for your photos on flickr.com

   We will use the name of our site on flickr so we have the same keywords. To take full advantage of Flickr, we will use a JavaScript-enabled browser and install the latest version of the Macromedia Flash Player.

9. Geo Target Pay Per Click (PPC) Campaign

   Available through Google Adwords program.

10. Post messages on Internet user groups and forums.

    Get involved with concierge related discussion groups and forums and develop a descriptive signature paragraph.

11. Write up your own LinkedIn.com and Facebook.com profiles.

    Highlight your background and professional interests.

12. Facebook.com Brand-Building Applications:

    As a Facebook member, we will create a specific Facebook page for our business through its "Facebook Pages" application. This page will be used to promote who we are and what we do. We will use this page to post alerts when we have new articles to distribute, news to announce, etc. Facebook members can then become fans of our page and receive these updates on their newsfeed as we post them. We will create our business page by going to the "Advertising" link on the bottom of our personal Facebook page. We will choose the "Pages" tab at the top of that page, and then choose "Create a Page." We will upload our logo, enter our company profile details, and establish our settings. Once completed, we will click the "publish your site" button to go live. We will also promote our Page everywhere we can. We will add a Facebook link to our website, our email signatures, and email newsletters. We will also add Facebook to the marketing mix by deploying pay-per-click ads through their advertising application. With Facebook advertising, we will target by specifying sex, age, relationship, location, education, as well as specific keywords. Once we specify our target criteria, the tool will tell us how many members in the network meet our target needs.

13. Blog to share our success stories and solicit comments

    Blogging will be a great way for us to share information, expertise, and news, and start a conversation with our customers, the media, suppliers, and any other target audiences. Blogging will be a great online marketing strategy because it keeps our content fresh, engages our audience to leave comments on specific posts, improves search engine rankings and attracts links. In the blog we will share fun

drink recipes and party tips. We will also provide a link to our Facebook.com page.   Resource: www.blogger.com
14. Other Embedded Links
We will use social networking, article directory postings and press release web sites as promotional tools and to provide good inbound link opportunities.
15. Issue Press Releases
We will create online press releases to share news about our new website.
Resources: Sites that offer free press release services include:
www.1888pressrelease.com and www.pr.com/press-releases.

7.2 Development Requirements

A full development plan will be generated as documented in the milestones. Costs that ____ (company name) will expect to incur with development of its new website include:

Development Costs
- User interface design $_____.
- Site development and testing $_____
- Site Implementation $._____

Ongoing Costs
- Website name registration $_____ per year.
- Site Hosting $_____ or less per month.

Site design changes, updates and maintenance are considered part of Marketing.

The site will be developed by ___ (company name), a local start-up company, under a partial barter agreement, so as not to impact of our cash flow position. The user interface designer will use our existing graphic art to come up with the website logo and graphics. We have already secured hosting with a local provider, _____ (business name). Additionally, they will prepare a monthly statistical usage report to analyze and improve web usage and return on investment.

The plan is for the website to be live by _____ (date).
Basic website maintenance, including update and data entry will be handled by our staff.
Site content, such as images and text will be maintained by _____ (owner name).
In the future, we may need to contract with a technical resource to build the trackable article download and newsletter capabilities.

7.3 Sample Frequently Asked Questions

We will use the following guidelines when developing the frequently asked questions for the ecommerce section of the website:
1. Use a Table of Contents: Offer subject headers at the top of the FAQ page with a hyperlink to that related section further down on the page for quick access.
2. Group Questions in a Logical Way and group separate specific questions related to a subject together.

3. Be Precise with the Question: Don't use open-ended questions.
4. Avoid Too Many Questions: Publish only the popular questions and answers.
5. Answer the Question with a direct answer.
6. Link to Resources When Available: via hyperlinks so the customer can continue with self-service support.
7. Use Bullet Points to list step-by-step instructions.
8. Focus on Customer Support and Not Marketing.
9. Use Real and Relevant Frequently Asked Questions from actual customers.
10. Update Your FAQ Page as customers continue to communicate questions.

The following frequently asked questions will enable us to convey a lot of important information to our clients in a condensed format. We will post these questions and answers on our website and create a hardcopy version to be included on our sales presentation folder.

How do I schedule a service?
Call _____ (company name) at _____ or e-mail us at _____.

I would like a service that I do not see on your site, can you assist?
Yes. _____ (company name) is constantly updating our service list. We will customize our service offerings to meet your needs and will do any service as long as it is legal, ethical and with good intentions.

Why should I try _____ (company name)?
____ (company name) is here to take the stress out of your day. We give you the peace of mind that your needs or those of your loved ones are being met.

What makes ___ (company name) different from other non-medical care providers?
We provide a wide range of non-medical homecare services. We are available 24 hours a day, 7 days a week, 365 days a year for any inquires, scheduling changes, or emergencies. We have no minimum hourly requirement of service per day and select only the most trusted and compassionate team members.

Can _____ (company name) take over management of my current household contracts such as gardeners and housekeepers?
Yes. _____ (company name) can assume management of the current contractors you have working in your home.

I need my prescription picked up, do you pay for it or do I?
It is preferred that you charge the prescription before we arrive to pick it up. If we have to pay at the point of purchase, an additional 5% is added to the service charge.

What are your normal hours of service?
_____ (company name) is on call 24 hours a day. Our normal business hours are from 8:00 a.m. to 6:00 p.m., Monday through Friday. After hours, weekends, and holidays are billed at a higher rate.

Do you review the work of your independent contractors for quality assurance?
Yes. We will do scheduled, and random onsite visits to ensure that the highest level of service is being given and distribute customer satisfaction surveys on a regular basis.

Where do you find your contractors?
Our contractors come from a variety of sources. Each contractor is interviewed and all references are checked. The performance of each contractor is reviewed quarterly based on your observations and our assessments.

How do you supervise your Caregivers?
We use an advanced Monitoring System that requires our service personnel to clock in and out through the telephone allowing us to effectively track hours and confirm attendance in real time. To ensure utmost client satisfaction, our system will notify us immediately if your concierge service provider has not clocked in or out as scheduled. In addition, we conduct satisfaction surveys, routine supervisory visits and random management quality assurance check-ins so our clients receive the best possible service.

How quickly can you dispatch a concierge service provider to my residence?
We understand the need for a service like ours to respond in an urgent manner. If you are in urgent need, we guarantee a highly qualified service provider will be at your residence within _____ (#) 3 hours of the initial request.

What areas do you service?
We service the greater _____ (city) area including but not limited to_____ .

Is _____ (company name) licensed, bonded and insured?
Yes. We are licensed, bonded and insured. Proof of coverage is available upon request.

How can a concierge help me?
We are available to assist you with both your everyday tasks and errands, as well as the out of the ordinary tasks.

Do I have to sign a contract to use your services on a regular basis?
No. If you require regular professional services, we would prepare a contract for you, if you require, but if you want to employ us on a single occasion, that's fine.

Why Should I Use _____ Concierge?
We are a client-driven service that strives to establish a lasting rapport with each and every client. Relationship building is our specialty and we will work closely with you, every step of the way, to ensure a satisfying and worthwhile experience. We know how busy you are and we understand how hard you work; that's exactly why we customize our services to suit your needs.

Why wouldn't I just put an ad in the paper and find someone on my own?
Working with our company affords you several major advantages. First, we are a licensed

and insured ___ (state) home health agency, offering you a great deal of protection. If something should happen to one of our senior home caregivers while on the job, we provide worker's compensation insurance and liability insurance. Anyone we send out to you is an employee of the company. We complete payroll, deducting the proper taxes so you do not get in trouble with the IRS. You may even be able to deduct these expenses as medical care, which you could not do if you were not properly following tax rules. We also supervise our home health caregivers; deal with scheduling and backup if a caregiver is sick or unable to make it to work. We relieve family members of a great deal of stress and headaches trying to manage senior caregivers on your own. And, all of our employees are thoroughly screened, trained, and run through a thorough background check.

How Much Notice Do You Need?
We will do our utmost to accommodate emergency requests. Although we prefer as much notice as possible, we can respond to most bookings within 24 hours.

What methods of payment do you accept?
We accept personal checks, certified checks, cash, MasterCard, and Visa.

Will my credit card be charged as a deposit?
No. We will only charge your credit card if we receive your authorization to debit or do not receive payment for services rendered upon completion.

How much do you charge for your services?
Our prices range from $___ to $_____ per hour, with a two-hour minimum.

Are materials, expenses and taxes included in your hourly rate?
No, the client is responsible for paying all additional charges on top of the hourly rate.

How will I know what additional service charges are?
We will provide receipts for all hourly charges and all additional service charges.

What happens if the caregiver is sick?

Your caregiver will be automatically replaced by another caregiver. We are here to assist you 24 hrs a day, 365 days a week in case of an emergency.

Do I need to be concerned about my personal information becoming public?
No. We are responsible professionals and all dealings will be kept confidential.

What is your pricing plan?
The level of value and quality services we offer is quite diverse and extensive. Because we provide unique services for our clients, our rates are based upon the number and variety of services needed, complexity of requirements, and projected length of time.

How does _____ (company name) work with my loved one's doctor?

Your caregiver will help organize all your doctors' information records. We will accompany them on their medical appointments and update you with the doctor's advice. These services offer you peace of mind, prevent overlapping tests and medications, and increase the effectiveness of medical care.

Will you administer medication?
Our insurance company says "no" but we can do medication counts and see that medication is on hand so that your senior can self-medicate.

How will I know how things are going?
The owner will follow up each contact with a telephone call to both the senior and to the designated family member. We also maintain a log of the time of arrival and departure, the name of the service provider and what took place during each visit. These logs can be left in the senior's home or a copy emailed or faxed to you on request.

7.4 Website Performance Summary

We will use web analysis tools to monitor web traffic, such as identifying the number of site visits. We will analyze customer transactions and take actions to minimize problems, such as incomplete sales and abandoned shopping carts. We will use the following table to track the performance of our website:

Category	2018 Fcst	2018 Act	2019 Fcst	2019 Act	2020 Fcst	2020 Act
No. of Customers						
New Subscribers						
Unique Visitors						
Bounce rate						
Page Views / Visit						
Avg. Time on Site						
Total Page Views						
No. of Products						
Product Categories						
Number of Incomplete Sales						
Conversion Rate						
Affiliate Sales						
Customer Satisfaction Score						

7.5 Website Retargeting/Remarketing

Research indicates that for most websites, only 2% of web traffic converts readers on the first visit. Retargeting will keep track of people who have visited our website and displays our ads to them as they browse online. This will bring back 98% of users who don't convert right away by keeping our brand at the top of their mind. Setting up a remarketing tracking code on our website will allow us to target past visitors who did not convert or take the desired action on our site. After people have been to our website and are familiar with our brand, we will market more aggressively to this 'warm traffic.'

Resource:
www.marketing360.com/remarketing-software-retargeting-ads/

8.0 Operations Plan

Operations include the business aspects of running our business, such as conducting quality assessment and improvement activities, auditing functions, cost-management analysis, and customer service. Our operations plan will present an overview of the flow of the daily activities of the business and the strategies that support them. It will focus on the following critical operating factors that will make the business a success:

1. We will enjoy the following advantages in the sourcing of our inventory: _____

2. We will utilize the following technological innovations in the customer relationship management (CRM) process: _____

3. We will make use of the following advantages in our distribution process: _____

4. We will develop the following in-house training program to improve worker productivity: _____

5. We will utilize the following system to better control inventory carrying costs. _____

6. We will implement the following quality control plan: _____

Quality Control Plan
Our Quality Control Plan will include a review process that checks all factors involved in our operations. The main objectives of our quality control plan will be to uncover defects and bottlenecks and reporting to management level to make the decisions on the improvement of the whole production process. Our review process will include the following activities:
    Quality control checklist
    Finished product/service review
    Structured walkthroughs
    Statistical sampling
    Testing process

Operations Planning
We will use Microsoft Visio to develop visual maps, which will piece together the different activities in our organization and show how they contribute to the overall "value stream" of our business. We will rightfully treat operations as the lifeblood of our business. We will develop a combined sales and operations planning process where sales and operations managers will sit down every month to review sales, at the same time creating a forward-looking 12-month rolling plan to help guide the product development and manufacturing processes, which can become disconnected from sales. We will approach our operations planning using a three-step process that analyzes the company's current state, future state and the initiatives it will tackle next. For each initiative, such as launching a new product or service, the company will examine the related financials, talent and operations needs, as well as target customer profiles. Our management team

will map out the cost of development and then calculate forecasted return on investment and revenue predictions.

Get Started Process
1. Client calls to request a free evaluation.
2. By asking questions and through careful observation, we mutually determine how much help is needed and how often.
3. We make a list of the day-to-day tasks that have become difficult to manage and the services that are needed.
4. We develop an individualized plan.
5. A schedule is arranged and one of our trained caregivers is assigned to provide individualized attention and services based on the plan.

We will develop a Concierge Operations Manual and treat it as an evolving document that taps our collective experience since the company's inception. It will outline operating procedures and processes, reporting guidelines, job descriptions, contact lists and a collection of forms and contracts.

We plan to write and maintain an Operations Manual and a Personnel Policies Handbook. The Operating Manual will be a comprehensive document outlining virtually every aspect of the business. The operating manual will include management and accounting procedures, hiring and personnel policies, and daily operations procedures, such as opening and closing the store, and how to _____. The manual will cover the following topics:

- Community Relations
- Media Relations
- Vendor Relations
- Competition Relations
- Environmental Concerns
- Intra Company Procedures
- Banking and Credit Cards
- Computer Procedures
- Quality Controls
- Open/Close Procedures
- Software Documentation

- Customer Relations
- Employee Relations
- Government Relations
- Equipment Maintenance Checklist
- Inventory Controls
- Accounting and Billing
- Financing
- Scheduling Procedures
- Safety Procedures
- Security Procedures

We plan to create the following business manuals:

	Manual Type	Key Elements
1.	Operations Manual	Process flowcharts
2.	Employee Manual	Benefits/Appraisals/Practices
3.	Managers Manual	Job Descriptions
4.	Customer Service Policies	Inquiry Handling Procedures

The plan is to place special emphasis on using software technology to make the transaction and interaction with customers more efficient and to accept a wide range of credit and debit card options. We will also encourage clients to set-up Concierge

Accounts and make pre-payment deposits to these accounts for their services.

We also plan to checkout specially designed software packages for concierges and the use of QuickBooks (www.quickbooks.com) to facilitate our record keeping and the acceptance of credit cards via PayPal (www.paypal.com).

We will work with our lawyer to develop a service contract that will spell out exactly what type of service we provide. It will also cover fees, how the client is billed, when payment is due (usually 30 days), who has the right to terminate the contract, how much notice is required and other relevant particulars.

We will set-up a training program to improve our staff's neighborhood knowledge and facilitate the sharing of local tips.

Because we depend upon our network of referral contractors, we will put all candidates through a rigorous selection process, to ensure they meet the following requirements:
- Current business license
- Clean Better Business Bureau record
- Adequate liability insurance
- Bonded (where applicable)
- Validated references
- A proven track record of entity success

Concierge Software Resources:
Liferro
http://www.liferro.com/products/concierge_software/concierge_software.htm
The Concierge Assistant http://goldkeysolutions.com
Virtual Assistant Manager
http://www.virtualassistantmanager.com/concierge_software.php

9.0 Management Summary

The Management Plan will reveal who will be responsible for the various management functions to keep the business running efficiently. It will further demonstrate how that individual has the experience and/or training to accomplish each function. It will address who will do the planning function, the organizing function, the directing function, and the controlling function. We will also develop an employee retention plan because there are distinct cost advantages to retaining employees. It costs a lot to recruit and train a new employee, and in the early days, new employees are a lot less productive. We will need to make sure that our employees are satisfied in order to retain them and, in turn, create satisfied customers.

Personal History

The owner has been working in the concierge industry for over ____ (#) years, gaining personal knowledge and experience in all phases of the industry. _____ (owner name) is the founder and operations manager of _____ (company name). He/she began his/her career as a _____ .

Over the last ____ (#) years, _____ (owner name) became quite proficient in a wide range of management activities and responsibilities, becoming an operations manager for _____ (former employer name) from _____ to _____ (dates). There he/she was able to achieve _____ (results realized). _____, owner of _____ (company name), has a degree in _____ from _____ (school name). He/she is an experienced entrepreneur with ____ years of small business accounting, finance, marketing and management experience. Education includes college course work in business administration and _____.

Duties and Responsibilities: Currently, _____ (owner name) will handle all aspects of planning, purchasing, sales, personnel, promotion, and production. As the company grows, a more formal management hierarchy will be developed.

These experiences, taken as a whole, provide _____ (owner name) with a wealth of practical knowledge to develop a high-quality service organization. His/her recognition that it requires time and money to properly train employees is essential to the profitability of _____ (company name).

Financial growth is monitored by _____ (owner name) and by an accountant who completes monthly statements used to make sound management decisions.

The owner will draw an annual salary of $_____ from the business although most of this goes to repay loans to finance business start-up costs. These loans will be paid-in-full by _____ (month) of _____ (year).

Advisory Resources Available to the Business Include:

	Name	Address	Phone
Accountant			
Attorney			
Insurance Broker			
Banker			
Business Consultant			
Wholesale Suppliers			
Trade Association			
Other			

Management Summary:

Ownership Structure _____ (owner name) is the owner of _____ (business name), which is a _____ (type of legal entity).

Owner Resume: He/she is an experienced _____ with over ___ years as a _____ with the _____ (organization name).

Prior experience includes_____.

Internal Mgt Team: Advisory team is comprised of ___(#) members and includes:
_____

Advisory team members bring the following talents and abilities to the table:
_____

The owner will oversee all marketing campaigns and operations.

Ext. Mgt Resources: Upon opening the business an accountant will be contracted. Our lawyer is _____ and our banker is _____.

Human Resource Needs: As soon as the business reaches $_____ in revenues, additional sales associates will be hired. Office staff will be added as annual sales revenue approaches $_____.

Note: Marketing and public relations will be handled mainly by the owner. If there is a greater need, a marketing consultant will be hired to help issues press releases and generate seminar and website content.

Management Matrix

Name	Title	Functions	Responsibilities

Outsourcing Matrix

Company Name	Functions	Responsibilities	Cost

Note: Marketing and public relations will be handled mainly by the owner. If there is a greater need, a marketing consultant will be hired to help issue press releases and generate seminar and website content.

9.1 Personnel Plan

Employee Requirements:
1. **Skills and Abilities**
   Staff must have a high school education, be self-motivating, and have strong customer service skills. Previous experience in the concierge industry is preferred.
2. **Recruitment**
   Experience suggests that personal referrals are an excellent source for employees. We have not had much success with published classified ads.
3. **Training and Supervision**
   Training is largely accomplished through a training program and hands-on experience. Additional knowledge is gained through industry books, magazines, and promotional materials. We will foster professional development and independence in all phases of our business. Supervision is task-oriented and the quantity is dependent on the complexity of the job assignment. More experienced employees are responsible for managing certain aspects of service production.
4. **Salaries and Benefits**
   We will pay from $___ to $____ an hour depending on experience. An employee discount of ____ percent on merchandise is offered. As business warrants, we hope to put together a benefit package that includes insurance, parking, and paid vacations.

Staffing Plan
The personnel plan is included in the following table. It shows the owner's salary and ___ full-time salaries for _____ (position title). There will be no benefits offered at this time.

A Board of Advisors will provide continuous mentoring support on business matters. Expertise gaps in legal, tax, marketing and personnel will be covered by the Board of Advisors. We will hire sales associates who are truly excited about what they do.

The owner will actively seek free business advice from SCORE, a national non-profit organization with a local office. This is a group of retired executives and business owners who donate their time to serve as business counselors to new business owners.

Personnel Plan
1. We will develop a system for recruiting, screening and interviewing employees.
2. Background checks will be performed as well as reference checks.
3. We will develop an extensive employee training program and conduct the course on an ongoing basis.
4. We will keep track of staff scheduling.
5. We will develop client satisfaction surveys to provide feedback and ideas.
6. We will develop and perform semi-annual employee evaluations.
7. We will "coach" all of our employees to improve their abilities and range of

skills.
8. We will employ temporary employees via a local staffing agency to assist with sales, deliveries and customer service prior to big holiday sales events.
9. We will pay a fair wage to increase employee morale and decrease turnover.

Note: We are cognizant of the fact that it costs far more to train a new employee rather than to maintain a current employee.

We will also develop a personnel manual. Its purpose is to set fair and equal guidelines in print for all to abide. It's the playbook detailing specific policies, as well as enforcement, thereby preventing any misinterpretation, miscommunication or ill feelings. This manual will reflect only the concerns that affect our personnel. A companion policy and procedure manual will cover everything else.

Our Employee Handbook will include the following sections:
1. Overview
2. Introduction to the Company
3. Organizational Structure
4. Employment and Hiring Policies
5. Performance Evaluation and Promotion Policies
6. Compensation Policies
7. Time Off Policies
8. Training Programs and Reimbursement Policies
9. General Rules and Policies
10. Termination Policies.

Job Description: Concierge Lifestyle Manager

This individual will have to have intimate knowledge of _____ (city), as well as global dining and nightlife venues, events and happenings, all while furthering their knowledge of their clients' needs and preferences. This individual must possess a polished appearance and be connected to the _____ (city) scene.

Responsibilities:
1. Develop in-depth relationships with clients to understand every possible need, like, and dislike.
2. Provide, explain, and promote Senior Concierge Services to current and potential buyers and brokers on-site at the sales office.
3. Create a customized welcome letter introducing the Senior Concierge Service to local residents.
4. Produce and distribute monthly newsletter with upcoming community events, schedules, and openings.
5. Fulfill client requests such as vacation destinations and last-minute reservations, in a timely fashion.
6. Research the most up to date trends and happenings in the _____ area.
7. Update and maintain daily activities to be able to report on time spent for weekly and monthly reporting requirements.
8. Initiative in understanding the luxury/high-end marketplace inclusive of restaurants, events, etc. specific to region and secondarily, key global cities in

order to meet/exceed clients requests.
9. Develop relationships with clients and vendors that establish trust and long-term ability to influence decision-making.

Requirements:
1. Bachelor's degree or the equivalent
2. 3-5 years minimum experience in public relations, sales, hospitality, or event-planning environment.
3. Excellent interpersonal skills at all levels
4. Conversant in City's perpetually evolving culture.
5. Strong communication skills verbally and written
6. Strong knowledge of Microsoft Office, internet and email/voice mail systems
7. Poised, confident, and comfortable in a public setting

Salary Guidance: The owner/manager wants to draw $_____ per month. Employees will start at $___/hour and ___% raises will come after the first year of operation. Only management personnel will qualify for fringe benefits.

Table: Personnel

	Number of Employees	Hourly Rate	Annual Salaries 2018	2019	2020
General Manager					
Errand Driver					
Personal Shopper					
Service Vendor Coordinator					
Field Sales Rep					
In-house Concierges					
Lobby Concierge					
Office Manager					
Relocation Manager					
Catering/Events Manager					
Bookkeeper					
Customer Service					
Marketing Coordinator					
Software Specialist					
Administrative Assistant					
Total People: Headcount					
Total Annual Payroll					
Payroll Burden (Fringe Benefits)		(+)			
Total Payroll Expense		(=)			

Salary Notes
The national average for a senior concierge is around $26 per hour, which is $52,000 per year. According to Genworth's 2013 Cost of Care survey, the national median hourly rate for home care is $19 per hour.

10.0 Risk Factors

Risk management is the identification, assessment, and prioritization of risks, followed by the coordinated and economical application of resources to minimize, monitor, and control the probability and/or impact of unfortunate events or to maximize the realization of opportunities. For the most part, our risk management methods will consist of the following elements, performed, more or less, in the following order.
1. Identify, characterize, and assess threats
2. Assess the vulnerability of critical assets to specific threats
3. Determine the risk (i.e. the expected consequences of specific types of attacks on specific assets)
4. Identify ways to reduce those risks
5. Prioritize risk reduction measures based on a strategy

Types of Risks:
_____ (company name) faces the following kinds of risks:

1. **Financial Risks**
    Our quarterly revenues and operating results are difficult to predict and may fluctuate significantly from quarter to quarter as a result of a variety of factors. Among these factors are:
    - Changes in our own or competitors' pricing policies.
    - Recession pressures.
    - Fluctuations in expected revenues from advertisers, sponsors and strategic relationships.
    - Timing of costs related to acquisitions or payments.

2. **Legislative / Legal Landscape.**
    Our participation in the concierge service arena presents unique risks:
    - Product and other related liability.
    - Federal and State regulations on business licensing, privacy and insurance.

3. **Operational Risks**
    For the past __ (#) years the owner has been dealing with computers so he is comfortable with technology and understands a wide array of software applications. However, the biggest potential problem will be equipment malfunction. To minimize the potential for problems, the owner will be taking equipment repair training from the manufacturer and will deal with basic troubleshooting and minor repairs. Beyond that, we have identified a service technician who is located close-by.

    To attract and retain client to the _____ (company name) community, we must continue to provide differentiated and quality services. This confers certain risks including the failure to:
    - Anticipate and respond to consumer preferences for partnerships and service.

- Attract, excite and retain a large audience of customers to our community.
- Create and maintain successful strategic alliances with quality partners.
- Deliver high quality, customer service.
- Build our brand rapidly and cost-effectively.
- Compete effectively against better-established concierge services.

4. **Human Resource Risks**

   The most serious human resource risk to our business, at least in the initial stages, would be my inability to operate the business due to illness or disability. The owner is currently in exceptional health and would eventually seek to replace himself on a day-to-day level by developing systems to support the growth of the business.

5. **Marketing Risks**

   Advertising is our most expensive form of promotion and there will be a period of testing headlines and offers to find the one that works the best. The risk, of course, is that we will exhaust our advertising budget before we find an ad that works. Placing greater emphases on sunk-cost marketing, such as our website storefront and on existing relationships through direct selling will minimize our initial reliance on advertising to bring in a large percentage of business in the first year.

6. **Business Risks**

   A major risk to retail service businesses is the performance of the economy and the small business sector. Since economists are predicting this as the fastest growing sector of the economy, our risk of a downturn in the short-term is minimized. The entrance of one of the three major chains into our marketplace is a risk. They offer more of the latest equipment, provide a wider array of products and services, competitive prices and 24-hour service. This situation would force us to lower our prices in the short-term until we could develop an offering of higher margin, value-added services not provided by the large chains. It does not seem likely that the relative size of our market today could support the overhead of one of those operations. Projections indicate that this will not be the case in the future and that leaves a window of opportunity for ___ (company name) to aggressively build a loyal client base.

The Company's start-up quarterly revenues and operating results are difficult to predict and may fluctuate from quarter to quarter as a result of a variety of factors, including changes in pricing to accommodate local market conditions, recession pressures and seasonal patterns of spending.

To combat the usual start-up risks we will do the following:
1. Utilize our industry experience to quickly establish desired strategic relationships.
2. Pursue business outside of our immediate market area.
3. Diversify our range of product and service offerings.

4. Develop multiple distribution channels.
5. Monitor our competitor actions.
6. Stay in touch with our customers and suppliers.
7. Watch for trends which could potentially impact our business.
8. Continuously optimize and scrutinize all business processes.
9. Institute daily financial controls using Business Ratio Analysis.
10. Create pay-for-performance compensation and training programs to reduce employee turnover.

Further, to attract and retain customers the Company will need to continue to expand its market offerings, utilizing third party strategic relationships. This could lead to difficulties in the management of relationships, competition for specific services and products, and/or adverse market conditions affecting a particular partner.

The Company will take active steps to mitigate risks. In preparation of the Company's pricing, many factors will be considered. The Company will closely track the activities of all third parties and will hold monthly review meetings to resolve issues and review and update the terms associated with strategic alliances.

Additionally, we will develop the following kinds of contingency plans:
Disaster Recovery Plan
Business Continuity Plan
Business Impact and Gap Analysis
Testing & Maintenance

The Company will utilize marketing and advertising campaigns to promote brand identity and will coordinate all expectations with internal and third-party resources prior to release. This strategy should maximize customer satisfaction while minimizing potential costs associated with unplanned expenditures and quality control issues.

10.1   Business Risk Reduction Strategy

We plan to implement the following strategies to reduce our start-up business risk:
1. Implement our business plan based on go, no-go stage criteria.
2. Develop employee cross-training programs.
3. Regularly back-up all computer files/Install ant-virus software.
4. Arrange adequate insurance coverage with higher deductibles.
5. Develop a limited number of prototype samples.
6. Test market offerings to determine level of market demand and appropriate pricing strategy.
7. Thoroughly investigate and benchmark to competitor offerings.
8. Research similar franchised businesses for insights into successful prototype business/operations models.
9. Reduce operation risks and costs by flowcharting all structured systems & standardized manual processes.

10. Use market surveys to listen to customer needs and priorities.
11. Purchase used equipment to reduce capital outlays.
12. Use leasing to reduce financial risk.
13. Outsource manufacturing to job shops to reduce capital at risk.
14. Use subcontractors to limit fixed overhead salary expenses.
15. Ask manufacturers about profit sharing arrangements.
16. Pay advertisers with a percent of revenues generated.
17. Develop contingency plans for identified risks.
18. Set-up procedures to control employee theft.
19. Do criminal background checks on potential employees.
20. Take immediate action on delinquent accounts.
21. Only extend credit to established account with D&B rating
22. Get regular competitive bids from alternative suppliers.
23. Check that operating costs as a percent of rising sales are lower as a result of productivity improvements.
24. Request bulk rate pricing on fast moving supplies.
25. Don't tie up cash in slow moving inventory to qualify for bigger discounts.
26. Reduce financial risk by practicing cash flow policies.
27. Reduce hazard risk by installing safety procedures.
28. Use financial management ratios to monitor business vitals.
29. Make business decisions after brainstorming sessions.
30. Focus on the products with biggest return on investment.
31. Where possible, purchase off-the-shelf components.
32. Request manufacturer samples and assistance to build prototypes.
33. Design production facilities to be flexible and easy to change.
34. Develop a network of suppliers with outsourcing capabilities.
35. Analyze and shorten every cycle time, including product development.
36. Develop multiple sources for every important input.
37. Treat the business plan as a living document and update it frequently.
38. Conduct a SWOT analysis and use determined strengths to pursue opportunities.
39. Conduct regular customer satisfaction surveys to evaluate performance.

10.2   Reduce Customer Perceived Risk Tactics

We will utilize the following tactics to help reduce the new customer's perceived risk of starting to do business with our company.

Status

1. Publish a page of testimonials. _____
2. Secure Opinion Leader written endorsements. _____
3. Offer an Unconditional Satisfaction Money Back Guarantee. _____
4. Long-term Performance Guarantee (Financial Risk). _____
5. Guaranteed Buy Back (Obsolete time risk) _____
6. Offer free trials and samples. _____
7. Brand Image (consistent marketing image and performance) _____
8. Patents/Trademarks/Copyrights _____

9. Publish case studies _____
10. Share your expertise (Articles, Seminars, etc.) _____
11. Get recognized Certification _____
12. Conduct responsive customer service _____
13. Accept Installment Payments _____
14. Display product materials composition or ingredients. _____
15. Publish product test results. _____
16. Publish sales record milestones. _____
17. Foster word-of-mouth by offering an unexpected extra. _____
18. Distribute factual, pre-purchase info. _____
19. Reduce consumer search costs with online directories. _____
20. Reduce customer transaction costs. _____
21. Facilitate in-depth comparisons to alternative services. _____
22. Make available prior customer ratings and comments. _____
23. Provide customized info based on prior transactions. _____
24. Become a Better Business Bureau member. _____
25. Publish overall customer satisfaction survey results. _____
26. Offer plan options that match niche segment needs. _____
27. Require client sign-off before proceeding to next phase. _____
28. Document procedures for dispute resolution. _____
29. Offer the equivalent of open source code. _____
30. Stress your compatibility features (avoid lock-in fear). _____
31. Create detailed checklists & flowcharts to show processes _____
32. Publish a list of frequently asked questions/answers. _____
33. Create a community that enables clients to connect with each other and share common interests. _____
34. Inform customers as to your stay-in-touch methods. _____
35. Conduct and handover a detailed needs analysis worksheet. _____
36. Offer to pay all return shipping charges and/or refund all original shipping and handling fees. _____
37. Describe your product testing procedures prior to shipping. _____
38. Highlight your competitive advantages in all marketing materials. _____

11.0 Financial Plan

_____ (company name) expects a profit margin of over ____ (60?)% starting with year one. By year two, that number should slowly increase as the law of diminishing costs takes hold, and the day-to-day activities of the business become less expensive. Sales are expected to grow at ____ % per year, and level off by year _____.

The initial investment in ___ (company name) will be provided by _____ (owner name) in the amount of $ _____. The owner will also seek a ___ (#) year bank loan in the amount of $ _____ to provide the remainder of the required initial funding.

The owner financing will become a return on equity, paid in the form of dividends to the owner.

Our financial plan includes:
    Moderate growth rate with a steady cash flow.
    Investing residual profits into company expansion.
    Company expansion will be an option if sales projections are met and/or exceeded.
    Marketing costs will remain below ___ (5?) % of sales.
    Repayment of our loan calculated at a high A.P.R. of ___ (10?) percent and at a 10-year-payback on our $_____ loan.

11.1 Important Assumptions

_____ (company name) sells very little on credit. The Personnel Burden is low because benefits are not paid to our staff. We will continue to work on a short-term interest rate that is lower. We are also assuming the economy will continue to grow after the current recession and there will continue to be an increased need for innovative Senior Concierge Services.

The following basic assumptions need to be considered:
1. The economy will grow at a steady slow pace, without another major recession.
2. There will be no major changes in the industry, other than those discussed in the trends section of this document.
3. The State will not enact 'impact' legislation on our industry.
4. Good access to the capital and financing to support our financial plan.
5. Sales are estimated at minimum to average values, while expenses are estimated at above average to maximum values.
6. Staffing and payroll expansions will be driven by increased sales.
7. Rent expenses will grow at a slow, predictable rate.
8. Materials expenses will not increase dramatically over the next several years, but will grow at a rate that matches increasing consumption.

Revenue Assumptions:

	Year	Sales/Month	Growth Rate
1.			
2.			
3.			
4.			

Resource:
www.score.org/resources/business-plans-financial-statements-template-gallery

11.2 Break-even Analysis

Break-Even Analysis will be performed to determine the point at which revenue received equals the costs associated with generating the revenue. Break-even analysis calculates what is known as a margin of safety, the amount that revenues exceed the break-even point. This is the amount that revenues can fall while still staying above the break-even point. The two main purposes of using the break-even analysis for marketing is to (1) determine the minimum number of sales that is required to avoid a loss at a designated sales price and (2) it is an exercise tool so that we can tweak the sales price to determine the minimum volume of sales we can reasonably expect to sell in order to avoid a loss.

Definition: Break-Even Is the Volume Where All Fixed Expenses Are Covered.

Three important definitions used in break-even analysis are:
- **Variable Costs** (Expenses) are costs that change directly in proportion to changes in activity (volume), such as raw materials, labor and packaging.
- **Fixed Costs** (Expenses) are costs that remain constant (fixed) for a given time period despite wide fluctuations in activity (volume), such as rent, loan payments, insurance, payroll and utilities.
- **Unit Contribution Margin** is the difference between your product's unit selling price and its unit variable cost.
  Unit Contribution Margin = Unit Sales Price - Unit Variable Cost

For the purposes of this breakeven analysis, the assumed fixed operating costs will be approximately $ _____ per month, as shown in the following table.

Monthly Fixed Costs:		**Variable Costs:**	
Payroll	_____	Cost of Goods	_____
Rent	_____	Labor	_____
Insurance	_____	Supplies	_____
Utilities	_____	Other	_____
Security.	_____		
Other	_____		
Total:	_____	Total	_____

A break-even analysis table has been completed on the basis of average costs/prices. With monthly fixed costs averaging $_____ , $____ in average sales and $_____ in average variable costs, we need approximately $_____ in sales per month to break-even.

Based on our assumed ___ % variable cost, we estimate our breakeven sales volume at around $ ___ per month. We expect to reach that sales volume by our _____ month of operations. Our break-even analysis is shown in further detail in the following table.

Breakeven Formulas:

Break Even Units = Total Fixed Costs / (Unit Selling Price - Variable Unit Cost)

_____ = _____ / (_____ - _____)

BE Dollars = (Total Fixed Costs / (Unit Price – Variable Unit Costs))/ Unit Price

_____ = (_____ / (_____ - _____)) / _____

BE Sales = Annual Fixed Costs / (1- Unit Variable costs / Unit Sales Price)

_____ = _____ / (1 - _____ / _____)

Table: Break-even Analysis

The break-even analysis is based on $_____ (20.00) as the average per unit revenue. This is based on the hourly rate charged to corporations, as they account for ____ (90?) % of our business. The charge for individuals is slightly higher, but since they only account for less than ____ (10?) % of our projected revenue, we are going to use the ____ ($21.00) figure.

Monthly Units Break-even   _____
Monthly Revenue Break-even $ _____

Assumptions:
Average Per-Unit Revenue $ _____   ($20.00)
Average Per-Unit Variable Cost $ _____   ($2.00)
Estimated monthly Fixed Cost $ _____   ($5,000)

Ways to Improve Breakeven Point:
1. Reduce Fixed Costs via Cost Controls
2. Raise unit sales prices.
3. Lower Variable Costs by improving employee productivity or getting lower competitive bids from suppliers.
4. Broaden product/service line to generate multiple revenue streams.

11.3 Projected Profit and Loss

Pro forma income statements are an important tool for planning our future business operations. If the projections predict a downturn in profitability, we can make operational changes such as increasing prices or decreasing costs before these projections become reality.

Our monthly profit for the first year varies significantly, as we aggressively seek improvements and begin to implement our marketing plan. However, after the first ___ months, profitability should be established.

We predict advertising costs will go down in the next three years as word-of-mouth about our Senior Concierge Service gets out to the public and we are able to find what has worked well for us and concentrate on those advertising methods.

Our net profit/sales ratio will be low the first year. We expect this ratio to rise at least _____ (15?) percent the second year. Normally, a startup concern will operate with negative profits through the first two years. We will avoid that kind of operating loss on our second year by knowing our competitors and having a full understanding of our target markets.

Our projected profit and loss is indicated in the following table. From our research of the personal services concierge industry, our annual projections are quite realistic.

This business plan assumes an eventual ____ (10?) % profit and is built using the following allocations of gross revenue:

- _____ (10?) % Profit
- _____ (50?) % Labor (including owner's draw)
- _____ (10?) % Inventory
- _____ (20?) % Overhead
- _____ (10?) % Cost of Merchandise

Key P & L Formulas:
Gross Margin = Total Sales Revenue - Cost of Goods Sold
Gross Margin % = (Total Sales Revenue - Cost of Goods Sold) / Total Sales Revenue
This number represents the proportion of each dollar of revenue that the company retains as gross profit.
EBITDA = Revenue - Expenses (exclude interest, taxes, depreciation & amortization)
PBIT = Profit (Earnings) Before Interest and Taxes = EBIT
A profitability measure that looks at a company's profits before the company has to pay corporate income tax and interest expenses. This measure deducts all operating expenses from revenue, but it leaves out the payment of interest and tax. Also referred to as "earnings before interest and tax ".
Net Profit = Total Sales Revenues - Total Expenses

Pro Forma Profit and Loss

	Formula	2018	2019	2020
Total Sales Revenue	A			
Direct Cost of Goods	B			
Other Costs of Goods	C			
Total Costs of Goods Sold	B+C=D			
Gross Margin	A-D=E			
Gross Margin %	E / A			
Expenses				
Payroll				
Payroll Taxes				
Delivery Labor				
Temp Labor				
Contracted Floral Designer				
Sales & Marketing				
Depreciation				
License Fees				
Dues and Subscriptions				
Rent				
Utilities				
Deposits				
Repairs and Maintenance				
Janitorial Supplies				
Office Supplies				
General Supplies				
Leased Equipment				
Buildout Costs				
Insurance				
Van Expenses				
Gas				
Merchant Fees				
Miscellaneous				
Total Operating Expenses	F			
Profit Before Int. & Taxes	E - F = G			
Interest Expenses	H			
Taxes Incurred	I			
Net Profit	G - H - I = J			
Net Profit / Sales	J / A = K			

11.4 Projected Cash Flow

The Cash Flow Statement shows how the company is paying for its operations and future growth, by detailing the "flow" of cash between the company and the outside world. Positive numbers represent cash flowing in, negative numbers represent cash flowing out.

The first year's monthly cash flows are will vary significantly, but we do expect a solid cash balance from day one. We expect that all our sales will be done in cash or by credit card and that will be good for our cash flow position. Additionally, we will stock only slightly more than one month's inventory at any time. Consequently, we do not anticipate any problems with cash flow, once we have obtained sufficient start-up funds.

A __ year commercial loan in the amount of $_____, sought by the owner will be used to cover our working capital requirement. Our projected cash flow is summarized in the following table and is expected to meet our needs. In the following years, excess cash will be used to finance our growth plans.

Cash Flow Management:
We will use the following practices to improve our cash flow position:
1. Become more selective when granting credit.
2. Seek deposits or multiple stage payments.
3. Reduce the amount/time of credit given to clients.
4. Reduce direct and indirect costs and overhead expenses.
5. Use the 80/20 rule to manage inventories, receivables and payables.
6. Invoice as soon as the service has been performed.
7. Generate regular reports on receivable ratios and aging.
8. Establish and adhere to sound credit practices.
9. Use more pro-active collection techniques.
10. Add late payment fees where possible.
11. Increase the credit taken from suppliers.
12. Negotiate extended credit terms from vendors.
13. Use barter to acquire goods and service.
14. Use leasing to gain access to the use of productive assets.
15. Covert debt into equity.
16. Regularly update cash flow forecasts.
17. Defer projects which cannot achieve acceptable cash paybacks.
18. Require a 50% deposit on custom framing orders, balance due on completed job.
19. Speed-up the completion of projects to get paid faster.
20. Ask for extended credit terms from major suppliers.
21. Put ideal bank balances into interest-bearing (sweep) accounts.
22. Charge interest on client installment payments.
23. Check the accuracy of invoices to avoid unnecessary rework delays.
24. Include stop-work clauses in contracts to address delinquent payments.
25. Speed up collection on receivables, either with incentives for early payment or by improving collections and invoicing earlier in the month.
26. Increase (speed up) your inventory turns per year.
27. Keep inventory at the minimum level necessary to sustain a given level of sales.

28. Reduce reliance on short-term borrowing to cover cash shortages will yield lower interest expense and increased profits.

Cash Flow Formulas:

Net Cash Flow = Incoming Cash Receipts - Outgoing Cash Payments
Equivalently, net profit plus amounts charged off for depreciation, depletion, and amortization. (also called cash flow).

Cash Balance = Opening Cash Balance + Net Cash Flow
We are positioning ourselves in the market as a medium risk concern with steady cash flows. Accounts payable is paid at the end of each month, while sales are in cash, giving our company an excellent cash structure.

Pro Forma Cash Flow

	Formula	2018	2019	2020

Cash Received
Cash from Operations

	Formula
Cash Sales	A
Cash from Receivables	B
Subtotal Cash from Operations	A + B = C

	Formula
Additional Cash Received	
Non-Operating (Other) Income	
Sales Tax, VAT, HST/GST Received	
New Current Borrowing	
New Other Liabilities (interest fee)	
New Long-term Liabilities	
Sales of Other Current Assets	
Sales of Long-term Assets	
New Investment Received	
Total Additional Cash Received	D
Subtotal Cash Received	C + D = E

Expenditures

	Formula
Expenditures from Operations	
Cash Spending	F
Payment of Accounts Payable	G
Subtotal Spent on Operations	F + G = H

	Formula
Additional Cash Spent	
Non-Operating (Other) Expenses	
Sales Tax, VAT, HST/GST Paid Out	
Principal Repayment Current Borrowing	
Other Liabilities Principal Repayment	
Long-term Liabilities Principal Repayment	
Purchase Other Current Assets	
Dividends	
Total Additional Cash Spent	I
Subtotal Cash Spent	H + I = J
Net Cash Flow	E - J = K

Cash Balance

11.5 Projected Balance Sheet

Pro forma Balance Sheets are used to project how the business will be managing its assets in the future. As a pure start-up business, the opening balance sheet may contain no values. The projected balance sheets must link back into the projected income statements and cash flow projections.

____ (company name) does not project any real trouble meeting its debt obligations, provided the revenue predictions are met. We are very confident that we will meet or exceed all of our objectives in the Business Plan and produce a slow but steady increase in net worth.

Long-term liabilities are projected to decrease steadily, reflecting re-payment of the original seven-year term loan required to finance the business. It is important to note that part of the retained earnings may become a distribution of capital to the owners, while the balance would be reinvested in the business to replenish depreciated assets and to support further growth.

All of our tables will be updated monthly to reflect past performance and future assumptions. Future assumptions will not be based on past performance but rather on economic cycle activity, regional industry strength, and future cash flow possibilities. We expect a solid growth in net worth by the year _____.

The Balance Sheet table for fiscal years 2018, 2019, and 2020 follows. It shows managed but sufficient growth of net worth, and a sufficiently healthy financial position.

Key Formulas:

Paid-in Capital = Capital contributed to the corporation by investors on top of the par value of the capital stock.

Retained Earnings = The portion of net income which is retained by the corporation rather than distributed to the owners as dividends.

Earnings = **Revenues - (Cost of Sales + Operating Expenses + Taxes)**

Net Worth = Total Assets - Total Liabilities
Also known as 'Owner's Equity'.

Pro Forma Balance Sheet

	Formulas	2018	2019	2020

Assets

Current Assets
Cash
Accounts Receivable
Inventory
Other Current Assets
Total Current Assets   A

Long-term Assets
Long-term Assets   B
Accumulated Depreciation   C
Total Long-term Assets   B - C = D

Total Assets   A + D = E

Liabilities and Capital

Current Liabilities
Accounts Payable
Current Borrowing
Other Current Liabilities
Subtotal Current Liabilities   F

Long-term Liabilities
Notes Payable
Other Long-term Liabilities
Subtotal Long-term Liabilities   G

Total Liabilities   F + G = H

Capital
Paid-in Capital   I
Retained Earnings   J
Earnings   K
Total Capital   I - J + K = L

Total Liabilities and Capital   H + L = M

Net Worth   E - H = N

11.6 Business Ratios

The following table provides significant ratios for the personal services industry. The final column, Industry Profile, shows ratios for this industry as it is determined by the Standard Industrial Classification (SIC) Index 7299, for comparison purposes.

Our comparisons to the SIC Industry profile are very favorable and we expect to maintain healthy ratios for profitability, risk and return. Use Business Ratio Formulas provided to assist in calculations.

Key Business Ratio Formulas:

EBIT = Earnings Before Interest and Taxes
EBITA = Earnings Before Interest, Taxes & Amortization. (Operating Profit Margin)

Sales Growth Rate =((Current Year Sales - Last Year Sales)/(Last Year Sales)) x 100
Ex: Percent of Sales = (Advertising Expense / Sales) x 100

Net Worth = Total Assets - Total Liabilities

Acid Test Ratio = Liquid Assets / Current Liabilities
Measures how much money business has immediately available. A ratio of 2:1 is good.

Net Profit Margin = Net Profit / Net Revenues
The higher the net profit margin is, the more effective the company is at converting revenue into actual profit.

Return on Equity (ROE) = Net Income / Shareholder's Equity
The ROE is useful for comparing the profitability of a company to that of other firms in the same industry. Also known as "return on net worth" (RONW).

Current Ratio = Current Assets / Current Liabilities
The higher the current ratio, the more capable the company is of paying its obligations. A ratio under 1 suggests that the company would be unable to pay off its obligations if they came due at that point.

Quick Ratio = Current Assets - Inventories / Current Liabilities
The quick ratio is more conservative than the current ratio, because it excludes inventory from current assets.

Pre-Tax Return on Net Worth = Pre-Tax Income / Net Worth
Indicates stockholders' earnings before taxes for each dollar of investment.

Pre-Tax Return on Assets = (EBIT / Assets) x 100
Indicates much profit the firm is generating from the use of its assets.

Accounts Receivable Turnover = Net Credit Sales / Average Accounts Receivable
A low ratio implies the company should re-assess its credit policies in order to ensure the timely collection of imparted credit that is not earning interest for the firm.

Net Working Capital = Current Assets - Current Liabilities
Positive working capital means that the company is able to pay off its short-term liabilities. Negative working capital means that a company currently is unable to meet its short-term liabilities with its current assets (cash, accounts receivable and inventory).

Interest Coverage Ratio = Earnings Before Interest & Taxes /Total Interest Expense
The lower the ratio, the more the company is burdened by debt expense. When a company's interest coverage ratio is 1.5 or lower, its ability to meet interest expenses may be questionable. An interest coverage ratio below 1 indicates the company is not generating sufficient revenues to satisfy interest expenses.

Collection Days = Accounts Receivables / (Revenues/365)
A high ratio indicates that the company is having problems getting paid for services.

Accounts Payable Turnover = Total Supplier Purchases/Average Accounts Payable
If the turnover ratio is falling from one period to another, this is a sign that the company is taking longer to pay off its suppliers than previously. The opposite is true when the turnover ratio is increasing, which means the firm is paying of suppliers at a faster rate.

Payment Days = (Accounts Payable Balance x 360) / (No. of Accounts Payable x 12)
The average number of days between receiving an invoice and paying it off.

Total Asset Turnover = Revenue / Assets
Asset turnover measures a firm's efficiency at using its assets in generating sales or revenue - the higher the number the better.

Sales / Net Worth = Total Sales / Net Worth

Dividend Payout = Dividends / Net Profit

Assets to Sales = Assets / Sales

Current Debt / Totals Assets = Current Liabilities / Total Assets

Current Liabilities to Liabilities = Current Liabilities / Total Liabilities

Business Ratio Analysis

	2018	2019	2020

Sales Growth

Percent of Total Assets
Accounts Receivable
Inventory
Other Current Assets
Total Current Assets
Long-term Assets
Total Assets

Current Liabilities
Long-term Liabilities
Total Liabilities
Net Worth

Percent of Sales
Sales
Gross Margin
Selling G& A Expenses
Advertising Expenses
Profit Before Interest & Taxes

Main Ratios
Current
Quick
Total Debt to Total Assets
Pre-tax Return on Net Worth
Pre-tax Return on Assets

Additional Ratios
Net Profit Margin
Return on Equity

Activity Ratios
Accounts Receivable Turnover
Collection Days
Inventory Turnover
Accounts Payable Turnover
Payment Days
Total Asset Turnover

Debt Ratios
Debt to Net Worth
Current Liabilities to Liabilities

Liquidity Ratios
Net Working Capital
Interest Coverage

Additional Ratios
Assets to Sales
Current Debt / Total Assets
Acid Test
Sales / Net Worth
Dividend Payout

Business Vitality Profile
Sales per Employee
Survival Rate

12.0 Summary

_____ (company name) will be successful. This business plan has documented that the establishment of _____ (company name) is feasible. All of the critical factors, such as industry trends, marketing analysis, competitive analysis, management expertise and financial analysis support this conclusion.

Project Description: (Give a brief summary of the product, service or program.)
_____

Description of Favorable Industry and Market Conditions.
(Summarize why this business is viable.)
_____

Summary of Earnings Projections and Potential Return to Investors:
_____

Summary of Capital Requirements:
_____

Security for Investors & Loaning Institutions:
_____

Summary of expected benefits for people in the community beyond the immediate business concern:
_____

Means of Financing:
A. Loan Requirements: $_____
B. Owner's Contribution: $ $_____
C. Other Sources of Income: $_____
Total Funds Available: $_____

13.0 Potential Exit Scenarios

Two potential exit strategies exist for the investor:

1. **Initial Public Offering. (IPO)**
   We seek to go public within ___ (#) years of operations. The funds used will both help create liquidity for investors as well as allow for additional capital to develop our _____ (international/national?) roll out strategy.

2. **Acquisition Merger with Private or Public Company.**
   Our most desirable option for exit is a merger or buyout by a large corporation. We believe with substantial cash flows and a loyal customer base our company will be attractive to potential corporate investors within five years. Real value has been created through the novel combination of home health care services as well as partnering with key referral groups.

APPENDIX

Purpose: Supporting documents used to enhance your business proposal.

- Tax returns of principals for the last three years, if the plan is for new business
- A personal financial statement, which should include life insurance and endowment policies, if applicable
- A copy of the proposed lease or purchase agreement for building space, or zoning information for in-home businesses, with layouts, maps, and blueprints
- A copy of licenses and other legal documents including partnership, association, or shareholders' agreements and copyrights, trademarks, and patents applications
- A copy of résumés of all principals in a consistent format, if possible
- Copies of letters of intent from suppliers, contracts, orders, and miscellaneous letters of intent
- In the case of a franchised business, a copy of the franchise contract and all supporting documents provided by the franchisor
- Newspaper clippings that support the business or the owner, including something about you, your achievements, business idea, or region
- Promotional literature for your company or your competitors
- Product brochures of your company or competitors
- Photographs of your product. equipment, facilities, etc.
- Market research to support the marketing section of the plan
- Trade and industry publications when they support your intentions
- Quotations or pro-forma invoices for capital items to be purchased, including a list of fixed assets, company vehicles, and proposed renovations
- References
- All insurance policies in place, both business and personal
- Operation Schedules
- Organizational Charts
- Job Descriptions
- Additional Financial Projections by Month

Helpful Resources

Associations

American Errand Runners Organization	www.errandinfo.com
National Association of Professional Organizers	www.napo.net
National Concierge Association	www.nationalconciergeassociation.com
The International Concierge and Errand Association.	www.iceaweb.org/

Offers networking, educational opportunities, resource directory and weekly chats.

Les Clefs d'Or International Concierge Association	
Meeting Professionals International	www.mpiweb.org
International Concierge Consultants	www.triangleconcierge.com
Yahoo Concierge Board	//groups.yahoo/group/conciergenet/

Children of Aging Parents (CAPS)   http://www.caps4caregivers.org
CAPS assists caregivers of the elderly with information and referrals, a network of support groups, and publications and programs that promote public awareness of the value and the needs of family caregivers.

Family Caregiver Alliance (FCA)   800-445-8106

Friends' Health Connection   http://www.48friend.org
Links persons with illness or disability and their family caregivers with others experiencing the same challenges.

National Alliance for Caregiving   http://www.caregiving.org
Helps family caregivers learn about information, videos, pamphlets, etc. that have been reviewed and approved as providing solid information.

National Family Caregivers Association   800-896-3650
A grassroots organization created to educate, support, empower and advocate for the millions of Americans who care for chronically ill, aged, or disabled loved ones. NFCA is the only constituency organization that reaches across the boundaries of different diagnoses, different relationships and different life stages to address the common needs and concerns of all family caregivers. NFCA serves as a public voice for family caregivers to the press, to Congress and the general public. NFCA offers publications, information, referral services, caregiver support, and advocacy.

Rosalynn Carter Institute for Human Development (RCI)   www.rci.gsw.edu
Provides educational programs for caregivers, conducts research, and disseminates information about caregiving.

Well Spouse Association   info@wellspouse.org
A national membership organization that gives support to husbands, wives and partners of the chronically ill and/or disabled. Well Spouse has a network of support groups and also a newsletter for spouses.

Aging Care   http://AgingCare.com

Helps people caring for elderly parents find support, resources and information, as well as a place to connect with other caregivers. Provides a community in which caregivers can connect with others in similar situations, to share ideas and help each other through the tough times.

AGIS Network   866-511-9186
AGIS.com provides education, support, expert advice, local resources and a vibrant community for caregivers and families of the elderly.

CareCentral
CareCentral is a personalized web service that allows users to create a private, secure online community for loved ones during significant health events. It is a free tool to update friends and family, organize and schedule offers to help, and encourage messages of hope, providing support when it is most needed.

CareConnection.com: www.careconnection.com
CareConnection.com is Website devoted to family caregivers, with up-to-date health news, elder care specialists, experts, insurance help, and coping advice. The site, owned by HealthCentral.com, offers in-depth resources from trusted sources, interactive tools, and connections to leading experts and caregivers who share their experiences and inspiration.

Caregiver.Com   800-829-2734
Caregiver.com produces Today's Caregiver magazine, the first national magazine dedicated to caregivers, the "Sharing Wisdom Caregivers Conferences", and Website which includes topic specific newsletters and online discussion lists.

Caregivinghelp.org   773.381.6008
CAREgivinghelp.org is free, interactive website featuring short video and text educational modules on a variety of caregiving topics, frequently asked questions that cover the different phases of caregiving, an online community monitored by a geriatric care specialist, exercises to help caregivers "take a moment" for themselves, and a comprehensive listing of resources.

CarePages   www.carepages.com
CarePages are free, private web pages that make it easy to reach out and receive messages of support and to stay connected to family, friends, co-workers and others who care about you and your loved one. The service is available to anyone caring for a loved one, but may be particularly helpful to those who have recently found themselves in a care giving role.

The National Family Caregivers Assoc.   www.thefamilycaregiver.org
The National Family Caregivers Association (NFCA) is America's premier organization for family caregivers reaching across the boundaries of diagnoses, age, and relationship to address the common needs and concerns of all family caregivers. Through education, support and advocacy NFCA empowers family caregivers to act on behalf of themselves and their loved ones, and works to remove the barriers that stand in the way of a family caregiver's health and well being.

Share the Care is a grassroots organization dedicated to preventing "caregiver burnout by promoting and educating people about the benefits of group caregiving using the SHARE THE CARE™ model."

Strength for Caring   http://www.strengthforcaring.com
Strength for Caring is an online resource and community for family caregivers that helps family caregivers take care of their loved ones and themselves. Strength for Caring is part of The Caregiver Initiative, created by Johnson & Johnson Consumer Products Company, Division of Johnson & Johnson Consumer Companies, Inc.

Caring for Elders
Vital information and possible support services for the elderly can be obtained by contacting your local county office of senior services or elder affairs as well as your local social service department. Area adult daycare centers may also provide information on resources for the elderly in your area. These numbers can be located in the governmental pages of the phone book or through a web query.

AARP   800-424-3410
AARP supplies information about caregiving, long-term care and aging, including publications and audio-visual aids for caregivers.

AGIS Network   866-511-9186   info@agis.com
AGIS.com provides education, support, expert advice, local resources and a vibrant community for caregivers and families of the elderly.

Eldercare Locator
National Association of Area Agencies on Aging   www.eldercare.gov
Eldercare Locator provides referrals to Area Agencies on Aging via zip code locations. Family caregivers can also find information about many eldercare issues and services available in local communities.

The National Association of Professional Geriatric Care Managers   520-881-8008
Geriatric care managers (GCMs) are health care professionals, most often social workers, who help families in dealing with the problems and challenges associated with caring for the elderly. This national organization will refer family caregivers to their state chapters, which in turn can provide the names of GCMs in your area. This information is also available online.

U.S. Administration on Aging   202-619-0724 http://www.aoa.gov
The Administration on Aging is the official federal agency dedicated to the delivery of supportive home and community-based services to older individuals and their caregivers. The AoA Website has a special section on family caregiving.
End-of-Life Planning, Hospice, and Bereavement Information

Aging with Dignity   888-5-WISHES (594-7437) http://www.agingwithdignity.org

Aging with Dignity publishes the Five Wishes Living Will document, a very user-friendly and comprehensive document that meets legal requirements in 35 states.

Caring Connections
Caring Connections provides free brochures on end-of-life topics including advance care planning, caregiving, hospice and palliative care, pain, grief and loss and financial issues. Caring Connections also provides Advanced Directives for all states.

HospiceDirectory.org
800-868-5171
Online consumer database that lists hospices in North America and the U.S. All hospices are listed at no cost. It is a free service that assists families and individuals in locating a hospice within their community quickly. Also provides reliable information about hospice and end-of-life care to consumers.

Hospice Foundation of America
800-854-3402
http://www.hospicefoundation.org
The National Hospice Foundation hosts an annual teleconference on issues of bereavement, and has publications on grief and bereavement.

The Compassionate Friends
877-969-0010
http://www.compassionatefriends.org
This group offers telephone support and understanding to families who have lost a child. They maintain a resource library and have a national chapter network and newsletter.
U.S. Department of Health and Human Services

National Clearing House for Long-Term Care Information
aoainfo@aoa.hhs.gov
The National Clearinghouse for Long-Term Care Information provides information on planning and financing long-term care including planning for end of life care, and all major types of public and private financing to help cover long-term care costs.

Health Insurance: Prescription Assistance Information
Family caregivers can contact their county or state Department of Health and Human Services for financial programs which may provide assistance for acquiring health insurance and prescription medications. Other possible financial resources may include social service agencies such as Catholic Charities, the Association of Jewish Families, and Children's Agencies. Local chapters of voluntary health agencies may also offer financial support programs and/or information on how to apply for such programs.

AGIS Network
866-511-9186
AGIS.com provides education, support, expert advice, local resources and a vibrant community for caregivers and families of the elderly.

Benefits Check-Up and Benefits Check-Up RX
http://www.benefitscheckup.org
A service of the National Council on the Aging, Benefits Check-Up and Benefits Check-UP RX help people over the age of 55 find federal, state, and local public and private programs that may pay for some of their medical care and/or prescription costs.

HealthInsurance.com
800-942-9019
http://www.healthinsurance.com
This website provides consumers and small businesses with quotes for health insurance and may help those who have lost their health insurance find an affordable alternative.

Medicare
http://www.medicare.gov
This is the official Website for the Centers for Medicare and Medicaid Services (CMS), the agency responsible for Medicare Rx. The toll-free number is 800/MEDICARE.

Medicare Rights Center
888-HMO-9050
http://www.medicarerights.org
This is an independent source of health care information and assistance for older and disabled Americans, their caregivers, and the professionals who serve them. Medicare Interactive (MI) is the one-stop source for information about health care rights, options and benefits and it is designed to help people find answers to all their Medicare questions. The website also has a list of phone numbers for each state's "State Health Insurance Assistance Program."

Medicare Rx Matters
http://www.MedicareRxMatters.org
Designed to help users make decisions about the new Medicare prescription drug plan, this site has three specific portals: one for family caregivers, one for people with Medicare, and one for professionals. The Website provides an overview, easy-to-understand steps, and information to assist users in making personal decisions about Medicare prescription drug coverage.

Medicine Program
573-996-7300
This program is for persons who do not have coverage either through insurance or government subsidies for outpatient prescription drugs and for those who cannot afford to purchase medications at retail prices.

RxCompare
Email: info@maprx.info
http://www.maprx.info
RxCompare™ is a free tool developed by Medicare Access for Patients-Rx (MAPRx) to

help users determine if they need to enroll in a Medicare drug plan and, if they do, to systematically compare the drug plans where they live and select the best option for their prescription needs. RxCompareTM works in tandem with Medicare's on-line "Prescription Drug Plan Finder" and with information available from plans or 1-800-MEDICARE.

Patient Advocacy Assistance and Programs
Patient Advocate Foundation
800-532-5274
http://www.patientadvocate.org
Patient Advocate Foundation serves as a liaison between patients and their insurer, employer and/or creditors to resolve insurance, job retention and/or debt crisis matters relating to a patient's condition.

Homecare Agencies
National Association for Home Care and Hospice
202-547-7424
http://www.nahc.org
This organization for home healthcare agency providers allows family caregivers to use the Internet to access a list of member agencies across the country.

Visiting Nurse Associations of America
617-737-3200
Website: http://www.vnaa.org
VNAA promotes community based home healthcare. Family caregivers can contact them to find their local VNA.

Assisted Living, Nursing Home, and Residential Care
Consumer Consortium on Assisted Living (CCAL)
703-533-8121
http://www.ccal.org
CCAL is a national consumer-focused organization that is dedicated to representing the needs of residents in assisted living facilities and educating consumers, professionals, and the general public about assisted living issues. Family caregivers can request the publication "Choosing an Assisted Living Facility: Strategies for Making the Right Decision," which provides helpful information and a concise checklist for those contemplating this next step.

National Citizens' Coalition for Nursing Home Reform
202-332-2275
http://www.nccnhr.org
This organization serves as an information clearinghouse and offers referrals nationwide for help with concerns about long-term care facilities.

NFCA Senior Housing Locator
206-575-0728

info@snapforseniors.com
NFCA Senior Housing Locator powered by SNAPforSeniors™ is a current, comprehensive and objective resource of all licensed senior housing in the U.S., including assisted living, residential care, nursing care and rehabilitation communities as well as Continuing Care Retirement Communities (CCRC) and a growing number of independent living retirement communities.
Medical Transport and Hospitality Housing

National Association of Hospital Hospitality Houses (NAHHH)
800-542-9730
NAHHH represents organizations that provide lodging (and service) for families receiving medical care away from home; furnishes information about hospitality homes in the caller's area; offers newsletter; and publishes an annual directory of facilities offering lodging.

National Patient Travel Center
800-296-1217
Family caregivers can receive help in locating air transportation for needy patients who need distant specialized medical evaluation, diagnosis or treatment. The National Patient Travel Helpline is available 24/7 and provides referrals to all major medical transport providers in the network.

Respite Resources

Easter Seals   http://www.easter-seals.org
Easter Seals provides a variety of services at 400 sites nationwide for children and adults with disabilities, including adult day care, in-home care, camps for special needs children and more.

Faith in Action   info@fiavolunteers.org
Faith in Action is an interfaith volunteer caregiving program of The Robert Wood Johnson Foundation. Faith in Action makes grants to local groups representing many faiths who volunteer to work together to care for their neighbors who have long-term health needs.

National Council on the Aging, Inc.   http://www.family-friends.org
This group provides respite (and other services) by matching men and women volunteers over the age of 50 with families of children who have disabilities or chronic illness. Programs are located throughout the country.

National Adult Day Services Association, Inc.   866-890-7357
This association provides information about locating adult day care centers in your local area.

National Respite Coalition (NRC)   703-256-9578
NRC provides a list of states that have respite coalitions. These state coalitions then list

respite services available in their state. The majority of the information is focused on helping families of children with special needs, but lately there has been an effort to enlarge their referral base to include lifespan respite information.

National Respite Locator Servicehttp://www.respitelocator.org/index.htm
Access a list of sites nationwide. While the vast majority focus on respite care for families of special needs children, the service now assists programs that provide respite for caregivers of adults and the elderly.

Shepherd's Centers of Americahttp://www.shepherdcenters.org
The organization provides respite care, telephone visitors, in-home visitors, nursing home visitors, home health aides, support groups, adult day care, and information and referrals for accessing other services available in the community. Services vary by center.

Training for Family Caregivers
Community-based resources may offer training and classes for family caregivers. Such resources may include: your local hospital; home care agencies; Area Agency on Aging, voluntary health agencies, and county and state departments of health.

American Red Crosshttp://www.redcross.org
American Red Cross has developed training programs for family caregivers. You will need to check with your local chapter to find out if there are classes in your area.

National Family Caregivers Associationhttp://www.thefamilycaregiver.org
NFCA has developed an educational workshop to teach family caregivers to communicate more effectively with healthcare professionals. Check out the NFCA Website to find out if there are workshops scheduled in your community.

Newsletters
The NCA News by the National Concierge Association
NAPO News by the National Association of Professional Organizers

Technology
Time Value Calculator//moneycentral.msn.com/investor/calcs/n_time/main.asp

Ticket Information/Entertainment
Celebrity Seatswww.celebrityseats.com
Ticket brokers specializing in hard-to-get tickets for all concerts, sporting events, etc.
Open Tablewww.opentable.com
The world's most popular website for making restaurant reservations online.

Miscellaneous
Employee Handbook - http://www.na.fs.fed.us/wihispanic/employee_handbook/
A template so that you can create your own employee handbook. .
http://www.logoyes.com/ - Create your own logo.
www.vistaprint.com - The Web's innovative e-printing site that lets you easily customize   and order your own FREE, high-quality, full-color business cards.
BigDates.com - It helps you remember and take action on the 'BIG DATES' in your client's lives, like birthdays, anniversaries, and holidays.
http://www.ezinequeen.com - How to publish an e-mail newsletter, or "e-zine."
http://www.prweb.com/ - Free online press release distribution services
www.score.org - Service Corps of Retired Executives
www.corporate.com - The Company Corporation can help you research and form an INC, LLC, Professional LLC, or Non-Profit Corporation.
Publicityinsider.com - PR Tips, Press Release Secrets, etc.
http://sbinfocanada.about.com/library/startbusinessquiz/blquestion1.htm
   This starting a business quiz will help you decide whether or not the time is right for you to start your own business.
www.LegalDocs.com - This site allows you to prepare customized legal documents and legal forms directly online.
www.copyscape.com - Dedicated to defending your rights online, helping you fight against online plagiarism and content theft.

Small Business Guides   www.smbtn.com/businessplanguides/
Open Office   http://download.openoffice.org/
US Census Bureau   www.census.gov
   Provides economic and demographic reports and information.
Federal Government   www.business.gov
   A one-stop shop for links to all federal sites that might be helpful to businesses.
US Patent & Trademark Office   www.uspto.gov
   This is a valuable resource for inventors and creators of new products, software and for companies seeking to protect trade names.
US Small Business Administration   www.sba.gov
   The federal agency that leverages its name to provide loans, information and other assistance to small business owners.
National Association for the Self-Employed www.nase.org
   A membership organization providing legislative updates, articles, insurance and more to micro business owners.
International Franchise Association www.franchise.org
   A member trade organization for franchisors, franchisees and suppliers to franchises.
Center for Women's Business Research www.cfwbr.org
   Compiles data on women-owned businesses.

Insurance Coverage
   Christine Wright & Erick Medina, Hanasab Insurance Services, Phone: 323-782-8452
   American Family Insurance - has a category for "errands and shopping
   Partner's USA Insurance - Partners USA Insurance Programs, (800) 382-5414

Sample Flyer Content

Does Your Holiday Gift List Include the Person Who has Everything?

Do you need the "Perfect Gift" that everyone can appreciate?

Give the "Gift of Time" to family, friends, and colleagues for all occasions with our Gift Certificates. _____ (company name) announces concierge Certificates that will make you the hero for your friends, loved-ones and colleagues.

_____ (company name) is a Senior Concierge Service designed to provide the retiree, sophisticated traveler, small business owner, senior corporate executive and busy families with the necessary and convenient components for a successful and well-balanced lifestyle. We offer Personal, Corporate, and Senior Concierge Services. Whether your concierge list includes a time-challenged individual, family, corporate executive, local celebrity, small business owner, single parent, or busy professional, we will partner with them to give back serenity and invaluable time for their lives.

Call _____ or visit our website at _____
for more information or to order our Gift Certificates.

Sample Sales Letter:

To: Residential Property Manager,

We are an upscale five-star concierge provider that offers both on- and off-site services to condominium buildings and upscale single-family communities. On-site services include the security, door man, bell hop, and valet you'd expect. Off-site offerings include the personal shopping, dog walking, plant watering, and valet dry cleaning (just to name a few) that go above and beyond the typical Senior Concierge Service suite.

In today's competitive real estate market, you need a concierge provider that will go beyond typical expectations. You want to distinguish your properties from the rest of the pack. When you partner with _____ (company name), you can expect our second-to-none services to attract, satisfy, and retain your residents, while building your reputation in the process.

Please contact the undersigned at _____ to discuss how our upscale Senior Concierge Services can improve your reputation and brand image.

Sincerely,

Internet Article Writing Template

1. Article Title

Maximum 100 characters (including spaces) - about 12 words.
Write it to catch the attention of readers and publishers. Start with your primary search engine keyword phrase. In printed media titles starting "How to…" or "10 top tips for…" are very popular, but they are not very helpful for search engines. The article title will go into the title of a web page.

2. Abstract

Maximum 500 characters - about 90 words but 50 or 60 is better.
Make it enticing to hook the publisher and make them want to read the full article. The abstract is primarily targeted at the publisher and will be displayed just below the title on the search pages in the directory, but is secondary to the title in getting attention. Some publishers may also use it.

3. Description – Meta Tag

Maximum 200 characters but preferably 150 – two lines of text.
This should be a shorter version of the abstract, which must contain your primary keywords. The Mega Tag is needed if you publish on your own website.

4. Keywords – Meta Tag

Maximum 100 characters - about 12 words comma separated
Start with your primary keyword of phrase then add the other relevant keywords that are used in the article.

5. Article Text

Length depends on your topic, market and writing style. Research suggests about 500 to 800 words, but some publishers want more of an in-depth analysis. Research your specific market and be flexible, with a prepared mix of lengths, including long and short versions of the same article. Write the basic article with no formatting. If you are using word, disable all the auto-formatting like smart quotes, automatic hypertext links and paragraph spacing because they will all cause problems later.

Include the 'Primary Keyword Phrase' into the first sentence. Include the liberal usage of keywords throughout the article, but don't overdo it. The article still has to be a good read. Remember that even though you are writing for several audiences, content must still be king. Do not promote your own products and services or your article will not be published. Also, do not include self serving links to your web site or affiliate sites in the body of the article, but rather save them for the 'Resource or Byline Box'. If you have links to resources show them as text, as many sites do not allow live html links in the body of the article.

Introduction
1. Brief outline of what will be covered in the article.
2. The motivating factor behind why this particular topic was selected and why you

are qualified to address the subject.
3. A brief statement on your credentials, experience and exposure.
4. What you have achieved from your experience to convince readers that you know the subject very well.

Core Subject Matter
1. Define the problem or address the subject areas that will define the gap between the uninformed and the knowledgeable.
2. Provide the benefits the reader will realize from reading the article.
3. Start with simple and general background knowledge, and gradually intensify the technicality of the subject matter.
4. State the expected challenges to be faced in tackling the problem.
5. Discuss the pros and cons of your proposed solution to create the link between the norm and the desired state.

Expand Upon Subject Matter
1. Add technical information to convince readers of the merits of your solution.
2. State a range of requirements needed to implement your solution and their options.
3. Compare players in the market and promote good practice.
4. Place emphasis on desired actions, taking a chronological approach to each stage.
5. Attempt to indirectly answer any questions you think your readers may have.
6. Give supporting points to gain confidence in the approach you recommend.
7. Suggest other options based on price and availability.

Conclusion
1. Summarize problem solution recommendations.
2. Refer readers to other helpful resources.

6. Copyright

Copyright, date, name, country. Few directories ask for this but it makes sense to put it at the bottom of the article or in the field requested.

7. Resource Box

Maximum 500 characters, "including spaces and html code."
This is your opportunity to promote yourself but limit content to 1 or 2 self-serving links. Refer to the links in the "Third Person." The directory publisher has to function with this link on their site or ezine so make it acceptable to them. Offer an incentive or reward for people to visit your web site, but make sure that live links show the web address not just keywords. If the publisher doesn't use live links, you still want to present your website address for later referral.

Advertising Plan Worksheet

Ad Campaign Title: _____
Ad Campaign Start Date: _____ End Date: _____

What are the features (what product has) and hidden benefits (what product does for consumer) of my products/services?

Who is the targeted audience?

What problems are faced by this targeted audience?

What solutions do you offer?

Who is the competition and how do they advertise?

What is your differentiation strategy?

What are your bullet point competitive advantages?

What are the objectives of this advertising campaign?

What are your general assumptions?

What positioning image do you want to project?
    __ Exclusiveness   __ Low Cost   __ High Quality
    __ Speedy Service   __ Convenient   __ Innovative

What is the ad headline?

What is the advertising budget for this advertising campaign?

What advertising methods will be used?
    __ Radio   __ TV/Cable   __ Yellow Pages
    __ Coupons   __ Telemarketing   __ Flyers
    __ Direct Mail   __ Magazines   __ Newspapers
    __ Press Release   __ Brochures   __ Billboards
    __ Other

When will each advertising method start and what will it cost?
    Method   Start Date   Frequency   Cost

_____

Indicate how you will measure the cost-effectiveness of the advertising plan?
Formula: Return on Investment (ROI) = Generated Sales / Ad Costs.

Viral Marketing

Definition: Also known as word-of-mouth advertising.
Objective: To prompt your customers to deliver your sales message to others.
Strategy: Encourage and enable communication recipients to pass the offer or message along to others.
Benefit: Provides an excellent advertising return on investment and builds the trust factor.

Methodologies:
1. Encourage blog comments and two-way dialogue.
2. Use surveys to solicit feedback.
3. Use refer-a-friend forms or scripts.
4. Provide discount coupon or logo imprinted giveaway rewards for telling a friend.
5. Utilize pre-existing social networks.
6. Participate in message boards or forums.
7. Add a signature line with a refer-a-friend tagline to all posts and emails.
8. Enable unrestricted access.
9. Facilitate website content sharing.
10. Write articles and e-books, and encourage free reprints with byline mention.
11. Submit articles with 'about the author' box to article directories, such as www.articlecity.com.
12. Develop attention-grabbing product line extensions to stay connected.
13. Do the unexpected by offering a surprise benefit.
14. Deliver a remarkable offering that exceeds customer expectations.
15. Provoke a strong emotional response by getting involved with a cause that is important to your customers.
16. Provide referral incentives.
17. Get free samples into the hands of respected opinion leaders.
18. Educate customers, as to your product benefits and competitive advantages, to act as spokespersons for your company.

Explain Your Viral Marketing Program
_____
_____
_____
_____
_____

Marketing on Social Networking Websites

1. Place banner ads or Pay-Per-Click ads on social networking sites.
2. Create an account on the website and add your company logo.
3. Encourage word-of-mouth exchanges by posting comments on friend's profiles.
4. Post surveys on your social networking pages to solicit feedback.
5. Create a profile that subtly and humbly tells everyone about you and your gift basket products and services.
6. Include links to your concierge basket business website.
7. Make your profile keyword rich with keyword phases from your business specialty.
8. Use a soft sell approach and focus on establishing your credibility and expertise as a concierge basket marketing guru, to be trusted by prospective clients.
9. Name your social networking page exactly as your organization is named.
10. Have a strong presence in one channel rather than all of them.
11. Make sure you give visitors a strong call to action to supply their email address, so you can contact them later.
12. Include a signature line with your website contact info.
13. Blog often, but make certain that instead of selling, you are sharing your concierge industry expertise.

Helpful Resources:
http://en.wikipedia.org/wiki/List_of_social_networking_websites
Examples: Facebook.com   Myspace.com
               LinkedIn.com   Ryse.com

Explain Your Online Social Networking Strategy
_____
_____
_____
_____
_____

Integrate Marketing into Daily Operations

Objective: To seamlessly integrate marketing processes into daily, routine operations.

Strategies:
1. Develop form to ask for referrals upon new customer registration and annual renewal.
2. Present a sales presentation folder upon registration or contract sign-up with needs analysis worksheets, testimonials, new product introduction flyers, innovative application ideas, etc.
3. Develop a second sales presentation folder version for presentation upon job completion or sale, with referral program details, warranty service contract blank, and accessory suggestions.
4. Include business cards and coupons with all product deliverables.
5. Install company yard signs during job set-up.
6. Include a thank you note/comment card with all deliverables.
7. Include flyers and helpful articles in all customer correspondence, especially mailed invoices and statements.
8. Attach logo and contact info to all finished products.
9. Conduct customer satisfaction surveys while clients are waiting to be served.
10. Develop enclosed warranty card to build customer database and feed drip marketing program.
11. Provide competitor product/service comparisons that highlight your strengths.
12. Incorporate feedback cards into merchandise displays.
13. Train all employees to also be sales and customer service agents.
14. Print your Mission Statement or slogan on all forms and correspondence.
15. _____
16. _____

Indicate how you will incorporate marketing into daily operations.

Sales Stage	Business Processes	Opportunities to Incorporate Marketing Techniques
Pre-sale		
Transaction		
Post Sale		

Monthly Marketing Calendar

Instruction: Use to plan your monthly marketing events or activities and evaluate individual event results and marketing lessons learned for the month.

Month/Year: _____

Event/Activity	Responsibility	Cost	Comments	Date	Results Evaluation

Monthly Evaluation of Lessons Learned:
_____
_____
_____

Form Strategic Marketing Alliances

Definition: A collaborative relationship between two or more non-competing firms with the intent of accomplishing mutually compatible and beneficial goals that would be difficult for each to accomplish alone. Also referred to as 'Collaboration Marketing'.

Note: Usually, potential alliance partners sell distinct or complementary products and/or services to the same target market audience.

Advantages: Improve marketing efficiency by achieving synergy in resource allocation with strategic partners.
Improve marketing effectiveness by creating a one-stop or wraparound shopping experience.
A way to inexpensively test the market for growth potential.

Types of Co-Ventures:
1. Informal Strategic Alliances
2. Contractual Relationships (Attorney review recommended)
3. New Business Entity (Set-up by attorney)

Informal Strategic Alliances
1. Most involve consultations regarding:
    a. Mutual Referrals
    b. Research for product improvements
    c. Promotion of products or services (affiliate programs).
    d. Creative product bundling arrangements.
2. May or may not require a written agreement.
3. May or may not require compensation.

Topics to be Covered:
1. The specific strategic goals and objectives of the alliance.
2. The performance expectations of the parties..
3. The scope of the alliance.
4. The period of performance.
5. Termination and renewal procedures.
6. Strategic marketing plan to promote the alliance.
7. Dispute resolution procedures.
8. Performance tracking methods.
9. Periodic evaluation of reciprocal benefits realized.
10. Website pages/links to promote alliance partners.

Example: The mutual referral relationship between a sports bar and a fitness club or physical fitness trainer.

Strategic Marketing Alliance Worksheet

Methodology:
1. Identify the assets and capabilities you can provide to the alliance.
2. Identify the assets and capabilities that the proposed partner will bring to the alliance.
3. Determine the benefits you are seeking from the alliance.
4. Determine the gaps in your offerings that the alliance partner can fill.
5. List any conflicting relationships with other businesses and benefits received.
6. Research the potential alliance for strategic fit and other opportunities.
7. List the ways in which your customers will benefit from this alliance.
8. Assess any alliance risks.
9. Determine the ongoing actions needed to maintain the alliance.
10. Design a marketing plan to promote the alliance.
11. Develop a Mission Statement for the alliance.
12. Develop the Management Plan for the alliance.
13. Design the alliance appraisal and renewal procedures.

Potential Alliance Partner	Partner Strengths Offered	Your Offering Gaps Filled	Customer Benefits	Alliance Risks

Referral Program Tips

Objective: To formalize your referral program so that it can be easily and consistently integrated into your operating processes.

1. Define the stages in the sales process when you will ask for a referral. Ex: Registration, Renewals, Annual Drive, etc.)

2. Document your referral asking script (include objection handling responses).

3. Include a request for referrals in your customer satisfaction survey and your registration forms.

4. Stress the dependence of your business on referrals in all your marketing communications.

5. Set-up a follow-up procedure and tracking form to convert referral leads into actual customers.

6. Publish your referral incentives, awards criteria and timetable for settlement.

7. Customize your referral program to the motivational needs of a select number of potential 'Bird Dogs' or 'Big Hitters'.

8. Educate potential referral agents as to the characteristics of your ideal prospect. (Develop Ideal Prospect Profile)

9. Set-up special, mutual referral arrangements with strategic business alliance partners and track the reciprocity of efforts.

10. Join or start a local lead group.

11. Set-up 'thank-you note' templates to facilitate your expression of gratitude.

12. Use logo imprinted giveaways, such as T-sheets, as referral thank you expressions.

Seminar Outline Worksheet

Objective: To establish your expertise on the subject matter and produce future possible networking contacts by offering a newsletter sign-up and/or business card exchange.

Warning: Make seminar information rich and not a sales presentation.

1. Start with Attention-Grabbing Headline
   Ex: Hard-hitting Quotation, Thought Provoking Question, Startling Fact

2. Introduce Yourself and Establish Your Credentials

3. Present Seminar Overview

4. Discuss Attendee Participation Guidelines

5. Solicit a sampling of attendee interests, backgrounds and concerns.

6. Establish Learning Objectives

7. Preview the Bulleted Topics To be Covered

8. Share a Relevant Success Story (Case Study).

9. Use analogies and comparisons to create reference points.

10. Use statistics to support your position.

11. Conclusion: - Summarize Benefits for Attendees / Appeal to Action

12. Hold Question and Answer Session

13. Final Thoughts
    - Appreciation for Help Received
    - Indicate after-seminar availability

14. Handout A Remembrance
    - Business Cards   - Glossary of Terms
    - Seminar Outline   - Feedback Survey

228

Seminar Planning

Opening Discussion
Canvas participants' previous experience in relation to the topic.

Introduction
Provide a brief introduction to establish the context, perhaps one or two references to relevant literature and a mention of the departmental context. Link back to the participants contribution to the opening discussion.

Outline
- what it is you have been doing
- what you learned
- the conclusions you have reached.

Discuss
- use the questions you developed in the planning phase to provide sequence and focus to the discussion

Learning Outcome:
- what is that you want participants to learn?
- how can you help them do that?

Time:
- develop a time frame for the session.
- mixture of input, activity and discussion.

Input:
- Refer to the questions you developed in the planning

Input
Establish a series of sub topic headings that will enable you to quickly get back on track after a question or discussion and that will keep you moving through the material in a logical sequence

Learning reflection
Develop a key question that will enable people to discuss the relevance and possible application of your findings into their own practice or context

Evaluation
Develop two to three key questions that will enable the participants to tell you in what ways the seminar was useful to them.

Seminar Evaluation Process

The following is a simple checklist to help you focus on your own contribution to the seminar. Write a brief note beside each question.

- Was the pre-seminar planning adequate?
- Was the session plan appropriate?
- Was there a balance between telling and discussing?
- Did the entire group participate?
- Were others able to contribute to the generation of new knowledge?
- Did I introduce the topic sufficiently?
- Did the first activity involve people in the topic?
- What was the highlight of the session? Why?
- What was the low point of the session? Why?
- How could I present this seminar differently next time?

YouTube Marketing Tips

YouTube has become a big marketing operation for businesses and there are even marketing agencies to help businesses gain exposure from YouTube using proven viral video strategies. With so much exposure possible from a single video clip, YouTube should become a part of every business marketing plan.

1. Focus on something that is funny or humorous, so that people will feel compelled to share it with friends and family.
2. Make the video begin and end with a black screen and include the URL of your originating website to bring traffic to your site.
3. Put your URL at the bottom of the entire video.
4. Clearly demonstrate how your product works.
5. Create how-to videos to share your expertise and develop a following.
6. Build contests and events around special holidays and occasions.
7. Run a search on similar content by keyword, and use the info to choose the right category and tags for your video.
8. Make sure the video is real, with no gimmicks or tricks.
9. Add as many keywords as you can.
10. Make sure that your running time is five minutes or less.
11. Break longer videos into several clips, each with a clear title, so that they can be selectively viewed.
12. Encourage viewer participation and support.
13. Take advantage of YouTube tags, use adjectives to target people searching based on interests, and match your title and description to the tags.
14. Use the flexibility provided by the medium to experiment.
15. Use the 'Guru Account' sign-up designation to highlight info videos and how-to guides.
16. Create 'Playlists' to gather individual clips into niche-targeted context so viewers can easily find related content.
17. Use 'Bulletins' to broadcast short messages to the world via Your YouTube Channel.
18. Email 'The Robin Good YouTube Channel' to promote a new video release.
19. Join a 'YouTube Group' to post videos or comments to the group discussion area and build your network of contacts.
20. Use 'YouTube Streams' to join or create a room where videos are shared and discussed in real-time.
21. Use 'Active Sharing' to broadcast the videos that you are currently watching, and drive traffic to your profile.
22. Use the 'Share Video' link found under each video you submit and then check the box 'Friends' to send your video to all your friends.
23. Create your own YouTube Channel when you sign-up for a new YouTube account.
24. Create video responses to existing videos.
25. Accept and welcome video responses.
26. Comment on other videos to build relationships and tactfully promote your video.

27. Use tags and descriptions to help google searches.
28. Do wear thought provoking clothing items to provoke viewer comments.
29. Post your Youtube.com link to Twitter and Facebook, and forum discussions.
30. Use video sitemaps and include title, description, play page, thumbnail and player or content location.
31. Transcribe your video content into the description field.
32. Produce videos on a regular basis and announce your future production schedule.
33. Make sure your videos are easy to share by providing sharing features like embed codes, 'tweet this' button and 'email this' links.
34. Publish to more than one location, including niche video sites.
35. Make videos about a subject you are passionate about to broadcast your expertise.
36. Provide viewers with a rare behind-the-scenes look at your operations.
37. Encourage viewers to comment back via text, audio, photo and/or video.
38. Incorporate credited viewer feedback into your video content.
39. Tell your story with emotion to elicit an emotional response from viewers and stimulate the viral sharing of your video.
40. Link your Youtube video to your website or blog by copying and pasting the Youtube Embed Code into your website code.
41. Create a YouTube video title that arouses curiosity in viewers and prompts them towards watching the shocking evidence.
42. Use unique tags that relate to your niche market.
43. Do not spoil the viral potential of the video by making it entirely an ad.
44. Embed your website's URL into the video.
45. Create a video that is simple enough to be remixed by others.
46. Reach out to individuals who run relevant blogs and actually encourage/reward them to post your embedded videos.
47. Start new forum threads and embed your videos into the dialogue.
48. Get permission to embed your YouTube videos right in the comments section of MySpace pages of friends.
49. On Facebook share your videos with your entire friends list.
50. On Facebook create an event that announces the video launch and invite friends, writing a note and tagging friends, or posting the video on Facebook Video with a link back to the original YouTube video.
51. Send the Youtube video link to your email database list.
52. Change the title of the video several times, from something catchy to something more relevant to your brand and niche market.
53. Engage in thumbnail optimization by creating a thumbnail or middle frame that is clear, which suggests a high video quality, and it should have a face or at least a person in it.
54. Create controversy in the comments section below the video by getting a few people to log in throughout the day and post heated comments.
55. Start by using some unique tags that are common to all of your videos and, then after a few days, add some more generic tags that draw out the long tail of a video.

Basic Monthly Marketing Plan Checklist

1. Send birthday greetings to existing clients. _____
2. Contact referral sources and express appreciation for their referrals. _____
3. Implement program to develop new referral sources. _____
4. Research new ways to solve more problems of your target clients. _____
5. Research possible new target audience needs. _____
6. Make your friends/family/associates/social contacts aware of your expanding capabilities. _____
7. Train all employees to assist in marketing efforts. _____
8. Conduct selected client interviews to assess performance, changing needs and suggestions. _____
9. Forward copies of articles of interest to contacts. _____
10. Take contact to breakfast, lunch or dinner. _____
11. Invite contact to sporting or cultural event. _____
12. Distribute articles that demonstrate your expertise. _____
13. Invite contacts to an informative seminar. _____
14. Send personal notes of congratulation. _____
15. Join organizations important to your contacts. _____
16. Update your mailing list. _____
17. Issue a press release on a firm accomplishment or planned marketing event. _____
18. Update your firm's list of competitive advantages. _____
19. Attend a networking event. _____
20. Update the helpful content on your website. _____
21. Arrange to speak on your area of expertise. _____
22. Become actively involved in the community. _____
23. Track your ad results to determine resource focus. _____
24. Develop alliances with complementary businesses. _____
25. Conduct customer satisfaction surveys. _____
26. Implement client needs analysis checklist. _____
27. Distribute newsletter featuring clients. _____
28. _____ _____
29. _____ _____
30. _____ _____

Networking Insights

Definition: A reciprocal process in which you share ideas, leads, information, and advice to build mutually beneficial relationships.

Networking Tips:
1. Start your own local referral group with other business owners.
2. Understand your long-term networking goals.
3. Become a helpful resource to networking members.
4. Research people and companies to know their goals and interests.
5. Offer referrals, resources and recommendations to receive same in return.
6. Consistently try to meet new people and make new friends.
7. Develop good listening skills.
8. Frequently express your gratitude for assistance.
9. Know what interests, strengths and availability you bring to the table.
10. Stay in touch with a newsletter, blog, postcards or email messages.
11. Keep asking questions to get others to tell you more about themselves.
12. Show warmth, display confidence, smile and shake hands firmly.
13. Explore organizations that offer accreditation and directory listings.

Entrepreneur Networking Possibilities

1. Meet Up — www.meetup.com
2. FaceBook, Friendster, Myspace — www.facebook.com
3. LinkedIn — www.linkedIn.com
4. Ryze — www.ryze.com
5. Int'l Virtual Women's Chamber of Commerce — www.ivwcc.org
6. Business Network International — www.BNI.com
7. Club E Network — www.clubENetwork.com
8. Local Chamber of Commerce
9. Rotary Club — www.rotary.org
10. Lion's Club — www.lionsclubs.org
11. Jaycees
12. Toastmasters — www.toastmasters.com
13. Woman Owned Network — wwwwomanowned.com
14. Alumni Associations
15. Parent Teacher Associations (PTA)
16. Trade Shows — www.tsnn.com
17. Trade Associations — www.associationscentral.com
18. EONetwork — www.eonetwork.org
19. Prof. Organizations, Economic Clubs, Charities, Churches, Museums, etc.

Perfect Your Elevator Pitch

A brief, focused message aimed at a particular person or niche segment that summarizes why they should be interested in your products and/or services.

I am a/we are _____(profession) and we help _____ (target market description) to_____(primary problem solved).

Press Release Cover Letter Worksheet
Instructions: Use this form to build a ready-to-use cover letter.

Your Letterhead.

Date

Dear _____,

As a company located in your coverage area, we thought the attached Press Release would be of special concern to your readers/viewers, as it touches upon something that we all have in common, an interest in
_____.

Brief overview purpose of the press release.
_____

I have also enclosed a media kit to give you background information on
_____ Company and myself. I hope to follow-up with you shortly.

I also possess expertise in the following related areas:
- _____
- _____
- _____

Should you wish to speak to me or require additional information, I can be reached at _____ or via email at _____.
Additional assistance with company supplied photos can be requested at the same number. This Press Release can also be downloaded from my company website at www. _____.

Thank you for your time and attention,

Contact Name
Company Title
Phone Number
Email Address

New Release Template

News Release

For Immediate Release
(Or Hold for Release Until …(date)….)

Contact:
Contact Person   _____
Contact Title   _____
Company Name   _____
Phone Number   _____
Fax Number   _____
Email Address   _____
Website Address   _____

Date: _____
Attention: _____   (Target Type of Editor)

Headline: Summarize Your Key Message:
                  _____

Sub-Headline: Optional: _____

Location of the Firm and Date.

_____

Lead Paragraph: A summary of the newsworthy content.
                      _____
                      Answers the questions:
                      Who: _____
                      What: _____
                      Where: _____
                      When: _____

Second Paragraph:
Expand upon the first paragraph and elaborate on the purpose of the Press Release.
_____
_____

Third Paragraph:
Further details with additional quotes from staff, industry experts or satisfied clients.
_____
_____

For Additional Information Contact:
_____
_____

About Your Expertise:
Presentation of your expert credentials
_____
_____

About Your Business:
Background company history on the firm and central offerings.
_____
_____

Enclosures: Photographs, charts, brochures, etc.

Special Event Release Format   Notes

1. Type of Event   _____
2. Sponsoring Organization   _____
3. Contact Person Before the Event   _____
4. Contact Person At the Event   _____
5. Date and Time of the Event   _____
6. Location of the Event   _____
7. Length of Presentation Remarks   _____
8. Presentation Topic   _____
9. Question Session (Y/N)   _____
10. Speaker or Panel   _____
11. Event Background   _____
12. Noteworthy Expected Attendees   _____
13. Estimated Number of Attendees   _____
14. Why readers s/b interested in event.   _____
15. Specifics of the Event.   _____
16. Biographies   _____

Track Ad Return on Investment (ROI)

Objective: To invest in those marketing activities that generate the greatest return on invested funds.

Medium	Cost	Calls Received	Cost/Call	No. Act. New Clients	Cost/New Client
Formula:	A	B	A/B=C	D	A/D=E
Newspaper					
Classified Ads					
Yellow Pages					
Billboards					
Cable TV					
Magazine					
Flyers					
Posters					
Coupons					
Direct Mail					
Brochures					
Business Cards					
Seminars					
Demonstrations					
Sponsored Events					
Sign					
Radio					
Trade Shows					
Specialties					
Cold Calling					
Door Hangers					
T-shirts					
Coupon Books					
Transit Ads					
Press Releases					
Word-of-Mouth					
Totals:					

Sample Thank-you and Referral Letter

Dear _____ (client name)

I wanted to take this opportunity to thank you for your business once again. If I can be of service to you in the future, I hope you will not hesitate to call.

In the meantime, I have enclosed a few business cards and referral cards. I would very much appreciate your passing them along to anyone in need of interior design services. As usual, I will mail you a referral fee for any business that comes my way from your efforts.

I have also enclosed a 'Customer Satisfaction Survey' with a self-addressed and stamped return envelope. Your feedback is invaluable in helping us to improve the services that we offer and we very much appreciate the time you will spend in completing the survey.

I hope you are enjoying your new surroundings and we look forward to serving you and your family in the future.

Please call me if I can be of any help. Thanks again.

Sincerely,

Complete Alphabetical List of Senior Concierge Services

A

Airlines Reservation & Charters   Airport shuttle information
Alterations for men and women   Apartment finders
Audiovisual rentals   Auto repair, inspection, and rental
Auto Rental   Auto detailing

B

Baby-sitting service   Bands and entertainment
Balloon bouquets   Barter arrangements
Beauty services   Bed and Breakfast reservations
Birthday and special occasion cakes   Boat & Yacht Charter
Business schedule organized/arranged   Business referrals

C

Cards sent for all occasions   Catering
Children's activities   Cigar dinners
Client and spouse itineraries   Coffee Service
Company outings   Conference planning and facilities
Corporate concierge shopping/delivery   Courier service
Computer lessons/repair   Customized travel itineraries
Customs handling   Car shopping, repairs, rentals
Cleaning services for home, office   Carpenters
Collecting estimates/house repairs   Cruises

D

Dinner parties planned and catered   Dog sitting, grooming, and walking
Dry cleaning   Dinner reservations
Delivery services

E

Entertainment information   Eyeglass repair/prescription filled
Event planning and execution   Equipment rental
Exotic foods   Exotic car purchase/rental/maintain
Exotic concierge   Exotic destinations
Errand services

F

Faxing/telexing/copying/printing   Federal Express
Fitness and Health Consultation   Flowers ordered and delivered
Flower design for home and office or special event

G

Grocery Shopping   Gardening and terrace planting
Garbage disposal and removal   Gourmet food, fruit, and gift baskets
Golf lessons and tee times   Gift shopping/wrapping/delivery

H

Hard to find items   Hotel reservations/recommendations
House/apartment sitting   House cleaning/move in/out/ etc
Homework assistance   Hair stylists

I

Information services (411)   Interior design

Invitation and calligraphy service

J

Jewelry Shopping Fine, antique, original, rare/unique

K

Kosher: Catering, foods, resources

L

Licensed massage therapy
Limousine service
Luggage and leather repair
Landscaping and gardening

Locksmith
Liquors and fine wines
Luggage transport and shipping
Laundry services

M

Manicure services
Meal preparation in home or office
Meeting planning and execution
Moving planning and execution
Mardi Gras balcony rentals

Makeup artists service/consultation
Medical service referrals
Messenger services
Museum and gallery info and tours

N

Nightlife recommendations/reservations
Nutritionist consultation/meal planning

Notary Public
Nanny Services

O

Office party planning and execution
Office organization

Overnight delivery

P

Private jets
Park and recreation information
Party and catering arrangements
Passport renewal
Pet services sitting grooming etc
Photographer/video for all occasions
Professional speakers
Personal shopper

Post office
Parking solutions (short/long term)
Party entertainment
Personal trainer - In office or home
Picture framing
Plumber
Property searches

Q

Quality control/assurance services

R

Reminder services
Real estate services

Restaurant recommendation/reservations
Romantic getaways

S

Secretarial services
Security services
Shoe shine and repair
Special events VIP tickets
Summer camp information

Sailing lessons and equipment
Shipping and packaging services
Ski lessons, trips, equipment
Sports events and training
Spa reservations

T

Tailoring services
Temporary staff
Tickets for theater/concert/opera

Telemarketing and conferencing
Tennis lessons and court reservations
Theme dinners

Translators   Travel planning/booking services

U V W

UPS   Uniform services

Vet appointments

Wine tasting   Wedding planners

Sample Press Release Content

FOR IMMEDIATE RELEASE

Headline: Concierges Are No Longer Just for Fancy Hotels!

_____ (city), ___ (state) — _____ (date)

_____ (company name) is pleased to announce the introduction of its new personal concierge and errand service to _____ (city), _____ (state), catering to the busy professionals, dual income families, new mothers, individuals recuperating from accident or illness, the elderly and small business owners.

_____ (company name) is just what the doctor ordered, giving you the prescription for more quality time to do the things you really enjoy doing.

_____ (company name) will look after those routine errands, such as grocery shopping, personal & concierge shopping, house sitting, going to the bank or post office, etc. We also organize quotes from skilled handymen and offer a waiting service for things to arrive or contractors to get the job done.

Anyone who is short on time or simply does not enjoy doing the running around and waiting in line will benefit from our service.

Hiring the services of _____ (company name) is very much like having your very own personal assistant. Our fees are affordable and new customers are invited to take advantage of our no obligation, free consultation and receive ____% off their first service fee.

concierge Certificates are also available for that special someone who has everything but time.

Contact _____ at _____ (phone number) or email _____ to arrange for a free, no obligation consultation or to sample our Senior Concierge Service at a 20% discount rate.

Contact Information:

Sample Press Release

FOR IMMEDIATE RELEASE

_____ (company name) Launches _____'s (city) First Personal Styling and Concierge Company

Owner _____, launches personal styling company to boost women's self-confidence, and offer expert style advice at an affordable price.
_____ (city), ___ (state) — _____ (date)
Committed to making women feel more confident and finding their own unique style, owner _____ (owner name) introduces _____ (company name), the city's first personal styling and concierge company.

A unique concept to the _____ metro area, _____ (company name) offers styling services such as closet editing, personal shopping, and personal styling. The company is devoted to providing clients with the tools they need to develop their own personal style.

_____'s (company name) closet editing service is an affordable luxury, designed not only to help women clean out their closets but also to boost self-confidence while saving time, money, and energy. _____ (owner name) works with clients to take an inventory of their closets and establish what they have, what they should keep, what they should donate, and what they need to create their own personalized style. Immediately following the closet edit, the client is given a list of items they actually need to help create the look they desire. A closet edit also teaches people better shopping skills so they buy less and wear more. After a closet edit, clients will be able to focus on what it is they need, how to use what they already have, and most importantly feel more confident in their style choices. The closet edit proves useful to anyone, whether a mom with no time to focus on herself or a new professional looking to step up her business wardrobe without breaking the budget.

_____ (company name) also offers personal shopping and personal styling services, which can be combined or customized to fit individual needs and budget. Drawing on years of experience as a _____, _____ (owner name) recognizes many women feel they lack personal style and the talent to develop one. _____ (company name) was created to bring women the tools they need to develop a unique personal image.

To learn more or to schedule a free consultation with the _____ (company name), please visit our website at _____ or call _____.

Contact Information:

Sales Letter Content

Corporate Senior Concierge Services

Target Markets:

    Hospitals   Real Estate Brokerages
    Law Firms   Major Corporations
    Medical Practices   Resorts

Use our services to enhance employee loyalty.
    Our Timesaving Work-Life Balance Programs improve employee productivity, morale and retention while reducing absenteeism and turnover.

Use our services to create customer loyalty
    Increase meaningful touch points and connections with your customers by giving them the most valuable gift of time.
    We provide high-touch, attentive service … and you get all the thanks.

Think of us as "on-call personal assistants".

You name it. There's no job too large or too small for our experienced, professional concierges. Plus, our convenient, web-based system makes service requests easy.

We help clients manage their busy schedules by taking care of their personal errands. We can arrange pet care, buy gifts and groceries, schedule car repairs and home maintenance, find the best tickets to events and concerts, and much more.

Sample Sales Letter

Are You Too Busy to Breathe?

Dear _____,

Did you ever think how wonderful it would be if someone took responsibility for all of your business and personal errands each day? Could you even imagine how much more time you would have for yourself and your family?

Well, there is good news. We can make this dream a reality for you. Our services range from the basic to the unusual. My company, _____ (company name) was founded to help professionals and busy people just like you.

We can do everything from getting your car washed or serviced while you are at work, to arranging a small dinner party at your home.

I would like to set up a meeting with you, at your convenience, to discuss in more detail all of the Senior Concierge Services my company offers. In the meantime, please fill-out the enclosed survey, which will give me a better idea of the types of services you might require.

I look forward to talking to you in the near future. Please don't hesitate to call me with any questions. I can be reached at _____ or by email at _____.

Sincerely,

P.S.   As a get acquainted special incentive for new clients, we are currently offering one free month of personal Senior Concierge Services. Please call for more details.   Thank you.

New Concierge Client Survey

Name _____
Phone Number _____
Address _____
City/State/Zip _____
Email Address _____

How did you hear about us? _____
Search Engine Keywords Used _____
How many people in your household? _____
What is your spouse occupation? _____
May we add you to our email list?   Yes / No

1. How often do you think you might use the services of a personal concierge?
   ___ Every day ___ Once a week ___ Once a Month ___ Several times a month.

2. What services would most interest you?
   ___ Errand services ___ Business-related services ___ Personal services
   ___ A Combination of All.

3. Which of the following statements best describes your situation?
   ___ I never have enough time in the day to get everything done.
   ___ With a helper, I could better manage my business.
   ___ I could use some occasional help with my personal errands.
   ___ All of the above.

Classified Ad Worksheet

Ad Budget: _____

Ad Objective: ___ Go to Website ___ Request More Info ___ Mail a Check
___ Introduce a new product/service ___ Announce a Sale
___ Increase awareness of product
___ Other _____

Target Market: _____

Target Market:
Demographics:
- Age _____
- Gender _____
- Income _____
- Education _____
- Location _____

Reading Interests:
- Daily Newspapers _____
- Weekly Magazines _____
- Magazines _____
- Trade Journals _____

Product. Knowledge Level _____

Purchase Motivators _____

Best Category Heading _____

Select Type of Message
- Strong Offer with Best Value for Money _____
- Point of Difference from Competitors _____
- Listing the Benefits _____

Product Price: $_____

Ad Cost: $_____

Number of Responses: _____
Cost/Response: _____
Number of Sales: _____
Cost/Sales: _____

Marketing Plan   Month: _____

Planned Accomplishments for month:
_____
_____

Describe target audience:
_____
_____
_____

Success Measures:
Number of New Prospects   _____
Number of New Contacts to Referral Network
Sales Revenues of _____ by _____
Other measure: _____

Referral Network Action Plan:
We will attend the following events:
    Event   Date   Objective
_____
_____

We will contact the following people in my network:
    Name   Date   Reason
_____
_____

We will meet the following people in person:
    Name   Date   Reason
_____
_____

We will keep in touch with the following people by sending them information, including articles and newspaper clippings:
    Name   Date   Information Type
_____
_____

Past Client Action Plan:
We will contact the following past clients:
Method Options: In-person, Mail, email, phone.
    Name   Date   Reason   Method
_____
_____

Prospecting Action Plan:

Distribution Methods: Publications, Website, Organizations, Email, etc.

Method   Date   Subject   Distribution
                                                     Method
Article   _____
Speech   _____
Newsletter   _____
Press Release   _____

Other Activities:
    Activity Type   Date   Target
_____
_____

Sample Flyer Template

Company Name
Address
City, State, Zip code
Website
Main Phone:
Email Address

Service Area:

What We Do:

Products:

Services:

Specialties:

Associations:

Awards / Certifications:

Open Hours

Special Offer:

Additional Info:

Coupon:

$_____ Off Any _____ Service

Name: _____
Address: _____
Phone: _____
Problem: _____
Expiration Date: _____

Offer valid for 90 days from _____ (date) . Limit one (1) coupon per contract. Cannot be combined with any other offer. Not redeemable on minimum service charge. Coupon must be presented at time of visit.

Made in the USA
Columbia, SC
01 December 2025

74517381R10146